TEACH YOURSELF

BUSINESS
GERMAN

A COMPLETE COURSE FOR BEGINNERS

Andrew Castley
and
Debbie Wagener

Hodder & Stoughton

A CIP catalogue record for this title is available from the British Library.

ISBN 0 340 54251 9

First published 1992

© 1992 Andrew Castley and Debbie Wagener

Typeset by Transet Typesetters, Coventry, England.
Printed in Great Britain for the educational publishing division of Hodder & Stoughton Ltd, Mill Road, Dunton Green, Sevenoaks, Kent by Clays Ltd, St Ives plc, Bungay, Suffolk.

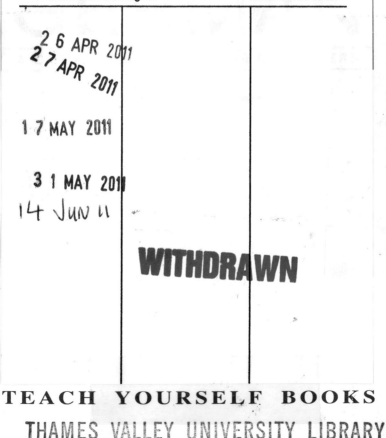

ty T E A C H Y O U R S E L F

THAMES VALLEY UNIVERSITY
Kings Road Learning Resource Centre
Kings Road, Reading, RG1 4HJ

Please return this item to the Issue Desk on or before the due date. Fines are charged on overdue loans.

If no-one else has reserved the item, you may extend the loan period up to three times without bringing it back. When renewing by telephone or through the learning resources catalogue, you will need your borrower barcode number and your *borrower* PIN number.

Issue Desk	0118 967 5060
24 hour automated renewals line:	020 8231 2703
Website and catalogue:	www.tvu.ac.uk/lrs

TEACH YOURSELF BOOKS

CONTENTS

—— ACKNOWLEDGEMENTS——

The authors and publishers would like to acknowledge the assistance of the following in the production of this book:

Lektion 3

Bayer AG, Leverkusen
Siemens AG, München
Friedrich Krupp GmbH, Essen

Lektion 9

Auma

Lektion 10

Frankfurter Allgemeine Zeitung GmbH, Frankfurt
Holzschuher & Gann GmbH, München
Berlitz Schule, München
Dr Werner Röhrs KG, Sonthofen
Ring-Treuhand GmbH, München

Lektion 17–24

Joachim Peters, Altes Schulhaus Verlag, Sulzbach
Swiss Embassy, London
Austrian Embassy, London

Language adviser

Olaf Matthies

—— INTRODUCTION ——

This course is intended for those who want to learn German for use in a practical business context. It has been designed to meet the basic needs of anybody involved in trade with German speaking people whether at managerial or secretarial level, or otherwise. Part-time or full-time students who are studying German as part of their secretarial or business courses will also find this book particularly useful in preparing for their examinations.

The book has been graded grammatically. Those who already have a basic knowledge of general German will have the opportunity of revising all the major grammatical points, in a step-by-step progression, from the simplest structures to the more advanced. This grading will also allow beginners to use the course without undue difficulty. The book does not cover all aspects of German grammar, so those who are starting German may find it useful to supplement this material with a basic grammar or general course. The reason for this is that the book emphasises practical communication, and the aspects of grammar presented here most directly serve this end.

The language and vocabulary have been selected with the aim of enabling learners to use their German in a wide range of commercial and social matters, in conversation and in writing (with special emphasis on business correspondence), and of building on their understanding.

—— The Course Structure —— and how to use it

The main objective of this course is to help you to achieve communicative competence in your own field. With this intention in mind, the first part of the book – Units 1–15 – has been organised around specific language functions. Each of these units brings in a particular language use, built around one or more themes or situations. Thus, for instance, Unit 1 will tell you how to introduce yourself and others, Unit 5 how to describe a product and process, Unit 7 how to discuss plans and commitments and so on.

Units 1–15 are each divided into two sections. One section normally aims at developing spoken competence through the use of dialogues (**Dialoge**), while the other concentrates mainly on the written language, helping to build understanding and giving guidance on writing, especially letter-writing. The model letters provide a source of standard commercial phraseology, and you should use them closely as a basis for creating your own business letters.

The layout of each section is approximately the same. Study the dialogue or passage noting all the new language forms and vocabulary. New words and expressions are listed immediately after the text and are also included in the German–English vocabulary at the end of the book. Any point which needs further explanation is dealt with under **Erklärungen.** Once you have grasped the meaning of the conversation, letter, reading passage, etc., read it through again until you are satisfied it is quite clear.

After the **Erklärungen** comes the grammar section, **Grammatik**, which highlights the main language points found in the preceding text and gives examples to illustrate each form or construction. All the sentences here appear with their English translation. In general, grammar is treated in layman's terms; where a technical grammatical term is used in the interests of brevity, it is always preceded by a brief explanation. Attention is drawn particularly to the list of strong verbs in the appendices.

Under the title of **Übungen** (*Exercises*) you will be able to apply what you have just learned through a series of exercises which call for different types of activities such as role-playing, letter-writing, writing messages, filling in forms, translating telexes or other material. Some of the exercises aim at reinforcing the grammar. You can check the answers in the key to the exercises.

In addition to the exercises set, you should revise the preceding text and identify examples of the grammar point dealt with in the lesson.

Symbols

 This indicates that the cassette is needed for the following section.

 This indicates dialogue.

This indicates exercises – places where you can practise speaking the language.

 This indicates key words or phrases.

 This indicates grammar – the nuts and bolts of the language.

 This indicates a reading section.

──── The Background Section ────

Units 16–23 give useful background information about German-speaking countries. The texts included in this section are of two different types. Some indicate a written register while others reproduce in written form a piece of oral language, which may be a talk or interview. From the point of view of language they aim at developing comprehension and you may proceed with each in the same way.

Study the texts carefully, trying to grasp the main ideas. They include a good deal of new vocabulary as well as drawing on what you have already learnt. This is to help you increase your passive vocabulary and improve your ability to read and understand written German. Try to determine what these new words mean by considering the context in which they occur, or their similarity with English words. Should this fail, look at the vocabulary list at the end of the reading passage or consult the vocabulary at the end of the book. A dictionary will also be useful at this stage.

Next, read the questions which follow the text, before you study it a second or even third time. Then you should be able to prepare your answers, either in English or German as required, without referring continually to the passage. You may check the answers in the key to the exercises. The text may be exploited further by considering other points not covered by the questions and by studying the passage in terms of the language which it contains. You can also look at the way in which various ideas are linked together within a paragraph or within the text as a whole.

Finally, a cultural briefing appears as part of the introduction. This is a brief but useful and informative section designed for the business person visiting Germany. It deals with social and business situations and related 'dos', 'don'ts' and 'what to look fors' to enable you to attune yourself readily to the more usual business and social situations.

Using the Course with the Cassette

Although the book has been designed in such a way that it is self-contained, you will find it of great benefit – especially if your aim is to speak and understand spoken German – to listen to the cassette which accompanies this course, as it provides an important practical aid for comprehension and pronunciation. The cassette contains versions of the **Dialoge,** which are not necessarily identical to those in the book, and the talks and interviews in the background section. There are also exercises and rôle-plays which will help you to practise your German in different situations.

We suggest that at the beginning of the course you start each unit by listening to the recording of the **Dialog** at the same time as you read it, paying special attention to the pronunciation and intonation of the speakers. Later on in the course you may well find that you can listen to the cassette without looking at the text. Then, when you have understood the gist of what was said, you can turn to the text and study the new language forms.

In the 'Background section', the talks and interviews can be used as a listening comprehension exercise, testing your ability to understand a longer piece of speech which contains a little unfamiliar language along with the familiar. Always try to understand the general meaning, rather than translate word for word, and guess the meaning of new words and expressions through their context. Then look at the questions which follow, and listen to the talk or interview again before answering them.

Pronunciation Guide

Vowels in German are monophthongs.

a	is pronounced as in *ah!* It can be short (as in *at*) e.g. **Wasser**, or long (as in *are*) e.g. **Vater**.
e	pronounced *ey* as in *bacon*, e.g. **gehen**.
i	as in *litter*, **bitte**.
o	can be short as in *top*, e.g. **Kopf**, or long as in *coal*, e.g. **Kohle**.
u	as in *loo*, e.g. **Fuß**.
ä	as in *gate*, e.g. **spät**.
ö	as in *er!*, e.g. **blöd**.
ü	say *ee*; now purse your lips and say *ee* again, e.g. **füllen**.
sch	as in *ship*, e.g. **Schiff**.
ch	hard as in the Scottish *loch*, e.g. **auch**, but softer after *i* (**ich**) or *e* (**echt**)
b	at the end of a word is pronounced *p*, e.g. **gelb**.
d	at the end of a word is pronounced *t* as in **Geld**.
sp	is pronounced *shp*, e.g. **spät** or **Sprechen Sie Deutsch?**
st	is pronounced *sht*, e.g. **stille Nacht**.
au	as in *drown*, e.g. **Traum**.
eu	as in *Oi!*, e.g. **Eule**.
äu	also as in *Oi!*, e.g. **Träumerei**.
ei	as in *eye*, e.g. **fein**.
ie	as in *eel*, e.g. **Liebe**.
s	as in English, unless at the start of a word when it is pronounced as *z*, e.g. **Sommer** or **so**.
z	pronounced *ts* as in *tents*, e.g. **zehn**.
ß	pronounced *ss* as in *stress*, e.g. **Straße**.

This is not intended as a comprehensive pronunciation guide. Remember that the best way to learn how to pronounce German is to hear it spoken. The cassette which accompanies this book is ideal for this purpose.

Abbreviations

masc.	masculine	nom.	nominative
fem.	feminine	acc.	accusative
neut.	neuter	dat.	dative
sing.	singular	subj.	subjunctive
pl.	plural	cond.	conditional

CULTURAL BRIEFING

The Federal Republic is a close neighbour of the UK and culturally quite similar. Political, social, economic and financial institutions are more remarkable for their basic similarity to those of the UK than for their difference. But there *are* differences and we should not ignore these just because most of the business and social world is conducted in Germany along similar lines to the UK. What follows is a series of snapshots of business practice and social manners which you might meet with, and which are different from what we are used to in Britain.

Custom and Practice

First, the working day begins earlier in Germany than in the UK. Office workers will begin at 8.00 a.m. or even 7.30 a.m. Hence the business person can schedule calls earlier – perhaps at 8.30 a.m. or 8.00 a.m. Whilst there is no particular pattern of finishing the working day earlier than in Britain, a good rule of thumb is not to schedule more than one call in the afternoon i.e. from 2.00 p.m. onwards.

It is not too surprising, therefore, that a German business partner may go to bed a little earlier than you normally do. This would never affect an evening's entertainment, but there might be occasions when consideration could be shown in this direction!

Shaking hands is much more widespread in Germany than in the UK. In a formal situation, for example a meeting, or when a newcomer is introduced to a group of people, it is quite usual for him to shake each of the group by the hand and say **Guten Tag** by way of greeting. In Britain this would be seen as overdoing it, but not in Germany.

If it is a one-to-one formal introduction, normal practice is to state your own name as you shake hands and add **sehr angenehm** (pleased to meet you) or **Guten Tag**.

On private visits, the guest always takes a gift for the host. If you are invited to a business partner's house (which might be as frequent as UK practice, or slightly less so), you might take flowers for the lady of the house. It would be safest to unwrap them before presenting them to her, but you are allowed to ask to dispose of the wrapping paper when you go in! (This wasn't always so!) In view of this practice you might take something suitable as a small gift – it might come in useful.

Whether on business or on a private visit, be absolutely punctual. It is a sign of politeness – and reliability.

Meals

Traditionally, the main meal is taken at midday, though nowadays there are plenty of exceptions to this. However, you will not find the equivalent of a ploughman's lunch generally being taken at midday. The lighter evening meal is referred to as **Abendbrot** unless it is something special. It often consists of bread with Wurst, cheese and trimmings.

If you are dining in company, remember these differences in table etiquette:

- The host is always the first person to lift his glass and say **Zum Wohl** or **Zum Wohlsein**. If you are the host, make sure you don't keep your guests waiting!
- Hands should always be visible when eating; not resting on the lap, for instance.
- Potatoes should never be cut with the knife, but with the fork with a scooping action.
- On the other hand, the bread roll *should* be cut with a knife and not broken as we do in Britain.
- The soup dish should be tilted *towards* rather than away from the eater (you eat soup in Germany, rather than drink or take it).

Attitudes

Generalisations should be avoided: usually exceptions far outnumber examples of a generalised statement. The following observations are offered as examples of what you may meet.

The Germans take work seriously and get paid well. The German business partner will almost certainly enjoy a quality of life significantly better than his contemporaries in many other countries in material terms.

Germans are health-conscious. It is surprising for visitors to note how frequently German colleagues suffer from **Kreislaufstörungen** (*circulatory problems*) in particular; in and to the south of Munich, the people are sensitive to the Föhn, an Alpine wind which saps the strength; it is common to take a few days' cure at one of the many spas, on prescription; you might hear **Es ist gesund** (*it's healthy/good for you*), said as some food or a drink is recommended to you.

Germans tend to be frank and open in their opinions and visitors sometimes see this as being brash or even rude (occasionally it is!) while the Germans see reticence in expressing opinions as not saying what you mean, or sometimes being hypocritical. Whilst you shouldn't modify your approach in the light of this, you might meet with the occasional uncompromising statement; it mightn't be as intentionally provocative as it seems.

German business people value flexibility in their partner organisations. You will probably soon hear the word **Flexibilität** and **flexibel**. The usual context is that of delivery dates or modifications to product specifications. It is useful to emphasise this aspect of your service, if it is indeed a feature of your organisation.

You may find there are fewer status symbols, or outward signs of a pecking order in working life in the Federal Republic than in many other countries. The incidence of managers having a company car is much lower; the company management will usually use the same dining facilities as the rest of the workforce; if flexitime is in operation, *everyone* will be subject to it.

You might notice the use of words suggesting partnership where the equivalent English terms do not: **Sozialpartner** (the two sides of industry); **Kollege** (used much more widely than *colleague*); **Mitarbeiter** (used much more widely than *fellow worker*); **Soziale Marktwirtschaft** (*social market economy*).

So these are a few snapshots of some customs and attitudes you might meet with in the Federal Republic.

Viel Erfolg!

1

INTRODUCING —— YOURSELF —— AND OTHERS

TEIL A

—— Dialog (Dialogue) ——

Herr Wolfgang Sieg, managing director of Sieg Metall GmbH, Düsseldorf, and Frau Müller, the sales manager, visit Herr Bauer at his office in Hamburg.

Herr Sieg Guten Tag.

Sekretärin Guten Tag. Kann ich Ihnen helfen?

Herr Sieg Ist Herr Bauer da? Ich bin Wolfgang Sieg aus Düsseldorf. Ich bin Betriebsleiter bei der Firma Sieg Metall GmbH.

Sekretärin Herr Bauer ist in seinem Büro. Kommen Sie bitte mit. (*The secretary announces their arrival.*) Herr Bauer, Herr Sieg und Frau Müller sind hier.
(*They meet Herr Bauer.*)

Herr Bauer Guten Tag, Herr Sieg. Wie geht es Ihnen?

Herr Sieg Sehr gut, danke. Das ist Frau Müller, unsere Verkaufsleiterin.

Herr Bauer Es freut mich Sie kennenzulernen, Frau Müller.

Frau Müller Gleichfalls.

Herr Bauer Nehmen Sie bitte Platz.

Guten Tag *Good day/hello*	**Sie sind hier** *They are here*
Kann ich Ihnen helfen? *Can I help you?*	**Wie geht's Ihnen?** *How are you?*
Ist Herr/Frau ... da? *Is Mr/Mrs ... there?*	**Sehr gut, danke** *Very well thank you*
Ich bin Betriebsleiter *I am the managing director*	**Das ist ... Herr/Frau** *This is ... Mr/Mrs*
bei der* Firma ... *with the ... company*	**unsere Verkaufsleiterin** *our sales manager* (fem)
Er ist in seinem* Buro *He is in his office*	**Es freut mich Sie kennenzulernen** *Pleased to meet you*
Kommen Sie bitte mit *Come this way, please*	**Gleichfalls** *Likewise*
	Nehmen Sie bitte Platz *Please take a seat*

*The dative case is covered in Lektion 4, Grammatik.

—— Erklärungen (Explanations) ——

1 **Guten Tag** also covers *good afternoon*, for which there is no German equivalent, other possible greetings are: **Guten Morgen**, *good morning*; **Guten Abend**, *good evening* and **Gute Nacht**, *good night*.

2 **Ich bin Betriebsleiter** – in the grammar section you will note that the German word for *the* (called the definite article) has three forms **der**, **die** and **das**, but remember that this is *not* used when describing your profession.

3 **Das ist ...** literally means *that is* but can be used as *this is* in simple introductions.

4 **Es freut mich Sie kennenzulernen** is fairly formal whereas abbreviations **es freut mich** or simply **freut mich** can be used in more informal situations. **Sehr angenehm** can also be used formally.

5 When describing people and their professions -**in** is often added to indicate the feminine form, for example:

> **Verkaufsleiter** *sales manager* (male)
> → **Verkaufsleiterin** *sales manager* (female)
> **Sekretär** *secretary* (male)
> → **Sekretärin** *secretary* (female)

— **10** —

6   It should be noted that, in the German business world, a handshake is customary, both on the initial introduction, as well as at subsequent meetings (See Cultural Briefing).

——— Grammatik (Grammar) ———

1   *Gender of nouns*

When *the* (called the definite article) is used with the name or title of a person, it is **der** for a masculine person and **die** for a feminine, for example:

der Mann	*the man*
die Frau	*the woman*
der Betriebsleiter	*the manager*
die Betriebsleiterin	*the manageress*

Note: One important exception is **das** Mädchen, *the girl* (see below for more on **das**).

Other nouns also have gender, for example:

Tag is masculine: **der** Tag   *the day*
Firma is feminine: **die** Firma   *the company*

and there is a third neuter gender which has **das** as its definite article, for example:

Büro: das Büro   *the office*

Plurals of all genders take **die** as the definite article, for example:

die Betriebsleiter	*the managers*
die Firmen	*the companies*
die Büros	*the offices*

(Note: German plurals rarely add 's', but rather various endings which are indicated in brackets in the vocabulary lists; this is dealt with in Lektioon 2, Grammatik, note 3.)

2 Present tense

(a) Regular verbs

This section deals with the infinitive of the verb, or the 'to do' part. All German verbs end in **-n** and mostly in **-en** in their infinitive form, i.e. *to go* is **gehen**, *to do* is **machen**, and their pattern (conjugation) in the present tense is as follows:

gehen *to go* (infinitive)		
ich geh**e** *I go/am going*		wir geh**en** *we go/are going*
du geh**st** *you go/are going**		ihr geh**t** *you go/are going**
*Sie geh**en** you go/are going**		Sie geh**en** *you go/are going**
er/sie/es geh**t** *he/she/it goes/is going*		sie geh**en** *they go/are going*

* See notes below.

(*i*)   There are three words for *you* in German depending on level of familiarity – **du** and **ihr** are used for family and friends, **du** being singular and **ihr** plural, whereas **Sie** covers both singular and plural and is used in more formal situations and is thus vital for the business context. For example:

Wohin gehst **du**, Hans?	*Where are you going, Hans?*
Wohin gehen **Sie**, Herr Sieg?	*Where are you going, Mr Sieg?*
Wohin geht **ihr**, Gabi und Bodo?	*Where are you going, Gabi and Bodo?*
Wohin gehen **Sie**, Herr Mayer und Herr Sucher?	*Where are you going, Mr Mayer and Mr Sucher?*

Note: The formal form is always written with a capital.

(*ii*)   There is only one form of the present tense in German for the two which we use in English. For example: **ich gehe** translates as *I go* or *I am going*.

(b) Irregular verbs

There are, however, some verbs which do not follow the regular conjugation and which are considered irregular:

sein *to be*			
ich bin	*I am*	wir sind	*we are*
du bist	*you are*	ihr seid	*you are*
Sie sind	*you are*	Sie sind	*you are*
er/sie/es ist	*he/she/it is*	sie sind	*they are*

3 My, your, his, her, etc (possessive adjectives)

mein	*my*	unser	*our*
dein	*your*	euer	*your*
Ihr	*your*	Ihr	*your*
sein	*his* (also *its*)	ihr	*their*
ihr	*her* (*its*)		
sein	*its*		

(*i*) Possessive adjectives have an **-e** ending when referring to a feminine noun, for example:

Herr Schmidt hat sei**ne** Firma in Hamburg.

(*ii*) **Ein**, the indefinite article, meaning *a* follows the same rule as you can see from the following examples:

ein Büro   *an office, one office*
ein**e** Bank   *a bank, one bank*

(*iii*) Where **sein** or **ihr** relate to masculine or feminine *objects*, they translate as *its*, for example:

Die Firma hat **ihren** Sitz in Bonn.   *The company has its head office in Bonn.*

——— Übungen (Exercises) ———

1 You are describing your company to a prospective customer: insert **der**, **die** or **das** as appropriate.

a) ... Firma ist sehr groß.
b) ... Büro ist in München
c) ... Verkaufsleiter ist Herr Sieg.
d) ... Betriebsleiterin ist Frau Müller.

sehr groß	*very big*

2 You are making conversation with your new German partners before lunch. Insert **mein**, **dein**, etc. (the possessive adjective) as indicated in brackets.

a) (*Our*) Firma ist ziemlich klein.
b) (*My*) Verkaufsleiter geht nach Hamburg.
c) (*His*) Sekretärin ist hier.
d) (*Her*) Platz ist leer.
e) (*Your*, formal) Büro ist sehr attraktiv.

---

ziemlich klein *fairly small*   **leer** *empty*

---

3 A client has just arrived from Munich. Select and insert the correct form of **gehen** (*to go*):

a) Wie ... es Ihnen?
b) Ich ... vor.
c) ... Sie ins Konzert?
d) Wir ... ins Theater.

Now insert the correct form of **sein** (*to be*):

e) Ich ... Betriebsleiter
f) Wir ... in meinem Büro.
g) ... Sie Verkaufsleiterin?
h) Frau Postler ... unsere Sekretärin.

4 You are the representative (**der/die Vertreter(in)**) of Johnson Ltd, a publishing house (**ein Verlag**), and you have come to see Frau Schmidt, general manager of a publishing house in Hamburg. You talk to her secretary.

Sekretärin	Guten Tag, kann ich Ihnen helfen?
Sie	*Say who you are. Say you are the representative of the Johnson Company in London. Say you are a publishing house. Ask whether Frau Schmidt is in.*
Sekretärin	Frau Schmidt ist in Berlin, aber sie ist morgen wahrscheinlich zurück. In welchem Hotel wohnen Sie?
Sie	*Say you are in Hotel Adler. You are in room 20.*
Sekretärin	Hotel Adler Zimmer Nummer 20. Sehr gut. Und die Telefonnummer?
Sie	(*Writing it down.*) *Here is the telephone number. Thank you.*
Sekretärin	Nichts zu danken. Auf Wiedersehen.
Sie	*Goodbye*

aber *but*	**Ich wohne im Hotel ...** *I am staying in Hotel ...*
wahrscheinlich *probably*	**das Zimmer (-)** *room*
sie ist morgen zurück *she is back tomorrow*	**und die Telefonnummer (-)?** *and the telephone number?*
In welchem Hotel wohnen Sie? *In which hotel are you staying?*	**nichts zu danken** *not at all*
	Auf Wiedersehen *Goodbye*

5   Complete the following exchanges with an appropriate phrase from the box.

a)   Ich bin Helmut Burg.

....

b)   Guten Tag, wie geht es Ihnen?

....

1   Es freut mich Sie kennen-
      zulernen.
2   Nein, ich bin Michael Laus.
3   Nein, ich bin Verkaufs-
      leiterin.
4   Gut danke, und Ihnen?
5   Ja, sie ist im Büro.

c)   Ist Frau Kessel da?

....

d)   Sind Sie Peter Kranz?

....

e)   Sind Sie Sekretärin?

....

TEIL B

The following letter extract was sent by Sieg Metall GmbH to a local businessman in Essen announcing the arrival of a new representative for the Ruhrgebiet, an industrial area in NW Germany.

SIEG METALL GmbH
KRAUSSTRASSE 30
4400 DUSSELDORF
TELEFON (0201) 96 32 13
TELEX 45 72 75

zu Händen
Herrn Schmidt
Einkaufsleiter
Brunnenstr. 6
4300 Essen 1

Ihr Zeichen: HPS. 21   unser Zeichen: DW/21/6   den 6. Mai 1991

Betreff: neuer Vertreter

Sehr geehrte Herren,

Es freut mich Ihnen mitzuteilen, daß unser Vertreter, Herr Kohl, aus Stuttgart
am 15 Mai ankommt.

Herr Kohl arbeitet für unsere Firma im Süden und besucht alle unsere
Kunden jeden Monat.

mit freundlichen Grüßen.

Wolfgang Sieg

Wolfgang Sieg
Betriebsleiter

---

zu Händen *for the attention of*	**ankommen** *arrive*
der Einkaufsleiter (-) *buying*	**arbeiten** *to work*
manager	**im Süden** *in the South*
unser/Ihr Zeichen *our/your*	(Also note **im Norden**, **im**
reference	**Westen** and **im Osten**)
neu *new*	**besuchen** *to visit*
Es freut mich Ihnen	**alle** *all*
mitzuteilen, daß *I am*	**der Kunde (-n)** *the customer*
pleased to advise	**jeden Monat** *every month*
you that	

Erklärungen

1 Company letterheads generally appear at the top centre or top right
of the letter. GmbH is the equivalent of a limited company and is the
most usual legal form. A German PLC is indicated by the initials **AG**
and partnerships by **OHG** or **KG** (limited partnership).

2 The date normally appears on the right beneath the sender's address and is often preceded by **den**. The number is followed by a full stop, for example **11. Januar.**

3 The recipient's name and address is written on the left-hand side. Note the addition of an **-n** to **Herr**, indicating 'to Mr'.

4 **Betreff** is the equivalent of re. and indicates the general content of the letter. It is normally underlined. There is, however a general trend now to omit the word **Betreff**.

5 The greeting used depends on the recipient, i.e. **Sehr geehrte Frau Braun**, or where no reference name is available, simply **Sehr geehrte Herren** or **Sehr geehrte Damen und Herren**.

6 The closing greeting – **mit freundlichen Grüßen** – covers both *Yours sincerely* and *Yours faithfully* and is the most frequent formula, often abbreviated to **mfg** on telexes.

7 As in English the sender's position in the firm goes below the name.

Grammatik

More about the present tense

Note that where the stem, for example the **arbeit-** part of **arbeiten** or the **find-** part of **finden,** of a verb ends in **t** or **d**, an **e** is added in the second and third person singular to enable the ending to be pronounced, for example:

arbeiten (*to work*) **finden** (*to find*)	**du arbeitest** *you are working* **du findest** *you find*	**er arbeitet** *he is working* **er findet** *he finds*

Übungen

1 The following dates represent an exchange of correspondence with your new German partners throughout the year. Write them as you would in a German letter.

a) 1st January 1992
b) 2nd March 1993
c) 3rd June 1994
d) 15th September 1995
e) 20th November 1996
f) 31st December 1997

Note: See Appendix 1 for a list of the months of the year in German.

2 Translate the following expressions which you might use in your correspondence.

   a) Dear Sirs
   b) Dear Mrs Braun
   c) I am pleased to advise you that
   d) Yours sincerely

3 You are introducing yourself and your company to a visitor. Insert the correct form of the verb in brackets in the sentences below.

   a) Ich (verkaufen) Metallprodukte.
   b) Wir (vertreten) Schmidt GmbH aus Düsseldorf.
   c) Unser Betriebsleiter (arbeiten) in einem Büro in Hamburg.
   d) Er (besuchen) die Firma jede Woche.
   e) Die Verkaufsleiterin (kommen) morgen.
   f) (Nehmen) Sie Milch in Ihrem Kaffee?

| **verkaufen** *to sell* | **jede Woche** *every week* |
| **vertreten** *to represent* | **morgen** *tomorrow* |

---

4 You are about to telephone your new German suppliers and are preparing a few notes in German for yourself as a prompt. You will find the new vocabulary in the box below the exercise.

I represent Smiths Ltd.
Our company is in the North.
We sell spare parts.
Your representative is coming tomorrow.
Our products are very good quality.
We visit our customers every week.

| **das Ersatzteil (-e)** *the spare part* | **gute Qualität** *good quality* |
| **das Produkt (-e)** *the product* | |

2

DESCRIBING A PLACE

TEIL A

Hamburg

Read this description of Hamburg, one of the main industrial centres in the Federal Republic.

Die Freie und Hansestadt Hamburg hat 1.5 Millionen Einwohner und liegt an der Elbe, etwa 120 Kilometer von der Nordsee. Hamburg ist ein wichtiger deutscher Hafen.

Es gibt in Hamburg viel Industrie, darunter Werften, Raffinerien, Verlage, die Presse, Chemikalien und Verbrauchsgüter.

Hamburg hat gute Verbindungen mit anderen Industriezentren Deutschlands, zum Beispiel Berlin, Frankfurt, Hannover, Düsseldorf und mit München in Süddeutschland. Die Deutsche Bundesbahn bringt Passagiere und Fracht; Passagiere fliegen auch mit Lufthansa nach Hamburg; das Autobahnnetz bringt Autos und Lieferwagen rund um die Uhr. Schiffe aus aller Welt bringen hauptsächlich Güter (aber auch Passagiere) in die Bundesrepublik.

Hamburg ist ein Stadtstaat, das heißt, sie ist gleichzeitig ein Bundesland.

der Einwohner (-) *inhabitant*	**das Zentrum (-en**
liegt an der Elbe *lies on the*	i.e. **die Zentren)** *centre*
river Elbe	**zum Beispiel** *for example*
etwa *about, approximately*	**die Deutsche**
wichtig *important*	**Bundesbahn** *German railways*
der Hafen (¨) *port*	**fliegen** *to fly*
es gibt *there is/there are*	**die Fracht** *freight*
viel *much, a lot*	**das Netz (-e)** *network*
darunter *among/of which*	**der Lieferwagen (-)** *delivery lorry*
der Werft (-en) *wharf, clock*	**rund um die Uhr** *round the clock*
der Verlag (-e) *publishing house*	**die Welt** *the world*
Chemikalien (plural only)	**hauptsächlich** *mainly*
chemicals	**in die Bundesrepublik** *to the*
das Verbrauchsgut	*Federal Republic*
(usu. plural ¨**er**)	**das heißt** *that is, i.e.*
consumer goods	**gleichzeitig** *simultaneously*
die Verbindung (-en)	
connection, communication	

--------------- **Erklärungen** ---------------

 1 **Die Freie und Hansestadt Hamburg.** Formerly a member of the medieval Hanse League of trading cities, Hamburg is still proud to refer to itself as the *Free and Hanseatic City*.

2 **Das Bundesland.** Germany comprises sixteen states called **Bundesländer**, which are broadly comparable in size to the regions of Britain. They also have a parliament which enjoys significantly greater decentralised powers than, say, County Councils in Britain. Hamburg and Bremen are both **Länder** as well as cities.

3 **Es gibt**, meaning *there is* or *there are* is a useful phrase for describing places and situations, for example: **Es gibt** ein Hotel in der Nähe.

--------------- **Dialog** ---------------

James Bent of Bent Aluminium Extrusions is considering establishing a manufacturing plant in Hamburg. He is visiting his agent, Andreas Peters to consider possible locations.

Bent	Also, Herr Peters, wo liegt das Industriegebiet genau?
Peters	Tja, es liegt in der Vorstadt im Westen. Die Bahn- und Straßenverbindungen sind sehr gut. Es gibt auch eine gute Busverbindung vom Busbahnhof. Und der Flughafen ist nur zwanzig Kilometer von dort.
Bent	Gibt es auch Hotels in der Nähe, Herr Peters?
Peters	Doch, auch ein paar Banken. Man kann dort auch Geld wechseln. Hamburg ist nämlich eine internationale Stadt! Aber es gibt kein Restaurant. Man fährt zwei Kilometer zu einem Restaurant. Die Hotels haben auch Konferenzräume.
Bent	Ausgezeichnet, Herr Peters! Also, was denken Sie?
Peters	Ja, ich glaube der Industriepark West ist richtig für uns.

---

wo   *where*
das Industriegebiet(-e)
  industrial zone
genau   *exactly*
die Vorstadt   *suburbs*
die Bahn   *railway*
die Verbindung (-en)
  communications
sehr gut   *very good*
der Busbahnhof(¨-e)   *bus station*
der Flughafen(-¨)   *airport*
nur   *only*
von dort   *from there*

auch   *also, too*
in der Nähe   *near*
ein paar   *a few*
man kann Geld
  wechseln   *one/you can exchange money*
nämlich   *so*
fahren   *travel, go, drive*
der Konferenzraum(-¨e)
  conference suite
ausgezeichnet   *excellent*
denken   *to think*
glauben   *to think, believe*
richtig   *right, correct*

Erklärungen

1   *Also*, *well* is often used at the beginning of a statement. **Tja**, *well* is actually a variation of **ja**.

2   Compound nouns like **Bahn- und Straßenverbindungen** are common. A characteristic of German is that it 'sticks words together' to form longer ones. You will constantly meet this. This example is of the reverse process: the element **Verbindung** (*connection*) belongs to both **Bahn** (*rail*) and **Straßen** (*roads*), and need only appear once. The hyphen shows that is has been omitted. A similar construction is used in the equivalent English *rail and road links*.

3 **Doch** is a strong form of *yes*, contradicting an (implied) negative.

4 **Eine gute Busverbindung.** You may have noticed that **ein, der, die** and **das** (articles) and adjectives like **gut** take endings to agree with the nouns with which they are associated. See **Grammatik** Lektion 6, note 2.

5 **Was denken Sie?** (or **Was meinen Sie?**) is used to ask someone's opinion. To give that opinion, **Ich glaube ...** is generally used.

——————— Grammatik ———————

♂ 1 *The verb* haben *(irregular)*

We have already met **sein** (*to be*). **Haben** (*to have*) is also irregular and takes these forms:

ich	habe	wir	haben
du	hast	ihr	habt
Sie	haben	Sie	haben
er, sie, es	hat	sie	haben

2 *Weak and strong verbs*

Almost all verbs in German belong to one of these categories; in addition a small number (e.g. **sein** and **haben**) are also irregular. Strong verbs have a sound change in the past tenses (c.f. English *sink, sank, sunk*), and also sometimes in the present tense; weak verbs do not.

Some strong verbs take an umlaut (¨) in their present tense **du** and **er, sie, es** forms. **Fahren** (*to travel*) is one of them.

Other verbs actually change the stem vowel in the **du** and **er, sie, es** forms. In all the following example, there is a vowel change in the **du** and **er, sie, es** forms. These are worth remembering:

	to travel	to take	to help	to represent	to give
ich	fahre	nehme	helfe	vertrete	gebe
du	fährst	nimmst	hilfst	vertrittst	gibst
Sie	fahren	nehmen	helfen	vertreten	geben
er, sie, es	fährt	nimmt	hilft	vertritt	gibt
wir	fahren	nehmen	helfen	vertreten	geben
ihr	fahrt	nehmt	helft	vertretet	gebt
Sie	fahren	nehmen	helfen	vertreten	geben
sie	fahren	nehmen	helfen	vertreten	geben

Note: All these strong verbs have in common a *sound* change in the **du** and **er, sie, es** forms.

An English/German dictionary will list all the strong verbs for your reference and the verb table in Appendix 2 contains the most common strong and irregular verbs.

3 Plurals

The plural of nouns in German is not uniform, and whilst there are patterns, the best thing is to learn the plural of any noun when you learn the noun itself. The various possibilities are:

No change (-)	das Mädchen	— die Mädchen
Add **e** (**-e**)	der Tisch	— die Tisch**e**
Add an umlaut and **e** (**-¨e**)	der Sack	— die S**ä**cke
Add **en** (**-en**)	die Funktion	— die Funktion**en**
Add **er** (**-er**)	das Feld	— die Feld**er**
Add an umlaut and **er** (**-¨er**)	der Mann	— die M**ä**nn**er**
Add **s** (**-s**)	das Büro	— die Büro**s**

4 Negatives

When you are making a negative, you will need one of two words. **Nicht** means *not*, and **kein** means *not a* or *no*. In some contexts it can be thought of as a negative of **ein**. It is very unusual to hear **nicht ein** meaning *not a*. Examples of negative sentences are:

Er trinkt **kein** Bier.	*He drinks no beer; he doesn't drink beer.*
Er geht **nicht**.	*He's not going.*
Ich fahre **nicht** nach Hamburg.	*I am not going to Hamburg.*
Es gibt aber **kein** Restaurant.	*But there is no restaurant.*

5 Agreement

In Lektion 1 we saw that **der, die, das** (the article) indicates the gender of a noun. We also saw that **ein** and **mein, dein,** etc. (the possessive adjectives) take **-e** when they precede a feminine noun, for example **meine Mutter**.

The articles also indicate the case of that noun. There are four cases in German, and we shall consider two of them here: the subject (also called the nominative case) and the object (also called the accusative case). We have dealt with the nominative case (subject) under number 4 above. The object of a sentence is the person or thing on which an action is carried out. For example:

Er trinkt **ein Bier.** *He drinks **a beer.***

So **ein** and **der, die, das** vary depending on their function in the sentence, or case of the noun with which they are associated.

	Masc	**Fem**	**Neut**
Nom	ein Mann	eine Frau	ein Kind
	der Mann	die Frau	das Kind
Acc	ein**en** Mann	eine Frau	ein Kind
	d**en** Mann	die Frau	das Kind

Note: The only new thing here is that **-en** is added in the masculine accusative of **ein**, **mein**, etc., and that **der** changes to **den** in the masculine accusative.

Nominative	**Accusative**
Ein Mann kommt	Hamburg hat **einen** Hafen
Meine Frau ist dort	Der Industriepark hat **eine** Bank
Der Direktor kommt	Die Firma hat **einen** Direktor
Der Flughafen ist groß	Es gibt **einen** Flughafen in der Nähe

Note: **Es gibt** takes the accusative case – i.e., the following noun (**Flughafen** above) is the object of the sentence.

Übungen

1 Read this passage about Hamburg and then, following the model,

write a similar text about Munich (**München**) using the notes provided.

Hamburg ist in Norddeutschland, ungefähr 350 Kilometer von Bonn entfernt. Die Stadt ist etwa so groß wie München mit ungefähr 1.5 Millionen Einwohnern. Hamburg liegt an der Elbe und ist ein großes Industriezentrum. Die wichtigsten Industrien dort sind Werften, Raffinerien und Verbrauchsgüter. Hamburg hat gute Flug-, Bahn- und Straßenverbindungen mit anderen deutschen Städten.

Notes on Munich:

Süddeutschland/Hauptstadt von Bayern/400 Kilometer/mit 1.2 Millionen Einwohnern/die Isar (*the river Isar*)/Maschinenbau, Elektrotechnik und Touristik/gute ... Verbindungen.../und Südeuropa.

die **Hauptstadt** *capital city*	**ungefähr** *about*
der **Maschinenbau** engineering	**Bayern** *Bavaria*

2 Complete the following dialogue about Munich. Any new words you need are in the box below the dialogue.

A Wo liegt München?
B
A In welchem Bundesland liegt München?
B
A Wieviele Kilometer ist München von Hamburg?
B
A Wieviele Einwohner hat München?
B
A Welche wichtigen Industrien hat München?

welch *which*	**wieviel** *how many*

3 Here are some questions about Industriepark West. Can you formulate the answers?

Q Wo liegt der Industriepark West?
A
Q In welcher Richtung?
A

Q Wie sind die Verkehrsverbindungen?
A
Q Welche Buslinie fährt von der Stadtmitte zum Industrie-
gebiet?
A
Q Wie weit ist das Industriegebiet vom Flughafen?
A
Q Gibt es ein Restaurant dort?
A
Q Gibt es auch eine Bank dort?
A
Q Kann man dort Geld wechseln?
A

4 Complete this information about a hotel in Hamburg, filling in the
correct form of **der, die, das, ein, eine** or **einen.**

D.. Hotel Nordstern ist in Hamburg. Es ist ein.. Hotel mit vier
Etagen und 100 Zimmern. Es hat ein.. Konferenzraum fur 150
Gäste. Ein.. Bar, ein.. Restaurant, und ein.. Garderobe sind hinter
dem Empfang. Es gibt ein.. Flughafen und ein.. Busbahnhof in der
Nähe. Es gibt also ein.. gute Busverbindung zur Stadt und gute
Flugverbindungen in alle Welt!

die Etage *floor*		**hinter** *behind*	
die Garderobe *cloakroom*		**der Empfang** *reception*	

5 James Bent's director is talking with the company's agent while
waiting for Mr Bent to arrive for a meeting. Replace the infinitives
with the correct form of the present tense:

D Was (denken) Sie von dem Industriepark West?
A Ich (glauben), er ist richtig fur uns.
D Herr Bent (kommen) oft nach Hamburg.
A Er (fahren) morgen nach England zurück.
D (Trinken) Sie ein Bier?
A Die Sekretärin (bringen) uns Kaffee.
D (Haben) Sie einen Plan von Hamburg?
A Ich (verstehen) nur wenig Deutsch.

6 You have arrived at your hotel to be met by your German agent.
Answer all his questions in the negative, beginning each answer
with **Nein,..**, for example, **Nein, ich trinke keine Milch; Nein,**

ich gehe nicht in die Stadt.

Q   Haben sie einen Koffer?

A

Q   Fahren Sie nach München?

A

Q   Gibt es hier ein Restaurant?

A

Q   Hat das Hotel einen Fitneßraum?

A

Q   Hat das Zimmer ein Radio?

A

---

der Koffer *suitcase*	**morgen** *tomorrow*	

TEIL B

—— Business Correspondence ——

Read this circular sent by the manager of the Hotel Nordstern in Hamburg announcing the new conferencing facility in the hotel.

Sehr verehrter Nordstern-Gast!

Es freut uns Ihnen mitzuteilen, daß das Hotel Nordstern jetzt neue Konferenzräume mit Platz fur 150 Gäste hat.

Die Konferenzräume finden Sie gleich hinter dem Empfang. Unser Hotelleiter zeigt Ihnen gerne diese neue Einrichtung. Wir freuen uns auf Ihren Besuch.

Mit freundlichen Grüßen,

G. Bergmann

G. Bergmann.
Hoteldirektor.

Es freut uns Ihnen mitzuteilen, daß *We are pleased to inform you that*	**der Leiter(-)** *manager, leader*
	zeigen *to show*
Ihnen (Wie geht es Ihnen?) *(to) you (How are you?)*	**dies** *this*
	die Einrichtung(-en) *(here) facility*
jetzt *now*	**Wir freuen uns (auf)** *we look forward (to)*
der Gast(-¨e) *guest*	**der Besuch(-e)** *visit*
gleich *immediately*	

Erklärungen

1 **Sehr verehrter Nordstern-Gast!** The word **verehrter** in lieu of **geehrter** is frequently used in open letters of this kind.

2 **daß** ... (*that*), a linking word joining two part-sentences or clauses, sends the verb in the following clause to the end. For example:

Es freut uns, daß Sie morgen **kommen.**	*We are pleased that you are coming tomorrow.*
Ich glaube nicht, daß das Hotel einen Konferenzraum **hat.**	*I don't think that the hotel has a conference room.*

3 The example below illustrates the rule that the (active) verb always appears as the second idea in a main clause.

Die Konferenzräume finden Sie...	*You (will) find the conference suite...*

4 **Gern** literally means *gladly* and when added to a statement it frequently means *to like to* (Ich trinke **gern** Bier, *I like drinking beer;* Ich höre gern Musik, *I like listening to music*).

In the letter, the sense would better be rendered by *gladly* or *be pleased to.*

Grammatik

Prepositions

Prepositions are expressions of time, place or some other relationship and occur before nouns. Note the following prepositions which we have already met.

von *from, of*	**um** *around, at*	**in** *in, into*
mit *with*		**ins** *into, to the* (with neuter nouns)
nach *after, to*		**an** *at*
		hinter *behind*
		auf *on, to*

We come back to prepositions in Lektion 4.

——————— Übungen ———————

1 You and your managing director are staying at the Nordstern. You write out a translation of the open letter on page 27 to draw your M.D.'s attention to it.

2 Write the German for:
   a) Dear Herr Braun
   b) We are pleased to inform you that...
   c) We look forward to your visit.
   d) You will find the firm in Ludwigstraße, no.10.
   e) Yours faithfully/Yours sincerely.

3

DESCRIBING
AN ORGANISATION

TEIL A

1 Read the following description of Bayer, a major chemical company in Germany:

Bayer ist eine große Chemiefirma in Deutschland. Sie ist ungefähr 130 Jahre alt und damit so alt wie Hoechst und älter als BASF. Ihr Hauptsitz liegt in Leverkusen aber sie hat Zweigstellen in der ganzen Welt, die meisten befinden sich in Europa. Heutzutage beschäftigt die Firma mehr als 170.000 Mitarbeiter und hat die höchste Beschäftigtenzahl von allen chemischen Firmen in Deutschland. Im Jahr verdient die Firma etwa DM 45.000 Millionen, d.h. ihr Umsatz ist niedriger als bei BASF und Hoechst, aber höher als bei ICI. Sie exportiert viele Waren in alle Länder der Welt. Die Firma spezialisiert sich hauptsächlich auf Arzneimittel und sie produziert etwa 600 Medikamente. Das Gesamtsortiment umfaßt rund 10.000 Produkte. Der Stand der Technologie in der chemischen Industrie in der Bundesrepublik wird immer höher und die Zukunft ist rosig.

das Jahr (-e) *year*	**der Umsatz (-¨e)** *turnover*
damit *therefore*	**niedrig** *low*
so alt wie *as old as*	**die Ware (-n)** *good(s)*
(**so ... wie** *as ... as*)	**in alle Länder der Welt** *to countries*
der Hauptsitz (-e) *head office*	*all over the world*
liegen *to lie, be situated*	**sich spezialisieren (auf)** *specialise*
die Zweigstelle (-n) *branch*	(*in*)
in der ganzen Welt *throughout the*	**hauptsächlich** *primarily*
(*whole) world*	**das Arzneimittel (-)** *medicine, drug*

die meisten *most, the majority*	**das Gesamtsortiment (-e)** *total*
sich befinden *to be situated*	*range of products*
beschäftigen *to employ*	**umfassen** *to include*
der Mitarbeiter (-) *employee,*	**rund** *around, approximately*
colleague	**der Stand der Technologie** *state of*
hoch *high*	*the art*
die Beschäftigtenzahl (-en)	**werden** *to become*
number of employees	**die Zukunft** *the future*
verdienen *to earn*	**rosig** *rosy*

———— Erklärungen ————

1 Generally, **d.h.** is used as an abbreviation for **das heißt** (in English *that means*) and is the equivalent of *i.e.*

2 German numbers exceeding one thousand use a full stop rather than a comma to indicate this, e.g. 17.000 (see the numbers section in Appendix 1). Conversely a decimal point is indicated by a comma, e.g. 2,5%.

———— Dialog ————

Herr Eisenhardt, managing director of Eisenwerke GmbH, a multi-national company with its head office in Duisburg, is interviewed by a journalist who is writing a report about the company.

Journalist	Guten Tag, Herr Eisenhardt.
Herr Eisenhardt	Guten Tag.
Journalist	Welche Rolle spielt Eisenwerke GmbH im internationalen Handel? Und wie groß ist die Firma im Vergleich zu anderen multinationalen Betrieben?
Herr Eisenhardt	Heutzutage erweitert sich die Firma überall in der Welt. Wir produzieren jetzt 1.000 Tonnen Blech pro Tag und haben Zweigstellen in vielen Ländern mit fast 50.000 Mitarbeitern aus aller Welt. Alle Abteilungsleiter sprechen

mindestens zwei Sprachen. Wir haben einen Vorsprung in der Technologie und sind also erfolgreich auf dem Weltmarkt. Wir handeln mit vielen Geschäftspartnern in Europa und wir freuen uns auf den europäischen Binnenmarkt.

ein Rolle (-n) spielen *to play a role*	**die Sprache (-n)** *language*
der Vergleich (-e) *comparison*	**einen Vorsprung haben** *to have an advantage, be ahead*
andere *other*	**erfolgreich** *successful*
der Betrieb (-e) *company*	**der Weltmarkt (-¨e)** *the world market*
sich erweitern *to expand*	**handeln** *to deal with*
überall in der Welt *all over the world*	**der Geschäftspartner (-)** *the business partner*
produzieren *to produce*	**sich freuen (auf)** *to look forward (to)*
das Blech (-e) *sheet metal*	
pro Tag *per day*	**der europäische**
der Abteilungsleiter (-) *department manager*	**Binnenmarkt** *the European single market*
sprechen *to speak*	
mindestens *at least*	

Erklärungen

1 Some plurals have added a final **-n**. This occurs when the plural noun is in the dative case which is discussed in Lektion 4. Examples are:

mit 50.000 Mitarbeiter**n**   *with 50 000 employees*
in vielen Länder**n**   *in many countries*

Grammatik

1 *Comparative and superlative*

When adjectives (e.g. *large/small* etc) are used in comparison (*larger/smaller*) or as a superlative (*largest/smallest*) they add the endings **er** and **st** plus the corresponding adjective ending (see Lektion 6) respectively. For example:

niedrig *low* → niedrig**er** *lower* → der/die/das niedrig**ste**
  the lowest

klein   *small* → klein**er**   *smaller* → der/die/das klein**ste**   *the smallest*

Note:

a)   There is no equivalent of the English **more** *interesting* for longer nouns, for example:

interessant → interessant**er** → der/die/das interessant**este**

Note also the additional **e** in **interessanteste** which enables adjectives ending in **t** or **d** to be pronounced.

b)   Some short adjectives add an Umlaut, for example:

alt   *old* → älter   *older* → der/die/das älteste   *the oldest*
groß   *big* → größer   *bigger* → der/die/das größte   *the biggest*

c)   Some common adjectives are totally irregular, for example:

hoch   *high* → höher   *higher* → der/die/das höchste   *the highest*
gut   *good* → besser   *better* → der/die/das beste   *the best*
viel   *much/many* → mehr   *more* → die meisten   *the most*

d)   The comparative is used with **als** to show dissimilarity:

Unser Umsatz ist niedriger **als** bei Siemens.	*Our turnover is lower than at Siemens.*
Unsere Firma ist kleiner **als** Daimler-Benz.	*Our company is older than Daimler Benz.*

e)   The use of **immer** (*always*) plus the comparative renders the repetition of a comparative in English, for example:

Die Produktion bei Siemens wird **immer höher.**   *Production at Siemens is getting higher and higher.*

2 *Reflexive verbs* (I dress myself, etc.)

Present tense

sich waschen *to wash oneself*	
ich wasche mich	*I wash myself*
du wäschst dich	*you wash yourself*
Sie waschen sich	*you wash yourself*
er/sie/es wäscht sich	*he/she/it washes him-/her-/itself*
wir waschen uns	*we wash ourselves*
ihr wascht euch	*you wash yourselves*
Sie waschen sich	*you wash yourselves*
sie waschen sich	*they wash themselves*

Note: Reflexive verbs are much more common in German and frequently translate non-reflexive verbs in English, as in the following useful phrases:

Unsere Firma **spezialisiert sich** auf chemische Waren.	*Our company specialises in chemical goods.*
Ich möchte **mich** mit Herrn Braun **verabreden.**	*I would like an appointment with Mr Brown.*
Setzen Sie **sich** bitte!	*Have a seat!*
Wir **interessieren uns** für Qualitätswaren.	*We are interested in quality goods.*

3 Interrogative or question form

(a) Word order

To ask a question in German, simply invert the subject and the verb of the sentence. The subject is in bold in the following examples:

Der Umsatz ist sehr hoch.	*The turnover is very high.*
Ist **der Umsatz** sehr hoch?	*Is the turnover very high?*
Der Hauptsitz liegt in Bonn.	*The head office is in Bonn.*
Liegt **der Hauptsitz** in Bonn?	*Is the head office in Bonn?*
Er fährt nach Hamburg.	*He is going to Hamburg.*
Fährt **er** nach Hamburg?	*Is he going to Hamburg?*

(b) Question words

The most common question words are:

wo?	*where?*	warum?	*why?*
wer?	*who?*	wieviel?	*how much?*
was?	*what?*	wieviele?	*how many?*
wie?	*how?*	was für ein?	*what sort of?*
wann?	*when?*		

The same word order is used after question words as in other questions and is similar to English, thus:

Wer sind Sie?	*Who are you?*
Was möchten Sie trinken?	*What would you like to drink?*
Wie produzieren Sie Ihre Maschinen?	*How do you produce your machines?*
Wie viele Mitarbeiter haben Sie?	*How many employees do you have?*

Was für eine Firma ist Siemens? *What sort of company is Siemens?*

Note: The same question word order applies to reflexive verbs where the subject is a pronoun as you can see in the example below:

Interessieren Sie sich für *Are you interested in our drilling machines?*
unsere Bohrmaschinen?

Note the difference, however, if the subject is a noun:

Wo befindet sich Ihr Büro? *Where is your office?*

As you can see, the reflexive pronoun **sich** comes before the subject **Ihr Büro**.

─────────── Übungen ───────────

1 Read through the passage about Bayer AG again and then without looking at the text, try to complete the missing words in this paragraph:

Bayer ist eine ... Chemie ... in Deutschland. Ihr Hauptsitz ... in Leverkusen aber sie hat ... in der ganzen ... Die meisten ... sich in Europa. Heutzutage ... die Firma mehr als 170.000 ... Im Jahr ... die Firma etwa DM 45.000 Millionen. Das Gesamt ... umfaßt rund 10.000 Produkte.

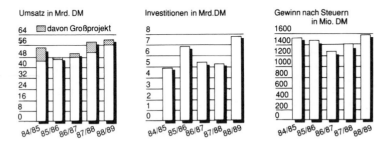

2 Read this description of Siemens AG, a company which manufactures electronic and electrical goods (**elektronische und elektrotechnische Produkte**).

Die Siemens AG. ist in der elektronischen und elektrotechnischen

Branchen tätig und produziert elektronische und elektrotechnische Produkte. Der Hauptsitz liegt in München. Sie ist eine sehr große Firma mit ungefähr 370.000 Mitarbeitern und hat einen hohen Umsatz von mehr als 60.000 Millionen DM. Sie spezialisiert sich auf Büromaschinen. Das Gesamtsortiment umfaßt auch Bordrechner für Autos und Mikrochips. Der wichtigste Markt für die Siemens AG ist Europa.

die elektrotechnische Branche *electronic engineering sector* **tätig sein** *to be active/operate in an area*	**die Büromaschinen** *office machinery/equipment* **der Bordrechner** *computerised dashboard*

Now write a similar description of Krupp GmbH, a company which manufactures machines and plant (**Maschinen und Anlagen**). Use this information:

Branche	Maschinenbau, Anlagenbau, Stahl (eg. die Stahlbranche)
Hauptsitz	Essen
Mitarbeiter	64.000
Umsatz	DM 20.000 Millionen
Sortiment	Kunststoffmaschinen, Werkzeuge, Magnete, Lokomotive, petrochemische Anlagen und Zement- und Förderanlagen
Markt	West Europa

der Maschinenbau *mechanical engineering* **der Anlagenbau** *plant making* **der Handel** *trade* **die Kunststoffmaschine(-n)** *plastics machinery*	**das Werkzeug (-e)** *tool* **die Zementanlage(-n)** *cement plant* **die Förderanlage (-n)** *conveyor*

3   You are discussing German industry with a colleague. Form the corresponding comparatives and superlatives using the adjectives in brackets:

Sie   Die Daimler Benz AG ist die (groß) Firma in der BRD.

Kollege	Ja, die Umsätze bei Autoproduzenten sind (hoch) als bei den chemischen Firmen.
Sie	Die chemischen Firmen sind aber (erfolgreich) als die elektrotechnische Branche.
Kollege	Die Beschäftigtenzahlen sind aber (niedrig) als in der Elektrotechnik.
Sie	Ja, und die Arbeitslosigkeit wird immer (schlecht).

die Arbeitslosigkeit	unemployment

4   You are the representative of an engineering company which has its main office in Newcastle. While attending a business conference in Germany you discuss your company with a German colleague (**ein Kollege/eine Kollegin**). Fill in your part of the conversation:

Kollege	In welcher Branche arbeiten Sie?
Sie	*Say you work for Carter Machines Ltd in the mechanical engineering sector in England.*
Kollege	Wie groß ist die Firma?
Sie	*Say it is the largest mechanical engineering company in England and has the highest turnover.*
Kollege	Wo liegt der Hauptsitz?
Sie	*Say it is in London but that you have branches in many countries.*
Kollege	Wie viele Mitarbeiter gibt es in London?
Sie	*Say there are 3000 employees in London.*
Kollege	Sind die meisten Engländer?
Sie	*Say yes, the majority are English, but there are many employees from all over the world.*
Kollege	Welche Sprachen sprechen Sie?
Sie	*Say you speak French and German.*
Kollege	Ich spreche nur etwas Spanisch. Ihr Deutsch ist ausgezeichnet!
Sie	*Say thank you!*

Vielen Dank/Danke schön	thank you

5   You are making a visiting journalist feel at home. Complete the sentences using the words in the brackets, taking care with the word order in the questions:

Sie	Möchten Sie (sich setzen)?
Journalist	Ja, danke! Ich (sich informieren) über Ihre Firma.
Sie	Sie (sich interessieren) für unsere Produkte?
Journalist	Ja, ich (sich freuen) auf die Besichtigung.
Sie	Wir (sich verabreden) am Montag, sagen wir um 9 Uhr?
Journalist	Ja, in Ordnung. Wo (sich befinden) Ihr Büro?
Sie	Sie (sich informieren) am besten beim Portier.

6 You want to find out some details about a competitive firm. Form the questions using the question word in the brackets:

   a) Die Firma ist groß (wie).
   b) Der Hauptsitz liegt in England (wo).
   c) Die Firma erweitert sich (wann).
   d) Der Betriebsleiter ist ein Engländer (wer).
   e) Die Firma hat viele Mitarbeiter (wieviele).
   f) Die Firma produziert Elektrogeräte (was).

TEIL B

Read these letters requesting and giving commercial references about a company.

1 **Die Anfrage** *The enquiry*

Sehr geehrte Damen und Herren,
Wir haben Ihren Namen als Referenz für die Firma 'Schmidt AG' und möchten gerne einige Informationen. Wir arbeiten bald mit dieser Firma und interessieren uns besonders für ihre finanzielle Lage, den Ruf von ihren Produkten und ihre Zuverlässigkeit. Wir wären Ihnen sehr dankbar, wenn Sie uns diese Auskunft schicken könnten.

Alle Einzelheiten bleiben natürlich vertraulich.

Vielen Dank im voraus

Mit freundlichen Grüßen

der Name (-n) *name*	**wenn Sie uns ... schicken**
einige *some*	**könnten** *if you could send*
arbeiten *to work*	*us ...*
bald *soon*	**die Auskunft (-¨e)**
die Lage (-n) *situation*	*information*
der Ruf (-e) *reputation*	**dies** *this*
von *of*	**die Einzelheit (-en)** *detail*
die Zuverlässigkeit *the*	**bleiben** *to stay, remain*
reliability	**vertraulich** *confidential*
Wir wären Ihnen sehr dankbar	**Vielen Dank im voraus** *many*
we should be very grateful	*thanks in anticipation*

2 Eine positive Referenz *A positive reference*

Sehr geehrte Damen und Herren,
wir danken Ihnen für Ihre Anfrage vom 12. Juli über die Firma Schmidt AG.
Es freut uns Ihnen mitzuteilen, daß ihre finanzielle Lage sehr günstig ist
und daß die Produkte einen sehr guten Ruf haben. Unserer Meinung nach
bringt eine Zusammenarbeit kein Risiko.

Mit freundlichen Grüßen

Wir danken Ihnen für *We thank*	**bringen** *to bring*
you for	**die Zusammenarbeit**
die Anfrage (-n) *enquiry*	*cooperation, working together*
günstig *favourable*	**das Risiko (-en)** *risk*
Unserer Meinung nach *In our*	
opinion	

3 Eine negative Referenz *A negative reference*

Sehr geehrte Damen und Herren,
Zu unserem Bedauern müssen wir Ihnen mitteilen, daß die finanzielle Lage
von dieser Firma ziemlich schlecht ist und daß sie schon mehrere
Schulden hat. Unserer Meinung nach ist eine Zusammenarbeit nicht
ratsam.

Mit freundlichen Grüßen

Zu unserem Bedauern *To our*	**schlecht** *bad*
regret	**mehrere** *several*
müssen *to have to*	**die Schuld (-en)** *debt*
ziemlich *rather*	**ratsam** *advisable*

Übungen

1 A German supplier, Herr Wolff, telephones you to find out about one of your clients. Fill in your replies:

Herr Wolff	Haben Sie eine gute Geschäftsverbindung mit Smith Books Ltd?
Sie	*Say yes, you have a very good business relationship.*
Herr Wolff	Haben sie einen guten Ruf?
Sie	*Say yes, they are very reliable.*
Herr Wolff	Und wie sind ihre Produkte?
Sie	*Say their products are of a high quality.*
Herr Wolff	Wie ist ihre finanzielle Lage?
Sie	*Say their financial situation is favourable.*
Herr Wolff	Bringt eine Zusammenarbeit ein Risiko?
Sie	*Say in your opinion cooperation does not involve any risk.*

---

die Geschäftsverbindung (-en)
business relationship

von guter Qualität *of a high quality*

---

2 You are asked to write a short letter in accordance with the following memo using the letters above as a guide:

Memo: we've received a letter from Bayer asking for references for Davies & Co., could you write and thank them for their enquiry (2nd June) tell them that in our opinion the company is very reliable and has a good reputation, and that their financial situation is favourable. Remind them this information is confidential.

4

DISCUSSING YOUR WORK

TEIL A

Dialog

Ingrid Kaufmann is being interviewed by a journalist, Werner Braun, about her job.

Braun Was sind Sie von Beruf?

IK Ich bin Diplom Kauffrau. Hier bei Firma Schmidt bin ich Abteilungsleiterin. Ich bin verantwortlich für den Einkauf und für die Disposition.

Braun Was ist Ihre Arbeit eigentlich?

IK Also das ist ganz unterschiedlich. Ich befasse mich mit der Einkaufsabteilung; das heißt, mit Beschaffung, Einplanung und Disposition. Wir brauchen alle Materialien rechtzeitig. Sonst haben wir Produktionsstopp. Das ist dann natürlich sehr teuer!

Braun Ah, der Verkauf ist also nicht Ihre Sache?

IK Nein, nicht direkt. Aber ich bin leitende Angestellte. Das heißt, ich spreche oft mit dem Verkaufsleiter, dem Personalleiter und dem Wirtschaftsprüfer. Wir besprechen dann ziemlich alle Aspekte unseres Betriebes.

Braun Fahren Sie oft zu Ihren Zulieferanten?

IK Ab und zu, ja. Das Reisen gefällt mir gut, aber ich führe auch ein normales Familienleben. Manchmal bin ich in Berlin, und am nächsten Tag in Paris! Aber ich bin selten in Großbritannien.

Braun Fur Sie ist gleitende Arbeitszeit nichts Neues!

IK Da haben Sie sicherlich recht! Hier in Hamburg beginne ich meine Arbeit um acht Uhr. Aber Feierabend ist kaum vor sieben Uhr abends.

Braun Aber es scheint mir, Ihre Arbeit gefällt Ihnen gut?!

IK Doch.

Braun Meine Güte, es ist schon acht Uhr. Sie sind bestimmt sehr müde.

IK Ja, ziemlich!...

Was sind Sie von Beruf? *What is your profession, job?*
Diplom Kaufmann/Kauffrau *qualified commercial executive*
die Abteilung(-en) *department*
die Leiterin(-nen) *manager* (female)
das heißt *that is, that means, i.e.*
verantwortlich *responsible*
der Einkauf *purchase*
die Einplanung *planning*
die Disposition *production control*
eigentlich *really, in fact*
unterschiedlich *various*
gehören (zu) *to belong to, to have to do with*
die Beschaffung *procurement*
teuer *expensive*
der Verkauf ist nicht Ihre Sache *sales is not your field*

leitende Angestellte (-n) *executive* (female)
der Wirtschaftsprüfer(-) *accountant*
besprechen *discuss*
ziemlich *rather, more or less*
der Betrieb(-e) *operation, factory*
der Zulieferant(-en) *supplier*
ab und zu *now and again*
manchmal *sometimes*
gleitende Arbeitszeit *flexitime*
der Feierabend *end of the working day*
kaum *hardly (ever)*
es scheint mir *it seems to me*
meine Güte *my goodness*
bestimmt *for sure, (you must be ...)*
ziemlich *rather*

Erklärungen

1 **Es gefällt mir** is one way of saying *I like* in relation to something specific:

Diese Musik **gefällt mir**.   *I like this music.*
Die Arbeit **gefällt mir**.   *I like the work.*

Grammatik

1 The Dative Case, or Indirect Object

This is the person or thing in a sentence which receives an action, for example:

He gave **her** *the flowers.*
She lent **him** *a book.*
They wrote **the firm** *a strong letter.*

The bold words are said to be in the dative case. In this function in German the word for *the* with the following noun changes as follows:

der → **dem**: Ich schreibe **dem** Chef einen Brief.	*I write the boss a letter.*
die → **der**: Er gibt **der** Einkaufsleiterin Blumen.	*He gives the buyer flowers.*
das → **dem**: Ich schenke **dem** Kind ein Teddybär.	*I give the child a teddybear.*

and:

ein → **einem**: Ich sage es **einem** Verkaufer.	*I tell a salesman.*
eine → **einer**: Sie gibt es **einer** Empfangsdame.	*She gives it to a receptionist.*

2 Dative prepositions

At the end of Chapter 2, we noted some prepositions. In this dialogue we meet some more:

bei	*with, at*	mit	*with*
seit	*since*	zu	*to*

These prepositions, and those in the first column on page 28 are always followed by the indirect object, or the dative case.
The full list is as follows:

aus (*out of*) bei mit nach seit	von zu außer (*except for*) gegenüber (*opposite*)

Ich arbeite bei **der** Firma. (fem.) *I work at the firm.*
Ich lerne Deutsch seit **einem** Jahr. (neuter) *I have been learning German for a year.*
Ich fahre mit dem Chef **zu der (zur)** Arbeit. (fem.) *I go to work with the boss.*
Er fährt mit der Sekretärin **zu dem (zum)** Büro. (neuter) *He drives to the office with the secretary.*

In the last two examples, **zu der** and **zu dem** have been abbreviated. This is usual. Other abbreviations are **am (an dem)**; **beim (bei dem)**. Check through the dialogue for examples.

3 Verbs taking the Dative

Finally, two common verbs are followed by the dative in German: **helfen** (*to help*), and **danken** (*to thank*).

Darf ich **Ihnen** helfen?   *May I help you?*
Wir danken **Ihnen** für Ihr   *We thank you for your letter*
  Schreiben vom ...   *of ...*

——————————— **Übungen** ———————————

1 Write five short sentences about Ingrid Kaufmann's areas of responsibility, business travel and work patterns, each beginning with '**Sie** (verb)...'.

2 Read the job description which follows. Then rewrite it as if Herr Boje were talking about his job to someone else (using the first person singular).

Herr Boje ist Kaufmann von Beruf und ist jetzt Verkaufsleiter bei der Firma Stemag in Hannover. Er fährt oft zu den Kunden überall in Europa. Manchmal vertritt er seine Firma auch in den USA. Er beginnt seine Arbeit in Hannover sehr früh morgens. Er hat Feierabend kaum vor sieben Uhr abends. Er hat oft Sitzungen mit anderen leitenden Angestellten.

3 Answer these questions about yourself:
  Either:
  a) Bei welcher Organisation arbeiten Sie?
  b) Was sind Sie von Beruf?
  c) Wo liegt Ihre Firma?
  d) Was ist Ihre Arbeit? (Ich bin verantwortlich für...)

  Or:
  a) Studieren Sie?
  b) Was studieren Sie?
  c) Wo studieren Sie?
  d) Was studieren Sie am liebsten?

4 Answer the following questions with **er/sie/es gefällt mir gut**:
  a) Wie gefällt Ihnen die Musik?
  b) Wie gefällt Ihnen dieses Bild?
  c) Wie gefällt Ihnen dieser Preis?
  d) Wie gefällt Ihnen das?

5 Complete the following passage by inserting **der, die** or **das** as necessary. Note that you will not only be using the nominative.

  Ich arbeite bei ... Firma Daube. Ich befasse mich mit ... Einkauf und mit ... Verkauf. Ich bin mit ... Arbeit sehr zufrieden. Ich komme öfters aus ... Büro. ... Betrieb ist nicht sehr groß, und ich bespreche jeden Tag mit ... Chef ziemlich alles. Aber ich weiß nicht sehr viel von ... Technik. Nach ... Arbeit gehen wir manchmal aus. Ich erzähle ... Chef von meiner Arbeit, und er erzählt mir von seiner.

TEIL B

Angelika Schneider, a secretary at Klöckner AG, wrote a letter to her friend describing her job. This is part of that letter ...

Liebe Beate,

Wir sehen uns schon seit langem nicht mehr. Ich schreibe Dir von dem Büro in meiner neuen Firma. Ich arbeite hier als Marketingassistentin. Wir sind in der Pharmazeutikabranche. Die Arbeit gefällt mir gut. Wie Du weißt, reise ich sehr gern, und ich besuche unsere Kunden ziemlich oft mit dem Chef. Nächste Woche fahre ich nach Madrid. Ich bin so gern in Spanien. Außerdem übersetze ich die Post aus Spanien und England, und telefoniere mit unseren Kunden dort. Ich mache die Post für meinen Chef und führe seinen Kalender. Die Arbeit ist sehr interessant und gefällt mir gut. Das Betriebsklima ist auch gut. Mittags gehen wir ins Restaurant. Es gibt auch gleitende Arbeitsstunden. Das ist sehr flexibel. Ich beginne die Arbeit um 7 Uhr in Sommer und um 8.30 Uhr im Winter. So habe ich in Sommer nachmittags frei...

reisen *to travel*	**ich führe seinen Kalender** *I*
oft *frequently*	*keep his diary*
außerdem *apart from that, in*	**das Betriebsklima** *working*
addition	*environment (climate)*
übersetzen *translate*	

Erklärungen

1 Note the following constructions which we have met with before and as revision, identify them in the above passages:

gern
es gefällt mir
es gibt

Übungen

1 Put the information contained in Angelika's letter in the third person, as though Beate were relating it to a mutual friend.

2 You have a new job and in a letter to a friend you include a paragraph describing what you do. Write as you might do in real life, using the following as a guideline:

Say you like your new work. It is interesting, the salary (**das Gehalt**) is good. Say you begin work at 8am and finish at 4.30pm. Your work is interesting; you translate the mail from Germany, you visit suppliers with your boss, you prepare the mail for the marketing director. The working environment is good, and you eat in the company restaurant at lunchtime.

3 Put the infinitives in the correct form of the present tense.

a) Wie Du (wissen), (reisen) ich sehr gern.

b) Wo (arbeiten) Du?
c) Ich (übersetzen) die Post.
d) Freitags (gehen) wir eins trinken.
e) Das (sein) sehr flexibel.
f) Ich (telefonieren) mit den Kunden.
g) Es (geben) gleitende Arbeitsstunden.

5

—— DESCRIBING —— A PRODUCT

Das Zeichen für Qualität!

Als einer der größten und bekanntesten Hersteller mit Niederlassungen und Vertretungen – weltweit– blieten wir eine umfang-reiche Produktpalette wie:

– Mikrofone

– Kopfhörer

– Elektroakustische Anlagen

– Beschallungs– systeme

– Personen – Führungsanlagen

für alle Einsatzbereiche.

Wenn Sie unser Programm kennenlernen möchten, schreiben Sie uns unter Angabe des Sie interessierenden Produktbereiches.

... mit weniger sollten Sie nicht zufrieden sein!

WL 31/90

Mikrofone · Kopfhörer · Beschallungssysteme
Theresienstr. 8·D–7100 Helbronn · Tel. (07131) 617–0 · Fax 6 04 59 · Telex 728771

TEIL A

1   Herr Sieg of Sieg Metall GmbH goes to a local car dealer to
purchase a new company car.

Herr Sieg   Guten Tag.

Verkäufer   Kann ich Ihnen behilflich sein?

Herr Sieg   Ich bin Betriebsleiter bei einer Firma hier in Düsseldorf und ich möchte ein Auto für die Firma kaufen. Ich
suche ein schnelles Auto und nicht zu groß. Können
Sie etwas empfehlen?

Verkäufer   Moment mal, schnell und nicht zu groß. Ich könnte
zum Beispiel das neue Opel Modell empfehlen. Es ist
ein sehr elegantes Auto, ist mittelgroß und verbraucht
wenig Benzin. Wenn Sie das Auto für die Stadt
benutzen, müssen Sie dieses Modell haben. Übrigens
ist es auch preisgünstig.

Herr Sieg   Wieviel kostet es?

Verkäufer   Wenn Sie bar bezahlen, kostet es DM 35.000. Wenn
Sie aber in Raten zahlen, ist es etwas teuerer.

Herr Sieg   Hat es ABS Bremsen und Allradsteuerung?

Verkäufer   Ja, und auch Zentralverriegelung und wir geben einen
Sonderrabatt von 5% für Firmen.

Herr Sieg   Also kostet es DM 33.750.

Verkäufer   Sie können vielleicht einen billigeren Wagen finden
aber es ist ein Qualitätswagen mit einem kraftvollen
Motor und die innere Ausstattung ist sehr bequem.
Wollen Sie die technische Ausstattung sehen? (*hands
him sheet*)

Herr Sieg   Das ist interessant, danke.

TECHNISCHE AUSSTATTUNG	
MOTOR:	92 KW (125 PS)
BREMSEN:	ABS SCHEIBEN
KATALYSATOR:	3-WEGE KATALYSATOR
TRANSMISSION:	5 GÄNGE
MAßEN:	LÄNGE 3.500 M
	BREITE 1.500 M
	HÖHE 1.400 M
ZENTRALVERRIEGELUNG:	√
ALLRADSTEUERUNG:	√
HINTERRADANTRIEB:	√

Herr Sieg   Ich nehme dieses Modell in rot, bitte!

behilflich *helpful*	**die Zentralverriegelung**
ich möchte/Sie möchten	*central locking system*
I would like, you would like	**der Sonderrabatt (-e)** *special*
kaufen *to buy*	*discount*
suchen *to look for*	**vielleicht** *perhaps*
empfehlen *to recommend*	**billig** *cheap*
Moment mal *just a moment*	**kraftvoll** *powerful*
mittelgroß *medium-sized*	**inner** *inner, interior*
verbrauchen *to consume, use*	**die Ausstattung** *fittings,*
(fuel)	*equipment*
benutzen *to use*	**bequem** *comfortable*
wenig *little, few*	**wollen** *to want*
das Benzin *petrol*	**sehen** *to see*
preisgünstig *inexpensive,*	**technisch** *technical*
value for money	**die Scheibe (-n)** *disc*
kosten *to cost*	**der Katalysator** *catalytic*
bar bezahlen *to pay cash*	*converter*
in Raten zahlen *to pay in*	**der Gang (-¨e)** *gear*
instalments	**das Maß (-e)** *dimension,*
teuer *expensive*	*measurement*
die ABS Bremse (-n) *ABS*	**der Hinterradantrieb** *rear-*
brake	*wheel drive*
die Allradsteuerung *four-*	
wheel drive	

Erklärungen

1 Note the alternative **Kann ich Ihnen behilflich sein?** for *Can I help you?*

2 Note that the words **Qualitäts-** and **Sonder-** can be used in front of nouns to give the additional meaning of *quality* or *special* respectively, for example:

> der **Qualitäts**wein   *the quality wine*
> das **Sonder**angebot   *the special offer*

Other common prefixes are **Haupt-** meaning *main*, **Gesamt-** meaning *total* and **Lieblings-** meaning *favourite*, for example:

> die **Haupt**straße   *the main street*
> der **Gesamt**betrag   *the total amount*
> meine **Lieblings**musik   *my favourite music*

3 **PS** stands for **die Pferdestärke** meaning *horsepower* which remains a typical engine measurement unit in Germany.

4 Note that **empfehlen** is a strong verb (Lektion 2) and alters its stem to **du empfiehlst** and **er/sie/es empfiehlt**.

—————— Grammatik ——————

Word Order

There are many instances in German where the word order differs considerably from English.

(a) Verbs + infinitive

Consider these sentences:

I want (1) to buy (2) a car.   Ich **will** (1) ein Auto **kaufen** (2).

You must (1) pay (2) cash.   Sie **müssen** (1) bar **bezahlen** (2).

Should (1) he buy (2) this car?   **Soll** (1) er diesen Wagen **kaufen** (2)?

In each case, the first verb (1) requires a second verb (2) to complete its meaning. Note that in each German equivalent the second verb stands at the end of the sentence or clause.

Verbs used in this construction (often referred to as modal verbs) are **können** *to be able*, **dürfen** *to be allowed to*, **wollen** *to want to*, **mögen** *to like to*, **müssen** *to have to* and **sollen** *to be* or *should*. These verbs are all irregular.

Mögen is most commonly used to say **Ich möchte** *I would like*, **Er möchte** *He would like*, etc. (See subjunctive forms, Lektion 13). For example:

Möchten Sie ein kleines Auto kaufen?   *Would you like to buy a small car?*

(b) Verbs + zu + infinitive

Some verbs require **zu** *to* before the second verb, for example:

Ich versuche ein billiges Auto **zu** finden.   *I'm trying to find a cheap car.*

Er verspricht einen
  Sonderrabatt **zu** geben.

*He promises to give a special
discount.*

(c) Dependent or subordinate clauses

Some main clauses complete their meaning by adding a dependent or subordinate clause, for example:

It is cheaper (main clause), *if you pay cash* (subordinate clause).
This stereo is better technically equipped (main clause) *although it is cheaper* (subordinate clause).
I want the small model/because it is cheaper.
I think/that this system comes with headphones.

These clauses are frequently signposted by one of the following subordinating conjunctions:

bevor	*before*	**obwohl**	*although*
da	*as*	**während**	*while*
daß	*that*	**weil**	*because*
nachdem	*after*	**wenn**	*if or when*
ob	*whether*		

Thus, following the above examples:

Es ist billiger, **wenn** Sie bar bezahlen.
Diese Stereoanlage hat eine bessere technische Ausstattung, **obwohl** es billiger ist.
Ich will das kleine Modell, **weil** es billiger ist.
Ich glaube, **daß** dieses System mit Kopfhörer angeboten wird.

Note:

(*i*) The verb in the subordinate clause moves to the end of the sentence, for example:

Sie nehmen das Auto.   *You take the car,* but
Sie müssen bezahlen, bevor   *You must pay before you take*
  Sie das Auto **nehmen.**   *the car.*

(*ii*) The main and subordinate clauses are separated by a comma.
(*iii*) The subordinate clause may precede the main clause, for example:

Wenn Sie bar bezahlen, wird es billiger.

(d) Position of verb

As indicated in Lektion 2 the verb in German must always be the second idea in a sentence or main clause:

Das neue Opel Modell (1st idea) ist (2nd idea) sehr preisgünstig.

The new Opel model is very good value for money.

Thus when another idea is placed at the beginning of the sentence, what was the first idea becomes the third idea:

Zum Beispiel (1st idea) ist (2nd idea) das neue Opel Modell (3rd) sehr preisgünstig.

In the same way when a subordinate clause precedes the main clause, the main clause verb (in bold below) must still come second, i.e. immediately after the comma:

Wenn Sie das Auto für die Stadt brauchen (1st idea), **müssen** (2nd idea) Sie dieses Modell haben. *If you need a car to use in town, you must have this model.*

Obwohl das Auto sehr teuer ist, **hat** es keine Zentralverriegelung. *Although the car is very expensive, it does not have central locking.*

———————— Übungen ————————

1 Study the dialogue and the **technische Ausstattung** again and answer these questions:
   a) Was für ein Auto will Herr Sieg kaufen?
   b) Welches Modell empfiehlt der Verkäufer?
   c) Was für Charakteristiken hat das neue Opel Modell?
   d) Wieviel kostet der Wagen?
   e) Wie will Herr Sieg bezahlen?
   f) Wieviel Rabatt bekommt er?
   g) Wieviele Gänge hat das Auto?
   h) Was für Bremsen hat das Auto?

2 You ask your colleague to accompany you to buy a new car and explain what you are looking for, taking care to use the correct word order.

Sie   *Say you want to buy a new car and invite him/her to come along.*

Kollege Ja bitte, wollen Sie ein großes Auto?

Sie   *Say yes, but you are also trying to find an inexpensive car.*

Kollege	Was für Charakteristiken suchen Sie?
Sie	*Say you would like an elegant car but comfortable with four-wheel steering.*
Kollege	Und was für ein PS möchten Sie?
Sie	*Say approximately 120 with rear-wheel drive.*
Kollege	Sie müssen aber für ein solches Auto viel bezahlen!
Sie	*Say you know, you have to pay in instalments and ask if he/she has got a car?*
Kollege	Ja, ich habe einen kleinen französischen Wagen mit Zentralverriegelung.

---

ein solches Auto   *such a car*   **mitkommen**   *to come along*

---

3 Study this advertisement which describes a new typewriter (**eine Schreibmaschine**).

Die neue elektronische Schreibmaschine TIPP208 von Bruder benutzt die neuste Technologie. Sie ist einfach zu verwenden, klein, leicht und elegant. Sie funktioniert mit Netzanschluß zu Hause oder im Büro und mit Batterien für die Geschäftsreise. Die TIPP208 Tastatur ist international und reagiert leise und blitzschnell. Die TIPP208 hat alle Vorteile der neusten Technologie: einen Speicher, ein Korrektursystem und austauschbare Schrifttypen für Ihren persönlichen Stil. DIE NEUE KLEINE TIPP208, AUCH DER PREIS IST BESCHEIDEN!

A colleague of yours has seen the advertisement above in a German magazine and has asked you to translate it. You will need the following vocabulary:

einfach *simple*	**der Vorteil (-e)** *advantage*
verwenden *to use*	**der Speicher (-)** *memory*
leicht *light, easy*	*(of computer)*
funktionieren *to operate*	**austauschbar** *interchangeable*
der Netzanschluß *mains*	*ble*
die Batterie (-n) *battery*	**die Schriftype (-n)** *typeface*
die Geschäftsreise (-n)	**bescheiden** *modest*
business trip	

4 In the following conversation a customer is buying a television set (**ein Fernsehen**), fill in the blank spaces with the verbs below:

Kunde	Guten Tag.
Verkäufer	Kann ich Ihnen …?
Kunde	Ich … ein Fernsehen kaufen. Können Sie mir etwas …?
Verkäufer	… Sie schwarz-weiß oder farbe?
Kunde	Farbe bitte.
Verkäufer	Dann … ich das Grundig. Es … von sehr guter Qualität.
Kunde	Kann ich es …?
Verkäufer	Ja,… Sie mit. Es ist sehr modern.
Kunde	Wieviel… es?
Verkäufer	Dieses Modell … wir zum Preis von DM 2.000.
Kunde	In Ordnung. Ich … es.

Verbs:

kommen	kosten
nehmen	empfehlen
mögen (möchten)	anschauen
sein	helfen
verkaufen	

schwarz-weiß *black and white*   **die Farbe (-n)** *colour*

5 Your colleague asks you for your opinion on a few cars. Translate your comments into German using the appropriate conjunction.

a) I think that the Opel model is very elegant.
b) The VW model is very comfortable although it is smaller.
c) I like the Mercedes model because its very big.
d) I don't know whether this model is good value for money.

TEIL B

Read the following letter which comprises a report on the German chemical industry.

Sehr geehrte Damen und Herren,
wir danken Ihnen für Ihr Interesse und können Ihnen folgendes über den
Export von Chemikalien aus der BRD berichten.

Deutsche Chemikalien werden hauptsächlich in Frankfurt und Köln
produziert. Hier wird auf pharmazeutische Produkte und Farben
konzentriert. Die pharmazeutischen Waren werden nach deutschen
Sicherheitsnormen streng kontrolliert. Mehr als 50% der Gesamtproduktion
wird dann exportiert. Die Fertigprodukte werden im allgemeinen über
Rotterdam transportiert und dann überall in die Welt geschickt. Wie in
anderen Branchen kauft man deutsche Chemikalien wegen ihrer Qualität.

Bitte wenden Sie sich an uns, wenn Sie weitere Informationen brauchen.

Mit freundlichen Grüßen

folgendes *the following*	**über Rotterdam** *via*
berichten *to report*	*Rotterdam*
die Farbe (-n) *dye*	**überall in die Welt**
nach *according to*	**schicken** *to send all over*
die Sicherheitsnorm (-en)	*the world*
safety standard	**die Branche (-n)** *the sector*
kontrollieren *to check,*	*(of industry)*
supervise	**wegen ihrer Qualität**
50% der Gesamtproduktion	*because of their quality*
50% of total production	**Bitte wenden Sie sich**
das Fertigprodukt (-e)	**an uns** *Please contact us*
finished product	**weiter** *further*
im allgemeinen *in general*	

Grammatik

1 Passive voice

Compare these two sentences

Die Firma exportiert viele Chemikalien. *The company exports many chemicals.*

Viele Chemikalien werden exportiert. *Many chemicals are exported.*

The first is an active sentence with the subject **die Firma** performing
the action **exportiert**. In the second sentence, the subject, **die
Chemikalien** receives the action; in other words the subject is
passive rather than active. This construction is called the passive voice.

The passive is formed with the verb **werden** (irregular) and the past participle (*produced, exported,* etc.) which is formed by adding a **t** to the stem and in most cases the prefix **ge**. For example:

geschickt   *sent*   *produziert   produced*
gemacht   *done/made*   konzentriert   *concentrated*

(See Lektion 10 for the past participles of irregular and strong verbs.)

Thus with the verb **fragen**, *to ask*

ich werde **ge**fragt *I am asked*	wir werden **ge**fragt *we are asked*
du wirst **ge**fragt *you are asked*	ihr werdet **ge**fragt *you are asked*
Sie werden **ge**fragt *you are asked*	Sie werden **ge**fragt *you are asked*
er/sie/es wird **ge**fragt *he/she/it is asked*	sie werden **ge**fragt *they are asked*

(*i*)   The most common forms are the third person singular and plural, for example:

Das Auto **wird** kontrolliert.   *The car is checked.*
Die Waren **werden** exportiert.   *The goods are exported.*

(*ii*)   The past participle is placed at the end of the sentence, for example:

Die Produkte **werden** über   *The goods are transported via*
    Rotterdam transportiert.   *Rotterdam.*

2   Man *as an alternative to the passive*

The passive can also be expressed by using the pronoun **man**, *one*, for example:

Man kauft viele Chemikalien.   *One buys many chemicals.*

instead of

Viele Chemikalien **werden**   *Many chemicals are bought.*
    gekauft.

Or:

Man transportiert die Waren   *One transports the goods via*
    über Rotterdam.   *Rotterdam.*

instead of

Die Waren **werden** über
Rotterdam transportiert.

*The goods are transported via
Rotterdam.*

Note: This construction is much more frequent in German than in English.

Übungen

1 You have received an enquiry from a trade gazette regarding your company which produces machine tools. Write a brief reply indicating that the products are primarily produced in Sheffield, that 25% of total production is exported and that the goods are transported to Europe (**Europa**) via Dover.

2 You are showing a German colleague around your manufacturing plant to explain the production process. You will find new vocabulary below the dialogue.

Sie	*Tell him that first the component parts are produced.*
Herr Braun	Und wie werden sie montiert?
Sie	*Tell him they are checked first then they are assembled by computer.*
Herr Braun	Was wird auf die Teile bespritzt?
Sie	*Tell him that all parts are sprayed with water during assembly.*
Herr Braun	Und dann?
Sie	*Tell him that the finished products are then transported to the dispatch department and are sent all over the world.*

---

zuerst *first*
der Bestandteil (-e)
 component part
montieren *to assemble*
mit Computer *by computer*
mit Wasser bespritzen *to spray with water*

während der Montage *during assembly*
nach der Versandabteilung *to the dispatch department*

---

3 You are describing a successful car business to a colleague. Change
   all the passive constructions to **man...**

   a) Die Autos werden in Hamburg produziert.
   b) 40% der Gesamtproduktion wird exportiert.
   c) Die Autos werden wegen Ihrer Qualität gekauft.
   d) 30% der Exporte wird nach den USA geschickt.

6

MAKING
—— ENQUIRIES AND ——
APPOINTMENTS

TEIL A

Read these letters making enquiries about the range of Perfekta typewriters.

Sehr geehrte Herren!
Bezugnehmend auf Ihre gestrige Anzeige in der Zeitschrift EDV bitten wir Sie um baldige Zusendung Ihres neuen Katalogs sowie Ihrer Preisliste.
Insbesondere interessieren wir uns fur die elektronische Schreibmaschine Perfekta 60. Mit freundlichen Grüßen,

Sehr geehrte Herren!
Für unsere Hauptverwaltung in Berlin brauchen wir elektronische Schreibmaschinen. Insbesondere interessiert uns die neue Serie Perfekta. Wir bitten um Ihre Preisliste und um Information über Ihre Produkte. Wir bitten ebenfalls um Angabe Ihrer Liefer- und Zahlungsbedingungen, sowie Ihrer besten Lieferzeiten.
Wir erwarten Ihre baldige Antwort mit Interesse.

Mit freundlichen Grüßen.

Bezugnehmend auf *With reference to*	**die Lieferbedingungen** *terms of delivery*
die Anzeige(-n) *advertisement*	**die Zahlungsbedingungen** *terms of payment*
die Zeitschrift(-en) *magazine*	**die Lieferzeit(-en)** *delivery time*
bitten (um) *request*	
insbesondere *in particular*	**baldig** *early*
die Hauptverwaltung(-en) *main office*	**erwarten** *await*

brauchen *need, require*
ebenfalls *similarly, also*
die Angabe(-n) (literally) *data, information (about)*

die Antwort(-en) *answer*

——— Erklärungen ———

The verb **bitten** means *to request*. For example:

1 Wir **bitten** Sie **um** (Zusendung).
   Wir **bitten** Sie **um** (Angabe).
   Wir **bitten** Sie **um** (Ihre Preisliste).

   The above sentences mean *We request ...* In correspondence it is the more formal way of saying *Please send us* or *Please indicate*. You can also write **Bitte schicken Sie uns ...**

2 The following are further examples of the verb occurring in second position in the sentence.

   Insbesondere interessieren wir uns ...
   We are especially interested ...

   Für unsere Hauptverwaltung in Berlin brauchen wir ...
   For our head office in Berlin we need ...

——— Grammatik ———

1 *Genitive case*

The genitive case shows possession: **the boss's** *car*; **the firm's** *results*; *the door* **of the office.**
Each bold word with its article is said to be in the genitive case. In German the above examples would be expressed as *the car of the boss, the results of the firm* and *the door of the office.* In each case *of the* would be expressed by varying **der, die** and **das** as follows:

   Das Auto **des** Chef**s** (masc.)
   Die Ergebnisse **der** Firma (fem.)
   Die Tür **des** Büro**s** (neut.)

Also, the masculine and neuter nouns themselves take an **s**, much the same as in English.

Similarly, **your** *boss's car,* etc. would be rendered by:

Das Auto Ihre**s** Chef**s**.
Die Ergebnisse Ihr**er** Firma.
Die Tür Ihre**s** Büro**s**.

Refer back to the letters to find further examples of the genitive case.

2 Adjectival endings

Look at these examples:

der neu**e** Katalog
Ihres neu**en** Katalogs
Ihre best**en** Preise
Ihre baldig**e** Antwort

Adjectives occurring before a noun take an ending depending on whether that noun takes **der, die** or **das.** In many instances, the right ending can be derived by noting the article **ein, eine, der, die** or **das,** or the possessive adjective (mein, dein, etc) which precedes the adjective, and using this chart:

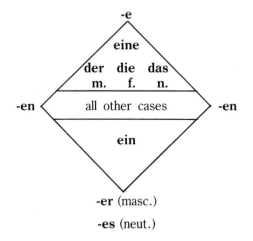

Locate the relevant preceding word on the inside corner of the diamond: the correct adjectival ending is shown on the outside of that corner. In the chart, **ein** stands also for **kein** and **mein, dein,** etc. **Der, die, das** stand also for **dies-**(*this*), **jen-**(*that*), **jed-**(*each, every*), **welch-**(*which*).

For example:

Der neue Katalog	**die** jung**en** Sekretärinnen (plural)
ein neu**er** Katalog	Zusendung **Ihres** neu**en** Katalogs
ein etablier**tes** Produkt	**des** alt**en** Chefs
Ihr neu**es** Büro	**Welche** elektronische
die junge Sekretärin	Schreibmaschine?

Note: All other cases in the diamond (ending **-en**) applies to **der** when used with a feminine dative noun, and to **die** when used with a plural. For example:

Ich gab **der** neu**en** Sekretärin den Brief.
I gave the new secretary the letter.

Die neu**en** Maschinen sind angekommen.
The new machines have arrived.

Übungen

This office furniture (**das Büromöbel**) is just what you need for your office in Hamburg. Write to the manufacturers following the model letters on page 60.

- Say that your company requires furniture for its office in Hamburg.
- Ask them to send you a catalogue and price list.
- Ask them to indicate their terms and delivery time.
- Close the letter by saying you await their answer with interest.

2 You are writing to a number of firms, soliciting a variety of information. Beginning each sentence with **Wir bitten um Zusendung** or **Wir bitten um Angabe**, request the following:

a) their catalogue.
b) their price list.
c) their terms of payment.
d) their terms of delivery
e) their delivery time.

3 Translate the following phrases:

a) The firm's car.
b) The boss's secretary.
c) The secretary's office.
d) The purchasing manager's computer.
e) The name of our general manager.
f) The door of your office.

4 Insert the correct endings in the following letter:

Sehr geehrt- Herren,
Wir danken Ihnen fur Ihr freundlich- Schreiben vom 12. dies- Monat-.
Es freut uns, daß Sie an der neu- Möbelserie "Exklusiva" interessiert
sind. Dieses modern- Büromobel ist nach den neuest- ergonomisch-
Prinzipien konzipiert; aus der beigelegt- Preisliste ersehen Sie, das wir
die best- Preise anbieten.
In Erwartung Ihres wert- Auftrag- verbleiben wir,
Mit freundlichen Grüßen,

beigelegt *enclosed*	**In Erwartung Ihres werten Auftrags verbleiben wir, ...** *In anticipation of your esteemed order, we remain ...*

TEIL B

—— Making Appointments ——

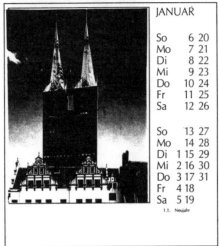

JANUAR

So		6	20
Mo		7	21
Di		8	22
Mi		9	23
Do		10	24
Fr		11	25
Sa		12	26
So		13	27
Mo		14	28
Di	1	15	29
Mi	2	16	30
Do	3	17	31
Fr	4	18	
Sa	5	19	

1.1. Neujahr

Colin Burrett, a British businessman, is in Leipzig. He telephones the newly-established subsidiary of Schick Mode GmbH to make an appointment to see Herr Meyer, the general manager. The telephone rings at Schick Mode (Leipzig) GmbH.

Empfang Schick Mode, Guten Tag.
Burrett Guten Tag. Hier Colin Burrett aus Birmingham. Ich bin auf der Durchreise in Leipzig und möchte Herrn Meyer sprechen.
Empfang Haben Sie eine Verabredung?
Burrett Leider nicht, aber ...
Empfang Es tut mir leid. Herr Meyer ist den ganzen Tag beschäftigt. Er betreut einen Kunden aus der Tschechoslowakei. Können Sie vielleicht morgen kommen?
Burrett Ja. Morgen früh bin ich frei.
Empfang Also, um 10 Uhr. Geht das in Ordnung?
Burrett Ja, in Ordnung, dankeschön. Auf Wiedersehen.

Colin Burrett telephones the sales manager of another Leipzig company. The telephone rings at Gebrüder Schein GmbH.

Sekretärin	Gebrüder Schein, Guten Tag?
Burrett	Guten Tag, ich möchte den Verkaufsleiter sprechen bitte.
Sekretärin	Einen Moment, ich verbinde. Wie ist Ihr Name, bitte?
Burrett	Ich heiße Colin Burrett von der Firma Barton Industries.
Sekretärin	Wie schreibe ich das, bitte?
Burrett	Beh, Uh, Ehr, Ehr, Eh, Teh, Teh.

(*The secretary talks to the sales manager's secretary on another line. She comes back to Burrett.*)

Sekretärin	Hören Sie?
Burrett	Ja, bitte?
Sekretärin	Es tut mir leid. Der Verkaufsleiter ist im Moment nicht da. Er ist zu Tisch. Können Sie um drei Uhr zurückrufen?
Burrett	Bitte, können Sie das wiederholen?
Sekretärin	Ob Sie um 3 Uhr zurückrufen können? Der Verkaufsleiter ist im Moment nicht da.
Burrett	Ja, in Ordnung. Bitte, wie heißt der Verkaufsleiter?
Sekretärin	Er heißt Herr Nußbaum.
Burrett	Herr Nußbaum. Dankeschön. Auf Wiederhören.
Sekretärin	Auf Wiederhören.

---

auf der Durchreise *passing through (the town)*		**Ich verbinde** *I am connecting you*	
beschäftigt *busy*		**Es tut mir leid** *I am sorry*	
betreuen *to look after, see to, take care of*		**Er ist zu Tisch** *He is at lunch*	
		wiederholen *repeat*	
Das geht in Ordnung *That is alright*		**zurückrufen** *call back*	
Gebrüder (Schein) *(Schein) Brothers*			

Erklärungen

1 The times of the day are as follows:

gestern *yesterday*		**morgen** *morning*	
heute *today*		**nachmittag** *afternoon*	
morgen *tomorrow*		**abend** *evening*	

These can be put together as needed: gestern morgen (*yesterday morning*); heute nachmittag (*this afternoon*); morgen abend (*tomor-*

row evening). The exception is **morgen früh**, which is the way of saying *tomorrow morning*.

2 **Auf Wiederhören** is used for *goodbye* on the telephone, unless it is understood that the next time the speakers meet, it will be in person, as in the first dialogue. In this case **Auf Wiedersehen** is used.

3 Listen to the tape and learn the alphabet in German. Below is an English version of the sounds you will hear:

a	i	ku	iks
be	jot	er	ipsilon
ce	ka	es	tset
de	el	te	Umlaut a
e	em	u	Umlaut o
ef	en	fau	Umlaut u
ge	o	we	estset
ha	pe		

ß is the German way of writing or printing **ss** in certain words. Notice that this is treated as a separate letter in the alphabet.

4 **Ob Sie um drei Uhr zurückrufen können.** When repeating a question which has not been understood the first time, a German speaker will usually use the form *I was asking whether (you can phone back at 3)*. This then becomes shortened to *Whether you can phone back at 3*. The German for *whether* is **ob,** which sends the verb to the end of the sentence. In all subordinate clauses like this, the verb occurs at the end. (Refer back to Lektion 5.)

————————— Übung —————————

1 You are travelling in Bavaria and you telephone a local company to make an appointment with the purchasing manager. You speak to the receptionist.

Empfang Guten Tag. Firma Jung.
You *Say a greeting. Identify yourself and where you are from, and say you would like to speak to the purchasing manager.*
Empfang Haben sie eine Verabredung?
You *Reply that you haven't an appointment but that you are*

	passing through and would like to make an appointment, if possible.
Empfang	Es tut mir leid, Frau Dr. Martens ist heute nicht da. Sie kommt erst heute nachmittag zurück.
You	*Say you are free tomorrow at 3 p.m.*
Empfang	Gut. Können Sie um 3.30 Uhr kommen?
You	*You did not catch the question; ask for her to repeat it.*
Empfang	Ob Sie um 3.30 Uhr kommen können?
You	*Yes, that will be fine.*
Empfang	Wie schreibe ich Ihren Namen, bitte?
You	*Spell your surname.*
Empfang	Gut. Auf Wiedersehen.
You	*Reply.*

Ich möchte einen Termin machen, bitte	*I would like to make an appointment, please*

7

DISCUSSING ——— PLANS AND ——— COMMITMENTS

TEIL A

——————— Dialog ———————

Ingrid Kaufmann, director of Schick Mode GmbH, discusses her plans and commitments for the day with a colleague. (Note the use of the familiar form.)

Januar 1992 21/22 Arbeitstage

1	
Do 2	
Fr 3	14·· Sozialgericht Münden
Sa 4	
So 5	
Mo 6	
Di 7	
Mi 8	
Do 9	14·· Treffen m. Einkleuterttsch/
Fr 10	
Sa 11	
So 12	
Mo 13	
Di 14	
Mi 15	10·· Intern. Funkaust. Berlin
Do 16	
Fr 17	
Sa 18	
Sa 19	
Mo 20	15·· Konferenz in · Handelspernt
Di 21	
Mi 22	
Do 23	
Fr 24	
Sa 25	
Sa 26	
Mo 27	
Di 28	
Mi 29	
Do 30	
Fr 31	

Februar 1992 20 Arbeitstage

Sa 1	
So 2	
Mo 3	
Di 4	
Mi 5	
Do 6	
Fr 7	
Sa 8	
So 9	
Mo 10	
Di 11	
Mi 12	
Do 13	
Fr 14	
Sa 15	
So 16	
Mo 17	
Di 18	
Mi 19	
Do 20	
Fr 21	
Sa 22	
So 23	
Mo 24	
Di 25	
Mi 26	
Do 27	
Fr 28	
Sa 29	

Klaus	Hallo Ingrid, wie geht's dir?
Ingrid	Hallo Klaus, mir geht's gut, danke.
Klaus	Ich muß mit dir über deine Geschäftsreise nach Österreich sprechen. Wir müssen die Termine und die Reisepläne besprechen. Bist du heute morgen frei?
Ingrid	Also, ich treffe mich um elf Uhr mit dem Vertreter von der pharmazeutischen Firma.
Klaus	Wie lange willst du mit ihm sprechen?
Ingrid	Ich weiß nicht eigentlich. Mindestens eine Stunde.
Klaus	Kann ich dich vielleicht während der Mittagspause sprechen?
Ingrid	Ja, warum nicht? Ich gehe zuerst einkaufen. Was ziehst du vor, sollen wir in der Kantine oder in einem Restaurant essen?
Klaus	Ich schlage vor, daß wir dieses neue Restaurant um die Ecke ausprobieren.
Ingrid	Ja gut, ich kenne es auch nicht. Ich muß aber um halb zwei wieder im Büro sein.
Klaus	Alles klar! Bis dann. Tschüß.

Österreich *Austria*
sprechen (über) *to talk, speak to (about)*
die Reisepläne (pl) *plans for the journey*
besprechen *to discuss*
heute morgen *this morning*
sich treffen (mit) *to meet (with)*
eigentlich *actually, in fact*

die Stunde (-n) *hour*
einkaufen gehen *to go shopping*
vorziehen *to prefer*
die Kantine (-n) *the canteen*
vorschlagen *to suggest, propose*
um die Ecke *around the corner*
ausprobieren *to try out*
bis dann *until then/see you later*

Erklärungen

1 Note the use of the familiar form between two colleagues. This is primarily a question of how well they know each other and personal attitudes, much in the same way as using first name terms in an English company. As a foreigner it is best to stick with the **Sie** form and then listen to which form the German speaker is using to address you and follow suit.

2 Note also the more casual expressions used here; **Alles klar** for *OK* or *Fine* and **Tschüß** for *Goodbye*.

3   The reply to **Wie geht's Ihnen/dir?** can use the same construction: **Mir geht's** followed by **gut/schlecht,** etc. This can be abbreviated to **Gut danke, Nicht so schlecht, danke,** etc.

4   Details on how to ask and tell the time are in Appendix 1. Most structures such as **Viertel vor eins,** *Quarter to one* are essentially the same as in English. Take care with *halb* ... though, which in German indicates half an hour before the hour not after as in English; thus **halb zwei** is *half past one.* Note also that in the context of time **um** means *at*: **um drei Uhr,** *at three o'clock.*

Dialog

Ingrid and Klaus are in the restaurant.

Ingrid Was hast du am Wochenende vor?
Klaus Ich nehme an, daß ich Samstag morgen wie üblich schwimmen gehe, am Nachmittag schaue ich Fußball mit meinen Freunden und dann verbringe ich den Abend mit ihnen im Weinkeller. Hast du etwas Interessantes vor?
Ingrid Ich bleibe zu Hause, um mich auf die Reise vorzubereiten. Ich fahre am Montag.
Klaus In welchem Hotel wohnst du in Wien?
Ingrid Ich reserviere ein Zimmer beim Hotel Ibis in der Nähe vom Bahnhof. Es gefällt mir gut dort.
Klaus Und an welchem Tag fährst du nach Salzburg?
Ingrid Ich komme am Sonntag nachmittag an und bleibe 3 Tage.
Klaus Du kommst also am Mittwoch zurück?
Ingrid Ja, hoffentlich! Es ist fünf vor halb, sollen wir?
Klaus Ja, wir müssen uns beeilen.

das Wochenende (-n) *the weekend*	**etwas Interessantes** *something interesting*
vorhaben *to plan*	**zu Hause** *at home*
annehmen *to suppose*	**sich vorbereiten (auf)** *to prepare oneself (for)*
schwimmen gehen *to go swimming*	**Wien** *Vienna*
üblich *usual, customary*	**ankommen** *to arrive*
der Fußball *football*	**zurückkommen** *to come back, return*
der Freund (-en) *friend*	
schauen *to watch*	**hoffentlich** *hopefully*
verbringen *to spend* (time)	**sich beeilen** *to hurry*

Erklärungen

1 Note that to express habitual time, i.e. what one does in general in the morning, an **s** is added. For example:

Morgens gehe ich immer einkaufen.
I always go shopping in the morning.

Abends gehe ich normalerweise in einen Weinkeller.
I usually go to a wine bar in the evening.

2 The expression **fünf vor halb** is actually the equivalent of *twenty-five past the hour* as it signifies *5 minutes to half before the hour*!

3 **Fahren** like **gehen** also means *to go* but implies using transport, whereas **gehen** is generally used where zu Fuß, *on foot* is implied.

4 The construction **um ... zu ...**, *in order to*, introduces an infinitive verb. For example:
Ich möchte nach London fahren, **um** meine Kunden **zu** treffen.
I would like to travel to London in order to meet my customers.
As always the infinitive with **zu** occurs at the end of the clause.

5 Expressions such as *something good, nothing special* are translated using the pronouns **etwas** (*something*) and **nichts** (*nothing*) with the relevant adjective. The adjective takes a capital letter and an **es** ending. For example:

etwas Besonder**es**   *something special*
nichts Interessant**es**   *nothing interesting*

Grammatik

1 Object pronouns

The object noun (for example **den/dem Vertreter**-the representative) can be replaced by one of two types of object pronoun (for example **ihn** or **ihm**-him) depending on whether it itself is in the accusative or dative:

ACCUSATIVE	MEANING	DATIVE
mich	*me*	mir
dich	*you*	dir
Sie	*you*	Ihnen
ihn	*him/it*	ihm
sie	*her/it*	ihr
es	*it*	ihm
uns	*us*	uns
euch	*you*	euch
Sie	*you*	Ihnen
sie	*them*	ihnen

For example in the accusative:

Ich sehe **den Vertreter** um 9 Uhr.　　*I am seeing the representative at 9 o'clock.*

becomes

Ich sehe **ihn** um 9 Uhr.　　*I am seeing him at 9 o'clock.*

In the dative the following would apply:

Ich spreche mit **dem Vertreter** morgen.　　*I am speaking with the representative tomorrow.*

would become

Ich spreche morgen mit **ihm**.

Look at the following examples and note that in German there may be more than one meaning depending on what has been said previously. Remember that the written difference of lower case 'sie/ihnen' and upper case 'Sie/Ihnen' is lost in speech.

Accusative

Sie besuchen **uns** nächste Woche.　　*They are visiting us next week.*

Wann können Sie **mich** sehen?　　*When can you see me?*

Ich rufe **sie** übermorgen an.　　*I'll telephone her/them the day after tomorrow.*

(in speech this could also be understood as *I'll telephone you* – Sie)

Dative

Kann ich **Ihnen** helfen?　　*Can I help you?*

(**helfen** always has a dative object)

Ich muß mit **ihr** sprechen　　*I must talk to her*

Notes:

(*i*)   Object pronouns precede other objects, for example:

Ich gebe **ihm** die Details später.   *I'll give him the details later.*

(*ii*)   Where two object pronouns occur the accusative precedes the dative, for example:

Ich gebe **sie** ihm später.   *I'll give them to him later.*

2   Separable verbs

In German some verbs are separable in that the prefix, like the **an-** in **ankommen** below, moves away from the stem, the **-kommen** part, and takes up a separate position at the end of the clause or sentence. Thus in the present tense.

ankommen   *to arrive*

Ich **komme** um vier Uhr in Birmingham **an.**   *I'm arriving at 4 o'clock in Birmingham.*

vorziehen   *to prefer*

Wir **ziehen** das Restaurant um die Ecke **vor.**   *We prefer the restaurant round the corner.*

anrufen   *to telephone*

Er **ruft** morgen **an.**   *He is phoning tomorrow.*

Note that this applies even in short clauses:

vorschlagen   *to suggest*

Ich **schlage vor**, daß wir um fünf Uhr gehen.

(*i*)   Where a separable verb moves to the end of the sentence it links up with its prefix again. For example:

Ich möchte das neue Hotel **ausprobieren.**   *I'd like to try out the new hotel.*

Sie müssen rechtzeitig **ankommen.**   *You must arrive on time.*

(*ii*)   Where a separable verb is used with a verb or conjunction requiring **zu,** the **zu** slips in between the prefix and the stem. For example:

| Ich versuche meine Sachen vorzubereiten. | *I am trying to prepare my things.* |
| Ich fahre mit dem Auto, um rechtzeitig anzukommen. | *I'm going by car in order to arrive on time.* |

—————— Übungen ——————

1 Study the two dialogues again and then answer the questions.

a) Warum muß Klaus mit Ingrid sprechen?
b) Was macht Ingrid um 11. Uhr?
c) Wie lange will sie den Vertreter sprechen?
d) Welches Restaurant möchte Klaus ausprobieren?
e) Was hat Klaus am Wochenende vor?
f) Wann fährt Ingrid?

2 Look at this page from a diary. It tells you which Austrian cities Ingrid is going to visit, on which dates and where she is going to stay.

> Besuch in Österreich
> 6. Juni Hinfahrt nach Wien
> Tage 6   10 Wien, Hotel Ibis
> Tage 11 13 Linz, Hotel Stadtwald
> Tage 14 16 Salzburg, Hotel Adler
> Rückreise 17. Juni

A colleague asks Ingrid about her travel plans. Give her answers using the above information.

a) Wann fährst du nach Österreich?
b) Welche Stadt besuchst du zuerst?
c) In welchem Hotel wohnst du?
d) Wann kommst du in Salzburg an?
e) Wieviel Tage verbringst du dort?
f) Wann fliegst du zurück?

3 During your visit to Austria, a German-speaking colleague asks you about your plans for the weekend.

Kollege Was machen Sie am Wochenende?
Sie *Say you are going swimming on Saturday morning. In the afternoon you are going shopping. You must buy*

presents for your wife/husband and children. In the evening you would like to try out the restaurant around the corner.

Kollege   Sind Sie am Sonntag frei?

Sie   *Say on Sunday you are hiring a car in order to visit the area. Ask your colleague if he wants to come with you.*

Kollege   Ja, gerne. Vielen Dank.

---

das Geschenk (-e)   *present*
das Kind (-er)   *child*
mieten   *to hire*

die Umgebung   *the environment, area*
mitkommen   *to come along, accompany*

---

4   You are going through your diary with your secretary. Replace the object nouns in brackets with the appropriate pronoun.

a)   Ich treffe (die Verkaufsleiterin) um 10 Uhr.
b)   Ich muß mit (dem Einkaufsleiter) um halb 12 sprechen.
c)   Ich will (die Mitarbeiter in der Versandabteilung) um viertel nach eins besuchen.
d)   Ich möchte mich mit (den Kunden) um 3 Uhr treffen.

Now imagine you are advising the parties concerned personally about the various arrangements and use the polite second person pronouns **Sie** and **Ihnen.**

5   You are giving details of your partner's trip to London. Put the verb in brackets into the correct form.

a)   Er (vorschlagen), daß er Montag fährt.
b)   Er (vorziehen) das große Auto
c)   Er (ankommen) um vier Uhr nachmittags.
d)   Er (annehmen), daß die Besprechung drei Stunden dauert.
e)   Er (zurückkommen) am Donnerstag.

TEIL B

Dagmar Janssen, a secretary at Schick Mode GmbH finds the following messages (**Nachrichten**) on her desk:

AKTENNOTIZ

AN: Dagmar   VON: Hilde Werner

Das Fotokopiergerät ist schon wieder kaputt. Können Sie den Techniker bitte anrufen. Er soll unbedingt heute kommen, um das Gerät zu reparieren.

AN: Dagmar Janssen   VON: Peter Braun

Können Sie bitte den Flug nach Linz für den 4. März bestätigen und mir die Platznummer mitteilen. Sie müssen das Reisebüro SCHWARZ anrufen und nach Bernd fragen. Sie sollen auch das Hotel Adler in Salzburg anrufen, um ein Einzelzimmer für den 7–9. März inklusiv zu reservieren. Die Telefonnummer ist 43. 23. 19.

AN: Dagmar Janssen   VON: Johannes Berg

Ich bin den ganzen Tag weg. Wenn es eine Nachricht für mich gibt, rufen Sie mich bitte an.
Die Nummer ist 87. 54. 3

an *to*	**von** *from*
das Fotokopiergerät (-e) *photocopying machine*	**der Flug (-e)** *flight*
schon wieder *yet again*	**bestätigen** *confirm*
kaputt *broken*	**mitteilen (+ dat)** *to inform, advise of*
der Techniker(-) *the technician*	**das Reisebüro (-s)** *travel agency*
anrufen *to telephone*	**fragen (nach)** *to ask (for)*
unbedingt *definitely, without fail*	**das Einzelzimmer (-)** *single room*
reparieren *to repair*	**weg** *away*

—————— Übungen ——————

1 Study the messages again and say whether the following sentences are true or false, (**wahr oder falsch**). Correct any false statements.

   a) Der Techniker soll morgen kommen, um das Fotokopiergerät zu reparieren

   b) Dagmar soll den Flug nach Linz für den 4. März bestätigen.

   c) Peter Braun möchte in Salzburg im Hotel Stadtwald wohnen.

   d) Johannes kommt heute nicht ins Büro.

   e) Dagmar muß Johannes nicht stören.

stören	*to disturb*

2   At the end of the day Dagmar has the following memos to send:

To Hilde Werner:
The technician isn't free today but he can repair the photocopier tomorrow. He is coming at two o'clock.

To Peter Braun:
Your seat number for the flight to Linz is 25B. The Hotel Adler is reserving a single room no. 215 for the 7–9 March inclusive.

To Johannes Berg:
Can you ring Klaus Schmidt, in order to confirm the business trip. He wants to know tomorrow without fail.
The telephone number is: 23 43 75

Write them out in German following the format of the sample memos.

8
MAKING
——— TRAVEL ———
ARRANGEMENTS

TEIL A

——————— Dialog ———————

Dagmar Janssen telephones the travel agency Globus Reisen to confirm flight reservations for her boss, Ingrid Kaufmann. The telephone rings at Globus Reisen...

Angestellte Globus Reisen, Guten Tag.
DJ Ich möchte Herrn Behr sprechen, bitte.
Angestellte Am Apparat.
DJ Guten Tag, hier Schick Mode; ich erkundige mich über einen Flug nach Wien.
Angestellte Unter welchem Namen, bitte?
DJ Unter dem Namen Ingrid Kaufmann.
Angestellte Und für wann ist der Flug?
DJ Montag, den 6. Juni.
Angestellte Ja, ich glaube, er ist schon bestätigt. Können Sie einen Moment warten, bitte? (*Coming back to Dagmar.*) Hören Sie?
DJ Ja, bitte.
Angestellte Also der Flug von Frau Kaufmann ist bestätigt. Abflug um 10.30 Uhr Flughafen Köln/Bonn. Frau Kaufmann muß sich eine Stunde im voraus am Flughafen anmelden. Ankunft 11.45 in Wien Schwechat. Sie kann die Flugkarte heute nachmittag abholen, wenn sie will.

DJ   In Ordnung. Das werde ich ausrichten. Dankeschön.
Angestellte   Gern geschehen. Auf Wiederhören.

Am Apparat *Speaking* (telephone)	**sich anmelden** *check in, register*
sich erkundigen über *enquire about*	**abholen** *pick up, fetch* (also: *meet*)
der Flug(-¨e) *flight*	**ausrichten** *pass on* (a message)
bestätigen *confirm*	**Gern geschehen** *A pleasure, Don't*
der Abflug (-¨e) *flight departure*	*mention it*
die Ankunft(-¨e) *arrival*	

Dialog

After confirming the flight, Dagmar telephones the Hotel Ibis in Vienna to book a single room for her boss.

Empfang   Hotel Ibis, Grüß Gott.
DJ   Guten Tag. Hier Firma Schick Moden in Köln. Unsere Generaldirektorin wird bald nach Wien fliegen, und ich möchte ihr ein Zimmer reservieren.
Empfang   Für wann, bitte?
DJ   Für Montag, den 6.Juni.
Empfang   Und für wieviel Nächte soll das sein?
DJ   Für sechs Nächte, vom 6. einschließlich bis zum 10. Sie wird am 11. abreisen.
Empfang   Soll das ein Einzelzimmer oder ein Zweibettzimmer sein?
DJ   Ein Einzelzimmer. Mit Bad und Dusche.
Empfang   Selbstverständlich. Ein Einzelzimmer mit Bad und Dusche für fünf Nächte vom 6. auf den 10.Juni.
DJ   Ja, so ist es.
Empfang   Wie heißt die Person noch?
DJ   Ingrid Kaufmann. Sie wird erst um 10 Uhr abends ankommen.
Empfang   Alles in Ordnung. Das Zimmer ist reserviert.
DJ   Dankeschön; auf Wiederhören.
Empfang   Ich danke auch; auf Wiederhören.

Grüß Gott *A South German greeting*	**einschließlich** *including*
abreisen *depart*	**die Dusche (-n)** *shower*
das Einzelzimmer(-) *single room*	**selbstverständlich** *of course*
das Zweibettzimmer(-) *double room*	**erst um** *not until, only* (of time)

Dialog

At the airport in Vienna, Ingrid Kaufmann is met by the company's agent for Lower Austria.

Agent Frau Kaufmann! Grüß Gott!
IK (*Expressing surprise.*) Grüß Gott! Das ist aber nett, daß Sie mich abholen.
Agent Erlauben Sie? Ich nehme Ihren Koffer.
IK Sehr freundlich. Danke, er ist sehr schwer.
Agent Wie war die Reise?
IK Sehr gut. Aber ich bin ein bißchen müde.
Agent Ich verstehe. Ich fahre Sie zu Ihrem Hotel. Sie können sich schön ausruhen, und morgen werden Sie wieder fit sein.
IK Vielen Dank. Ist alles auf morgen vorbereitet?
Agent Doch, alles ist vorbereitet. Wir werden Herrn Fleth morgen früh um acht Uhr bei mir im Büro treffen. Ich werde Sie um Viertel vor acht vor dem Hotel abholen.
IK Dankeschön
Agent Wie lange bleiben Sie in Wien?
IK Bis zum 11. Am elften werde ich nach Linz fahren.
Agent Bitte, gehen wir hier durch. Ich habe den Wagen drüben geparkt.

Erlauben Sie? *Would you permit me ...?*
der Koffer(-) *suitcase*
war *was*
die Reise *journey*

ein bißchen *a little*
sich ausruhen *to relax, have a rest*
vorbereitet *prepared*
drüben *over there*

Erklärungen

1 Schwechat is Vienna's airport.

Grammatik

1 Numbers

The ordinal numbers are made by adding **-te** to the cardinal numbers up to **neunzehn,** after which add **-ste.** Thus:

der siebzehn**te,** der achtzehn**te,** der neunzehn**te,** der zwanzig**ste,** der einundzwanzig**ste,** der zweiundzwanzig**ste,** and so on.

The exceptions are:

der erste	*the first*
der dritte	*the third*
der siebte	*the seventh*

Ordinal numbers are of most practical use in dates. When giving the straightfoward date, use the accusative, which means the number taking an **-n** ending. For example:

den erste**n** April
den sechste**n** Februar
den zwölfte**n** Juni
den einunddreissigste**n** Dezember

On the (date) is expressed as **am** as in the examples below:

am ersten April	*on the first of April*
am fünften Juni	*on the fifth of June*

2 The future tense

This is formed, as in English, by using an auxiliary verb (*will*) and the infinitive (*to go*). The auxiliary verb is **werden,** and the infinitive goes to the end of the clause:

Ich **werde** morgen **kommen.**	*I shall come tomorrow.*
Sie **wird** nächste Woche nach Halle **fahren.**	*You/She will go to Halle next week.*

For the conjugation of **werden,** see Lektion 5.
Identify any occurrences of the future tense in the dialogues.

——————— Übungen ———————

 1 Study the dialogues again and answer these questions:

    a) Wann wird Frau Kaufmann nach Wien fliegen?
    b) Wann wird sie von Wien nach Linz fliegen?
    c) Um wieviel Uhr wird sie im Hotel ankommen?
    d) Um wieviel Uhr wird der Agent sie vom Hotel abholen?

e) Wieviel Nächte bleibt sie im Hotel Ibis?

f) Wer holt sie vom Flughafen in Wien ab?

2 You are manning an exhibition stand in Hanover and are phoning to make the hotel reservations.

Empfang	Hotel Bellevue, guten Tag?
You	*Say hello, you wish to reserve two single rooms.*
Empfang	Ja, für wann?
You	*Say for the 5th March.*
Empfang	Und für wieviel Nächte bitte?
You	*You require the room for five nights.*
Empfang	Ja, das geht in Ordnung. Zwei Einzelzimmer – mit oder ohne Bad?
You	*With a bath.*
Empfang	Ja, unter welchem Namen, bitte?
You	*Say your name and spell your surname.*
Empfang	Können Sie das schriftlich bestätigen, bitte?
You	*Yes, you can confirm in writing.*
Empfang	Dankeschön. Um wieviel Uhr werden Sie am 5. ankommen?
You	*Say you will arrive in the evening, at 6 p.m.*
Empfang	Dankeschön. Geht in Ordnung. Auf Wiedersehen.
You	*Goodbye.*

3 You are discussing your first trip to Germany with a German-speaking colleague. Answer her questions using the following guidelines.

K	Guten Tag, wie geht es? Ist alles auf Ihre Deutschlandreise vorbereitet?
S	*Say yes, you will leave Birmingham on Friday, 13th at 6 a.m. and arrive in Berlin at 9 a.m.*
K	Und haben Sie ein Hotel?
S	*Say yes, you will be staying at the hotel Kempinski. The room is confirmed.*
K	Werden Sie Herrn Schramm von Siemens besuchen?
S	*Say yes, you will be meeting Herr Schramm. He will be meeting you at the airport: he lives near the airport. You will be going to Siemens, then you will be visiting two new customers near Berlin.*

K   Sehr interessant. Ich hoffe, es wird ein erfolgreicher Besuch in
Berlin sein!
S   *Thank your colleague.*

4   Listen to the questions on the tape and answer by stating the date
written out below:

a)   (Wann kommen Sie wieder?) Am 1. Dezember.
b)   (Für wann ist das Zimmer?) Den 3. Februar.
c)   (Wann kommt die Lieferung an?) Am 7. Juni.
d)   (An welchem Tag trifft er ein?) Am 31. September.
e)   (Wann fahren Sie ab?) Am 25. Oktober.
f)   (Den Wievielten haben wir heute?) Give today's date.
g)   (Wann ist Ihr Geburtstag?) Give your birthday.

TEIL B

Read the following exchange of telexes between Floform plc and
their German agent, Dieter Wolf:

Floform: LIEFERUNG FUER SIEMENS KOMMT AM 10. IM
FLUGHAFEN TEMPELHOF AN STOP FLUG NR LH 876 AN-
KUNFTSZEIT 09 OOH STOP BITTE ABHOLEN UND UNVER-
ZUEGLICH AN DIE FIRMA SIEMENS WEITERBEFOERDERN
STOP BITTE UM IHRE RUECKWENDIGE BESTAETIGUNG
STOP MFG ROONEY

Wolf: IN ORDNUNG: WERDE AM 10TEN MAERZ ACHT
KISTEN VOM FLUGHAFEN ABHOLEN UND ZU DER FIRMA
SIEMENS BRINGEN STOP MFG WOLF

Floform, am 10.3: FLUG LH876 HAT VERSPAETUNG STOP
ANKUNFT IN BERLIN WIRD VORAUSSICHTLICH UM 14.00
ERFOLGEN STOP BITTE HERRN SCHRAMM BENACHRICH-
TIGEN STOP DIE KISTEN BITTE BIS 16.00 UNBEDINGT BEI
SIEMENS AUSLIEFERN STOP OHNE DIE WAREN KOENNEN
SIE NICHTS ANFANGEN STOP MFG ROONEY

Wolf: MUSS HEUTE MITTAG LEIDER NACH MUENCHEN
STOP WERDE AM 11TEN ALLES ERLEDIGEN STOP KEINE
SORGEN STOP MFG WOLF

Floform: IN ORDNUNG. LIEFERSCHEIN NICHT VERGESSEN STOP OHNE DEN LIEFERSCHEIN KEIN GELD STOP MFG ROONEY

Wolf, am 11.3.: KISTEN BEI SIEMENS GUT ANGEKOMMEN STOP HERR SCHRAMM LAESST GRUESSEN UND DANKT FUER DEN PROMPTEN VERSAND STOP MFG WOLF

---

die Lieferung(-en) *delivery*	**anfangen** *to start*
weiterbeförden *to forward*	**leider** *unfortunately*
rückwendig *by return*	**erledigen** *to sort out, do*
Verspätung haben *to be late*	**Keine Sorge** *Don't worry*
erfolgen (here) *to take place*	**der Lieferschein (-e)**
benachrichtigen *to inform*	*delivery note*
unbedingt *at all costs,*	**Herr S.läßt grüßen** *Herr S*
definitely	*sends his regards*
ausliefern *deliver*	**der Versand** *despatch*

Erklärungen

1 **Bitte abholen.** This is a polite form of the command form (imperative). Simply the infinitive with **Bitte** (see Lektion 9).

2 **MFG** means **mit freundlichen Grüssen** and is used to sign off letters and telexes.

3 Telex machines do not have the umlaut character, which is therefore indicated by including **e** after the appropriate vowel.

Grammatik

1 An, in, um, von, nach, zu

We first met prepositions in chapters 2 and 4. Locate them in the passage above and in the dialogues in Teil A of this Lektion.

In Lektion 4 we saw that some prepositions are always followed by the dative case. Some, however, always take the accusative case. They are:

durch *through*	**ohne** *without*
für *for*	**um** *at, around*
gegen *against*	**wider** *against*
bis *until*	**entlang** *along*

For example:

> **ohne** den Lieferschein   *without the receipt*
> **für** den Versand   *for dispatch*

Yet others take the accusative if they indicate motion towards and the dative if not. They are:

an *at*	**über** *over*
auf *on*	**unter** *under*
hinter *behind*	**vor** *in front of, before*
neben *next to*	**zwischen** *between*
in *in, into*	

For example:

Ich gehe **in die** Stadt.   *I am going into town* (motion towards).

Ich bin **in der** Stadt.   *I am in town* (no motion towards).

Ich gehe **ins** (=**in das**) Theater.   *I am going to the theatre.*

Ich bin **im** (=**in dem**) Theater.   *I am in the theatre.*

Sie legt die Akten **auf den** Tisch.   *She is putting the files on the table.*

Die Akten liegen **auf dem** Tisch.   *The files are on the table.*

Übung

 1   Rewrite the first and last telexes as if they had formed part of an exchange of letters.

Erklärung

🔑 **1** **Mit der Bahn:** if, however, you are travelling by train this is the type of Deutsche Bahn timetable that you will need.

60   **Deutsche Bundesbahn**

DB Winterfahrplan vom 30. September 1990 bis 1. Juni 1991		

12.42	D 2027	Frankfurt (Main)
15.02	D 2021	Frankfurt (Main)
18.49	D 2803	Saarbrücken

Zeichenerklärung: **DB**

Abfahrt Bonn Hbf:
Richtung Koblenz

0.01	D 2115	München Ost +
0.20	D 217	Klagenfurt
0.28	D 203	Basel
0.34 b	D 1203	Basel
0.56 b	D 219	Salzburg
1.05 c	D 2111	München
6.18	EC 29	Wien
7.18	EC 13	Klagenfurt
7.22	EC 5	Sestri
		Levante
7.50	FD 1917	Tegernsee
8.18	EC 21	Budapest
8.24	EC 11	Milano
8.54	FD 1913	Oberstdorf
9.11 D	IC 811	München
9.18	IC 129	Mittenwald/
		Seefeld
9.22	EC 15	Klagenfurt
9.28 b	D 1293	Skopje
9.35	D 2701	Freudenstadt
10.11	IC 113	Stuttgart/
		Innsbruck
10.18	IC 621	München
10.22	EC 7	Brig
11.11 Dc	IC 813	Stuttgart
11.18	EC 25	München/
		Innsbruck
11.24	IC 515	München
11.33	FD 1903	Konstanz
12.11	IC 815	Stuttgart
12.18	IC 521	München
12.24	EC 3	Chur
12.36	D 2027	Frankfurt (Main)
13.11 Dc	IC 711	Stuttgart
13.18	IC 523	München
13.22 Bc	IC 619	München
14.11	IC 713	Stuttgart
14.18	EC 27	München
14.24	EC 9	Chur
14.56	D 2021	Frankfurt (Main)
15.11 D	IC 715	Stuttgart
15.18	IC 525	München
15.22	IC 615	München
16.11	IC 817	Stuttgart/
		München
16.18	IC 527	München
16.22	IC 817	München
16.43	D 2803	Saarbrücken
17.11 Bc	IC 819	Koblenz/
		Stuttgart/
		München
17.18 Bc	IC 721	Regensburg
17.22	IC 619	München
18.11	IC 630	Frankfurt (Main)
18.18	IC 623	Nürnberg
18.22	IC 517	Stuttgart
19.11	EC 30	Frankfurt (Main)
19.18	IC 723	Nürnberg
19.22	IC 601	Basel
19.42	D 1305	Karlsruhe/Rom +
20.01 b	D 1252	Irun — nur Liege-
		wagen
20.18 Bc	IC 527	Würzburg
20.22	IC 519	Stuttgart
21.10	D 223	Wien
21.18 Bc	IC 503	Karlsruhe
21.23	EC 23	Frankfurt (Main)
21.34	D 201	Milano/Ventimiglia
21.49	D 1323	Meran
22.26 Bc	IC 544	Koblenz

Abfahrt Bonn Hbf:
Richtung Köln

23.01 b	D 1217	Innsbruck
23.26 Bc	IC 640	Koblenz
+ = Schlaf- und Liegewagenzug		

Abfahrt Bonn Hbf:
Richtung Köln

4.48 c	D 2110	Norddeich
4.54 b	D 218	Oostende
5.18 b	D 1202	Oostende
5.24	D 202	Dortmund
5.41	D 218	Amsterdam
5.59 b	D 1216	Utrecht
6.38 Dc	IC 641	Dortmund
7.33 Dc	IC 545	Hannover
8.18	D 222	Amsterdam
8.34	EC 22	Oostende
8.40Dc	IC 502	Hannover
8.47	IC 631	Westerland
9.34	IC 518	Hannover
9.40	IC 626	Dortmund
10.26	D 2802	Dortmund
10.34	IC 600	Dortmund
10.40	IC 722	Hannover
10.47	EC 31	Kopenhagen
11.34	IC 618	Dortmund
11.40 Dc	IC 720	Hannover
12.01	D 2020	Dortmund
12.34	IC 616	Dortmund
12.40	IC 526	Hannover
13.47	IC 818	Hamburg
13.34	IC 614	Dortmund
13.40	IC 524	Hannover
13.47	IC 816	Kiel
14.16	D 2700	Dortmund
14.34	EC 8	Hannover
14.40 Dc	IC 628	Dortmund
14.47 B	IC 714	Hamburg
15.34	IC 516	Hannover
15.40	EC 26	Amsterdam
15.47	IC 712	Hamburg
16.22	FD 1902	Münster
16.34	EC 2	Amsterdam
16.40	IC 520	Hannover/
		Braunschweig
16.47 Bc	IC 710	Hamburg
17.19	FD 1916	Dortmund
17.34	IC 514	Dortmund/
		Hannover
17.40	EC 24	Braunschweig
17.47	EC 14	Amsterdam
18.34	EC 6	Kiel
18.47	IC 128	Hannover
18.47 Bc	IC 812	Dortmund
19.17	FD 1922	Hamburg
19.34	IC 512	Dortmund
		Dortmund/
		Hannover
19.40	EC 20	Dortmund
19.47	IC 112	Hamburg
20.34	EC 10	Dortmund
20.40	EC 12	Dortmund
20.47	IC 810	Dortmund
21.22	D 2026	Dortmund
21.34	EC 4	Dortmund
21.40	IC 822	Dortmund
22.34 B	IC 812	Dortmund
22.40 Bc	IC 820	Dortmund
23.50	EC 28	Köln

Abfahrt Bonn-Bad Godesberg:
Richtung Koblenz

9.42	D 2701	Freudenstadt

Abfahrt Bonn-Bad Godesberg:
Richtung Köln

10.19	D 2802	Dortmund
11.54	D 2020	Dortmund
14.06	D 2700	Dortmund
21.15	D 2026	Dortmund

Abfahrt Bonn-Beuel:
Richtung Koblenz

8.20	FD 1923	Berchtesgaden
9.50	FD 1921	Passau
10.01	D 2121	Frankfurt (Main)
14.19 b	D 1173	Straßbourg/
		Ventimiglia
19.40 b	D 13005	Bourg St. Maurice
21.59 b	D 1225	Wien
22.21 b	D 1417	Innsbruck
22.28 b	D 1213	Augsburg/Villach
22.54 b	D 1315	Bozen
23.59 b	D 1419	Innsbruck

Abfahrt Bonn-Beuel:
Richtung Köln

5.19 b	D 1418	Dortmund
5.39 b	D 1416	Dortmund
6.05 b	D 1314	Dortmund
7.15 c	FD 1943	Bad Harzburg
7.32 b	D 1224	Oostende
8.11 b	D 1322	Dortmund
17.08	FD 1912	Dortmund
17.57	FD 1920	Dortmund
18.49	D 2120	Dortmund

Zeichenerklärung:

Alle Züge 1. und 2. Klasse
(außer D 1252 — nur Liegewagen)

A = verkehrt montags bis freitags
B = verkehrt täglich außer samstags
C = verkehrt samstags, sonn- und feiertags
D = verkehrt montags bis samstags
b = verkehrt nur während bestimmter Tage oder Zeitabschnitte; bitte Aushangfahrpläne auf den Bahnhöfen beachten.
c = verkehrt nicht während bestimmter Tage oder Zeitabschnitte; bitte Aushangfahrpläne auf den Bahnhöfen beachten.

Weitere Informationen durch die Zentrale Reiseauskunft Bonn Hbf., Telefon (0228) 194 19.
Alle Angaben ohne Gewähr.

Zentrale Reiseauskunft	☎ 194 19
Richtung Köln, Dortmund	☎ 115 31
Richtung Mainz, Hannover, Berlin	☎ 115 32
Richtung Frankfurt, Nürnberg, Karlsruhe, Basel	☎ 115 33
Richtung Stuttgart, München, Oberstdorf	☎ 115 34
Hauptbahnhof Bonn	☎ 715-1
Bahnhof BN-Bad Godesberg	☎ 36 32 46
Bahnhof Bonn-Beuel	☎ 46 44 96
Bahnhof Bonn-Mehlem	☎ 36 32 46

9

GIVING DIRECTIONS, —— INSTRUCTIONS —— AND ADVICE

TEIL A

———————— **Dialog** ————————

Anton Milovic is visiting the Electronica exhibition in Munich. He enquires at the hotel reception about how to get there.

Milovic   Guten Tag. Wie komme ich am besten zum Messe-platz?

Electronica Haben Sie ein Auto?

Milovic   Nein.

Electronica Nehmen Sie also am besten die U-Bahn. Vor dem Hotel gehen Sie rechts. Nehmen Sie die zweite Straße links, und am Ende ist die U-Bahn Station.

Milovic   Ja, und welche Linie?

Electronica Linie 3. Richtung Sendlinger Tor. Steigen Sie am Messeplatz aus. Sie können sich nicht verfehlen.

Milovic   Gut. Vielen Dank!

die Messe(-) *trade fair, exhibition*	**aussteigen** *to alight*
die U–bahn *underground*	**einsteigen** *to board*
rechts *(to the) right*	**sich verfehlen** *to miss one's way*
links *(to the) left*	

Christoph Zarakovitch is also visiting the exhibition. He has hired a car during his stay in Munich. On his way to the exhibition he gets lost and asks a passer-by (**ein Passant**) the way.

Zarakovitch Entschuldigen Sie bitte, wie komme ich am besten zum Messeplatz?

Passant Oh, einen Moment. Ja. Fahren Sie hier geradeaus bis zur zweiten Ampel. Fahren Sie dann rechts 'rein, und weiter bis zur nächsten Querstraße. Dort rechts und über die Brücke geradeaus weiter. Sie sehen dann das Messegebäude auf der rechten Seite.

Zarakovitch Und wie weit ist das, bitte?

Passant Ungefähr drei Kilometer.

Zarakovitch Dankeschön. Auf Wiedersehen.

Passant Bitte sehr. Auf Wiedersehen.

die Ampel *traffic light*	**die Brücke(-n)** *bridge*
nächst *next, nearest*	**wie weit** *how far*
die Querstraße *crossroads*	**geradeaus weiter** *straight on*
'rein *(turn) into*	**das Gebäude** *building*
die Kreuzung(-en) *crossroads*	

Philippe Gaultier is already at the fair, but has left his catalogue at the hotel. He is looking for the stand of Formflo plc and speaks to a receptionist (**eine Empfangsdame**).

Gaultier Guten Tag, Ich suche den Stand der Firma Formflo.

Empfangsdame Moment, ich muß mal nachsehen. Ja, hier ist er. Gehen Sie durch diese Tür, dann rechts. Gehen Sie an dem Restaurant vorbei und Sie werden den Stand auf der rechten Seite sehen.

Gaultier Darf ich mal auf den Katalog sehen? Dankeschön.

Empfangsdame Bitte.

suchen *to look for, seek*	**vorbeigehen an** (dat.) *to go past*
nachsehen *to look up (reference)*	

Two young colleagues, Peter Fink and Olaf Köfer, arrive on the first day to man their stand.

Peter Du, ich kenne mich hier gar nicht aus!

Olaf Ich war natürlich gestern hier. Ich muß schnell telefonieren. Geh' doch zum Stand – es ist schon spät! Ich komme in zehn Minuten.

Peter Gut, aber wie komme ich hin?

Olaf   Geh' mal hier geradeaus, und dann rechts!

Peter   Gut. Gib mir mal den Messekatalog und den Schrankschlüssel! Ich will nämlich Kaffee kochen.

Olaf   Eine gute Idee. Bis gleich. Und vergiß nicht, die Broschüren auszulegen!

Ich kenne mich hier nicht aus *I don't know my way around*	**auslegen** *to set out*
Wie komme ich hin? *How do I get there?*	**die Broschüre(-n)** *brochure*
vergessen *to forget*	**der Schrankschlüssel(-)** *cupboard key*

——————— Grammatik ———————

🔊 *The command form of the verb*

When giving an instruction, you will be using the polite form of *you* (**Sie**) or the familiar form (**du**, in the singular, **ihr** in the plural). There are therefore three forms of the imperative:

(*a*) The polite form

This is simply constructed by inverting the subject and verb:

Steigen Sie ein!	*All aboard!*
Gehen Sie geradeaus!	*Carry straight on.*
Kommen Sie herein!	*Come in.*

(*b*) The familiar form, singular

Du is omitted (as in English) and an **e** is added to the verb stem:

    du gehst becomes **gehe!**
    du kommst becomes **komme!**

Frequently this **-e** is omitted in speech.

With irregular verbs taking a vowel change in the **du** form, this **-e** is always omitted:

Vergiß die Kataloge nicht!	*Don't forget the catalogues.*
Gib mir die Flasche!	*Give me the bottle!*

The familiar form, plural

Simply omit **ihr,** exactly as in English, for example when you are dealing with two or more friends or relatives, you might wish to say:

Kommt pünktlich nach Hause!	Come home on time.
Geht weg!	Go away.
Hört doch auf!	Stop it.

As the last examples suggest, the plural familiar form is relatively unusual in business contexts. The imperative form is always followed by an exclamation mark.

—————— Übungen ——————

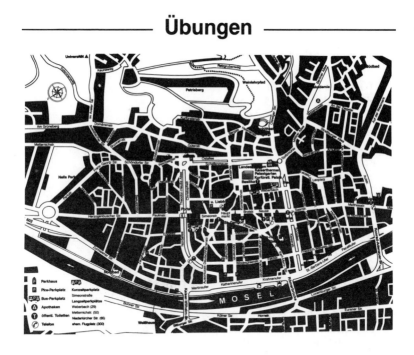

1 Look at the map of Trier. You are at the main station. Ask the way to:

der Hauptmarkt
das Karl Marx Haus
die Porta Nigra
the **Zurlauben** quay and harbour (der Hafen)

2   You are still at the station, waiting for a colleague who caught a later train, and some passers-by ask you for directions to:

die Europahalle
die St. Gandolf Kirche
die St. Paulin Kirche
der Alte Kran (a Roman crane by the river)

3   Below are some instructions. Tick the Right or Wrong column depending on whether the translation is correct or not.

Right   Wrong

a)   Steigen Sie am Messeplatz aus!
(*Get out at the exhibition*)
b)   Steigen Sie am Sendlinger Tor ein!
(*Get out at the Sendlinger Tor!*)
c)   Fahren Sie geradeaus weiter!
(*Give it a wide berth!*)
d)   An der dritten Ampel links!
(*Left at the second lights!*)
e)   Fahren Sie zurück bis zur Querstraße!
(*Go back to the crossroads!*)
f)   Gehen Sie am Stadttheater vorbei!
(*Go to the theatre!*)

4   Give the appropriate instruction:

a)   There is a knock at the door; you wish the person to enter.
b)   You invite your guest to take off her coat (**ablegen,** *to take off one's coat*).
c)   You invite your guest to take a seat.
d)   You ask your assistant to bring two coffees.
e)   Your friend phones: tell him not to forget the beer for this evening. (There is to be a party.)
f)   In return, he asks you to pick up the food from a mutual friend; you ask him to give you the address.
g)   Finally, returning to your guest, you ask her to forgive (**Entschuldigen**) the interruption (**die Unterbrechung**).

TEIL B

A group of English students is visiting Hamburg on an exchange. A

tutor from the Fachschule Hamburg-Harburg is welcoming them on
a guided tour of the city by coach.

Bitte einsteigen!
Platz nehmen, bitte! Also, meine Damen und Herren. Herzlich
Willkommen in Hamburg. Unser Fahrer kommt gleich, aber ich
möchte vorher ein paar Worte sagen.
Zunächst, darf ich mich vorstellen. Ich heiße Herr Beecken,
Vorname Olaf; ich gebe Englisch auf der Fachschule in Hamburg-
Harburg.
Ja; wir wollen gesund bleiben und die Umwelt verschonen, also
unterwegs bitte nicht rauchen!
Kaffee wird unterwegs serviert, aber bitte den Platz nicht
verlassen!
Hallo! – Aufpassen, bitte!
Ja, und am Ende unserer Reise, ein Trinkgeld für unseren Fahrer
nicht vergessen! Ich wünsche einen schönen Aufenthalt in Ham-
burg. Oh, da kommt unser Fahrer schon...

gleich *very soon, immediately*	**verschonen** *spare, save*
ein paar *a few*	**unterwegs** *en route*
zunächst *first of all*	**Kaffee wird serviert** *coffee is served*
Darf ich mich vorstellen *May I introduce myself*	**verlassen** *leave*
Ich gebe Englisch *I teach English*	**aufpassen** *pay attention, take care*
gesund *healthy, fit, good for you*	**das Trinkgeld (-er)** *tip*
bleiben *stay, remain*	**die Reise (-n)** *trip, journey*
die Umwelt *environment*	**wünschen** *to wish*
	der Aufenthalt(-e) *stay*

Grammatik

More about the imperative

In a polite, public situation, instructions are often given in the form of an
infinitive phrase: **Bitte nicht rauchen; Bitte Platz nehmen,** and so
on. The infinitive occurs at the end of the phrase in German.
(Refer to the telex in Lektion 8.)

Übungen

1 Read the passage above and write out all the infinitive phrases you can find which convey an instruction.

2 A party of Germans is visiting your home town. You are asked to welcome them. Make a short speech of welcome along the following lines:

Greet the group. Bid them welcome in your town. Introduce yourself. You would like to say a few words. Indicate they should not smoke, please, in this area (**der Raum**). This evening there is a party (**die Party**). Tomorrow at 10 a.m. there is a guided tour (**die Rundfahrt**). Tomorrow afternoon there is a visit to (a tourist attraction in your area). Wish them a pleasant stay in your town. Point to the buffet table and invite them to help themselves (**sich bedienen**).

10

APPLYING
—— FOR A ——
JOB

TEIL A

1 Eine Anzeige

 Study this advertisement from the **Süddeutsche Zeitung** (a newspaper printed in Munich). A German publishing company (**ein Unternehmen der Verlagsbranche**) is looking for a buyer (**ein Einkäufer**).

Für unseren Beratungskunden, ein bekanntes, international operierendes Unternehmen der Verlagsbranche, mit Sitz im Raum München, suchen wir einen international versierten

Einkäufer

Ihre Qualifikation
- Sie sind in vergleichbarer Position tätig.
- Sie haben umfassende Erfahrung im internationalen Einkaufs-Marketing und beherrschen demzufolge die englische Sprache perfekt.
- Sie sind sicher in den Bereichen Wertanalyse, Lieferantenbewertung und Kalkulation.
- Sie beherrschen die Verhandlungs-Strategie und -Taktik.
- Sie können teamorientiert arbeiten und führen.

Die ausgeschriebene Position ist leistungsorientiert dotiert und bietet gute Entwicklungschancen.
Wenn Sie das Angebot interessiert, bewerben Sie sich bitte mit vollständigen Unterlagen und Gehaltsangabe bei

Werbeagentur GmbH, Pegnitzstraße 8, 8000 München 19

bekannt *well-known*	**teamorientiert** *as part of a team*
versiert *experienced, practised*	**führen** *manage, lead*
vergleichbar *comparable*	**ausgeschrieben** *advertised,*
(in) ... tätig sein *to be/work (in)*	*announced*
(a sector/field, etc.)	**leistungsorientiert dotiert** *paid on*
umfassend *comprehensive*	*performance*
das Einkaufsmarketing *purchase*	**bieten** *to offer*
marketing	**die Entwicklungschance (-n)**
beherrschen *to master, to speak*	*opportunity for promotion*
(language)	**das Angebot (-e)** *offer*
demzufolge *therefore*	**sich bewerben (um)** *to apply (for)*
sicher *confident, sure*	**vollständig** *complete*
der Bereich (-e) *domain, field*	**die Unterlage (-n)***document*
die Wertanalyse (-n) *value, analysis*	**die Gehaltsangabe** *salary*
die Lieferantenbewertung *supplier*	*requirement*
analysis/assessment	
die Verhandlungsstrategie (-n)	
negotiating strategy	

Erklärungen

1 This advertisement has been placed by an advertising agency (**eine Werbeagentur**) on behalf of their client (**der Beratungskunde**).

2 Note the many English words used in business jargon; **Marketing, Taktik, Team.** This is a result of the adoption of many American management theories and ideas.

2 Ein Bewerbungsbrief

Many people applied for the job above including Martina Dorn who sent the following letter together with her curriculum vitae (**der Lebenslauf**).

Werbeagentur GmbH,
Pegnitzstraße 8
8000 München 19.

München, den 23. April

Sehr geehrte Damen und Herren,

ich habe Ihre Anzeige in der Süddeutschen Zeitung vom 21. April mit
Interesse gelesen und möchte mich um die Stelle als Einkäuferin bewerben.
Wie Sie aus dem beigefügten Lebenslauf ersehen, habe ich mein Abitur im

Jahre 1985 bestanden. Ab Oktober 1985 habe ich an der Münchener Universität studiert. Ich habe Betriebswirtschaftslehre als Hauptfach gewählt und habe mein Studium im Jahre 1990 abgeschlossen.

In September 1990 habe ich eine Stelle als Einkäuferin bei Salamander aufgenommen und habe viele Geschäftsreisen gemacht.

Jetzt bin ich als Einkäuferin bei Wertheim tätig und habe also die nötige Erfahrung in Lieferantenbewertung und Verhandlungs-Taktik bekommen.

Ich habe auch EDV Erfahrung, und spreche fließend Englisch. Meine Referenzen zeigen, daß ich gerne als Teil eines Teams arbeite.

Ich hoffe, daß diese Bewerbung Ihr Interesse erweckt und stehe Ihnen für ein Interview gerne zur Verfügung.

Ich freue mich auf Ihre baldige Antwort.

Mit freundlichen Grüßen.

Martina Dorn

Martina Dorn

---

lesen *to read*	**das Studium** *studies* (in
die Stelle (-n) *post, job*	higher education)
ersehen (aus) *to see/gather*	**abschließen** *to conclude,*
(*from*)	*finish*
das Abitur *German equivalent*	**aufnehmen** *to take on* (a job)
of A levels	**die Erfahrung** *experience*
bestehen *to pass*	**die EDV** = elektronische
(*examination*)	Datenverarbeitung *electron-*
die Betriebswirtschafts-	*ic data processing*
lehre *business*	**die Bewerbung (-en)** *the*
administration	*application*
das Hauptfach (¨er) *main*	**erwecken** *to arouse*
subject	**baldig** *in the near future*
wählen *to choose, select*	

———————— Erklärungen ————————

1   Note that in German it is not possible to say *in 1990*. The year may simply stand alone as a figure, for example:

> **1985** habe ich das Gymnasium besucht.
>
> *In 1985 I attended the grammar school.*

or must be preceded by **im Jahre**, *in the year of*, for example:

> Ich habe mein Studium **im Jahre 1990** abgeschlossen.
>
> *I completed my studies in 1990.*

Grammatik

🎬 1 Perfect tense

In order to refer to events in the past we use the perfect tense. This is
formed primarily using the present tense of **haben** followed by the past
participle which is invariable (refer to Lektion 5, the passive voice). For
example:

	machen *to make, do* (regular)
ich habe gemacht	*I have done, I did*
du hast gemacht	*you have done, you did*
Sie haben gemacht	*you have done, you did*
er/sie/es hat gemacht	*he/she/it has done, he/she/it did*
wir haben gemacht	*we have done, we did*
ihr habt gemacht	*you have done, you did*
Sie haben gemacht	*you have done, you did*
sie haben gemacht	*they have done, they did*

(*i*) In German the perfect tense is used commonly in speech and
letters to cover both the English *I have done* and *I did.*

(*ii*) Note that the past participle, in this case **gemacht,** is placed at the
end of a clause or sentence. For example:

Ich **habe** mein Abitur in einer   *I did my Abitur at a school in*
  Schule in Berlin **gemacht.**   *Berlin.*

(*iii*) Strong verbs have irregular past participles which nevertheless
follow a distinctive pattern, thus **aufnehmen** becomes **aufgenommen** in the same way as **nehmen** becomes **genommen,** and
genießen becomes **genossen** in the same way as **abschließen**
becomes **abgeschlossen.** Identify other irregular participles in the
sample letter and note related verbs in the verb table (Appendix 2).

(*iv*) Verbs with a prefix which does not become separate from the
stem (for example **be-, emp-, ent-, er-, ge-, mi-, ver-, zer-**) do not
generally add **ge** to the past participle. For example, **erwecken**
becomes **erweckt, bestehen** becomes **bestanden, bekommen**
remains as **bekommen. Bestanden** and **bekommen** are of course
also irregular in that they do not conform with the stem + **t** ending.

(*v*) Verbs ending in **-ieren** also form the past participle without the
ge, for example **studieren** becomes **studiert.**

(*vi*) In separable verbs the **ge** is placed between the prefix and the
verb stem, for example, **abschließen** becomes **abgeschlossen**

(irreg.) and **aufnehmen** becomes **aufgenommen** (irreg).

Übungen

 1 Martina Dorn is telling a colleague about the advertisement she saw and answering the following questions.

a) Wo haben Sie die Anzeige gesehen?
b) Was für eine Stelle ist es?
c) Was brauchen Sie für Erfahrung?
d) Sollen Sie Sprachkenntnisse haben?
e) In welchen Bereichen müssen Sie Fachkenntnisse haben?
f) Was für Entwicklungschancen bietet die Firma an?

Fachkenntnisse	*specialist knowledge*

2 You're explaining to a German business partner about the new branch (**Zweigstelle**) you have opened. Put the verb in brackets into the perfect tense.

a) Wir (gründen) eine neue Zweigstelle in Hamburg.
b) Der Betriebsleiter (engagieren) 50 Mitarbeiter.
c) Die Firma (mieten) drei Büros.
d) Sie (*they*) (haben) schon viel Erfolg.
e) Sie (verkaufen) viele Produkte.
f) Ich (besuchen) die Zweigstelle letzte Woche.

3 Draft out an application for one of the four following job advertisements using Martina Dorn's letter as a guide.

Frankfurter Allgemeine
ZEITUNG FÜR DEUTSCHLAND

Für die Bildredaktion der Frankfurter Allgemeinen
Zeitung suchen wir eine/n

Bildredakteur/in

Unser neuer Mitarbeiter oder unsere neue Mitarbei-
terin sollte redaktionelle Erfahrung (Agentur oder
Tageszeitung) und umfassende Kenntnisse in der
aktuellen Bildbeschaffung haben.
Wir erwarten Initiative und zuverlässiges Arbeiten im
Team. Ein gutes Auge für Bilder wird vorausgesetzt.
Schicken Sie bitte Ihre vollständigen Bewerbungs-
unterlagen unter der Kenn-Nr. 6/90 an die

Frankfurter Allgemeine Zeitung GmbH
Personalabteilung
Hellerhofstr. 2-4
6000 Frankfurt am Main 1

TEIL B

This is the cv sent by Martina Dorn with her letter of application.

LEBENSLAUF

Familienname: Dorn   Vorname: Martina

Anschrift: Wittenbergstr. 14, 1000 München 2.

geb. am: 10 Oktober 1966   in: Köln, Nordrhein Westfalen

Vater: Johann Josef Dorn

Beruf: Bildredakteur

Mutter: Gertrud Dorn, geb. Beck

Beruf: Hausfrau

BILDUNG:

Gymnasium: von 1978 bis 1985 – Abitur mit 2,4 – Dalberg Gymnasium, Köln

Studium: von 1985 bis 1990 – Münchener Universität – Diplom Betriebswirt

BERUFLICHE ERFAHRUNG:

September 1990 –   Oktober 1991 Einkäuferin bei Salamander Schuhen AG, München Oktober 1991 bis heute Einkäuferin bei Wertheim GmbH, München

REFERENZEN: Herr Zimmermann (Einkaufsleiter), Wertheim, Rosastraße 15, 8000 München 20

---

die Anschrift (-en) *address*
der Bildredakteur (-e) *picture editor*
die Hausfrau (-en) *housewife*
die Bildung *education*
das Gymnasium (Gymnasien) *grammar school*

das Diplom (-e) *equivalent of a British degree*
Diplom Betriebswirt *degree in business administration*
beruflich *professional*

Erklärungen

 1 Contrary to English custom, German cvs are generally requested handwritten since this can be more revealing than a typewritten copy!

2 Note that German cvs generally give brief details of the parents.

3 **Geb.** is the abbreviation of **geboren** meaning *born*, for example:

Ich bin im Jahre 1959 geboren.   *I was born in 1959.*

4 After **die Grundschule**, *primary school*, there are three different types of secondary school in Germany:

- **Das Gymnasium** which is the approximate equivalent of the British grammar school and which generally leads on to **die Universität.**
- **Die Realschule** which is a technical school which concentrates on more vocational courses and which often leads to **die Fachhochschule** which is comparable to a polytechnic.
- **Die Hauptschule** which is equivalent to a former secondary modern school and less academic, generally leading straight into work or an apprenticeship (**die Lehre**).

Dialog

Two executives of the publishing company are shortlisting the candidates and are considering Martina's application.

Frau Feder   Gerd, hast du diese Bewerbung von Martina Dorn gesehen? Sie hat die richtigen Qualifikationen.

Herr Fuchs   Nein, sie ist gerade mit der Post gekommen.

Frau Feder   Also, sie hat neulich ein Diplom Betriebswirt abgeschlossen und ist auch bei Salamander tätig gewesen.

Herr Fuchs   Ja? und was hat sie dort für Aufgaben gehabt?

Frau Feder   Sie hat mit den ausländischen Lieferanten verhandelt und hat alle Entscheidungen in Bezug auf Importe getroffen.

Herr Fuchs   Hat sie auch ihre Referenzen geschickt?

Frau Feder   Ja, sie sind sehr gut. Sie hat sich gut in ihr Einkaufsteam integriert und sich als sehr zuverlässig bewiesen.

---

die Aufgabe (-n) *task, job*	**in Bezug auf** *relating to, with reference to*
verhandeln *to negotiate*	**sich beweisen (als)** *to prove oneself (as)*
eine Entscheidung (-en) treffen *to make a decision*	

Grammatik

1 *Perfect tense with sein*

As a rule, verbs like **kommen, gehen, fahren** and **laufen** (*to run, walk*) which show a change of place (movement) or **sterben** (*to die*) and **werden** (*to become*) which show a change of state, form the perfect tense using the present tense of **sein** rather than **haben**. For example:

---

werden *to become*	
ich bin geworden	*I have become, I became*
du bist geworden	*you have become, you became*
Sie sind geworden	*you have become, you became*
er/sie/es ist geworden	*he/she/it has become, he/she/it became*
wir sind geworden	*we have become, we became*
ihr seid geworden	*you have become, you became*
Sie sind geworden	*you have become, you became*
sie sind geworden	*they have become, they became*

(*i*) Whether a verb takes **haben** or **sein** in the perfect tense is indicated in most dictionaries by **h** or **s**.

(*ii*) **Bleiben** and **sein** also both form the perfect tense with **sein**.

(*iii*) Many of these verbs are also strong and have irregular past participles, for example:

kommen	gekommen	laufen	gelaufen
gehen	gegangen	bleiben	geblieben
fahren	gefahren		

Again these can be noted as following a similar change to strong verbs of the same type; for example, **bleiben** and **beweisen** make the same vowel change to become **geblieben** and **bewiesen,** and **werden** and **bewerben** become **geworden** and **beworben.** Study the verb tables in Appendix 2 for further examples.

(*iv*) **Sein** itself forms the totally irregular participle **gewesen.**

Übungen

1 Answer the following questions about Martina.

    a)   Wann ist Martina geboren?
    b)   Was ist ihr Vater von Beruf?
    c)   Wann hat sie das Gymnasium besucht?
    d)   Wann hat sie ihr Studium abgeschlossen?
    e)   Wann hat sie bei Salamander gearbeitet?
    f)   Wann hat sie ihre Stelle bei Wertheim gefunden?

2 You're expecting a new German colleague and you ask a few questions about his background.

Sie	*Ask what sort of degree he has completed.*
Herr Grünwald	Er hat ein Diplom in Chemie bekommen.
Sie	*Ask where he has worked until now.*
Herr Grünwald	Er hat bei Daimler Benz gearbeitet.
Sie	*Ask what sort of work he did.*
Herr Grünwald	Er war im Verkauf tätig.
Sie	*Ask if he has had experience in negotiation.*
Herr Grünwald	Ja, er hatte persönlichen Kontakt mit vielen Kunden.

3 Complete the following conversation between two colleagues by inserting the past participle of the verbs in brackets.

Ralf Braun	Wo bist du am Wochenende (sein)?
Klaus Schmidt	Ich bin nach Hause (fahren).
Ralf	Hast du Freunden (besuchen)?
Klaus	Nein, ich habe eine Geschäftsreise (machen).
Ralf	Hast du Erfolg (haben)?
Klaus	Ja, die Firma hat 100 Maschinen (kaufen)

4 Fill in this form with information about yourself.

Familienname: Vorname:

Anschrift:

geb. am: in:

Vater:

Beruf:

Mutter:

Beruf:

Bildung:

Berufliche Erfahrung:

Referenzen:

11
ATTENDING
— AN —
INTERVIEW

TEIL A

Martina Dorn received the following letter from Frau Feder:

Sehr geehrte Frau Dorn,

Stellenangebot: Einkäuferin

Wir danken ihnen fur Ihren Brief, der gestern hier eingegangen ist. Ich möchte Sie zu einem Gespräch einladen, das am 18.3.um 10.00h.hier in meinem Büro stattfinden wird. Herr Gibowski, der auch am Gespräch teilnehmen wird ist unser Betriebsleiter.

Wollen Sie bitte kurz bestätigen, daß Sie am 18.3. anwesend sein werden.

Mit freundlichen Grüßen,

Dorothea Feder

Dorothea Feder

Stellenangebot (-e) *job vacancy*	**einladen** *invite*
eingehen *to arrive* (of goods, mail)	**stattfinden** *to take place*
das Gespräch(-e) *conversation,*	**teilnehmen an** (+dat.) *to take part in*
interview	**anwesend** *present*

———— Erklärungen ————

1 **Danken,** *to thank*, takes the dative case, hence: **Wir danken Ihnen für...**

Refer to Lektion 6 on this.

Martina replied:

Sehr geehrte Frau Feder,

Haben Sie vielen Dank für Ihren Brief vom 12.3., den ich erst heute aber erhalten habe, und der mich zu einem Gespräch einlädt. Ich werde am 18.3. um 10.00h. bei Ihnen vorsprechen.

Mit freundlichen Grüßen,

M. Dorn

M. Dorn

erst heute *not until today*	**vorsprechen** *to present*
erhalten *to receive*	*oneself* (for a meeting)

Erklärungen

 1 **Haben Sie vielen Dank für...** is not as formal as **Wir danken Ihnen für...,** but is acceptable in professional communications.

Grammatik

1 *Relative clauses*

These are clauses which describe or qualify a noun. They begin with *which, that* or *who* in English. These words are called relative pronouns. The equivalent words in German are **der, die,** and **das** and their variants. **Der, die** and **das** render *who, which* or *that*. For example:

*The firm **which makes teddybears** has gone bankrupt.*
*The man **who ran it** now makes dolls.*
*The product **(that) we make** is popular.*

would be expressed in German as follows:

Die Firma, **die Teddybäre herstellt,** hat Pleite gemacht.
Der Mann, **der sie führte,** produziert jetzt Puppen.
Das Produkt, **das wir herstellen,** ist populär.

The form of the word for *which* and *who* depends on the gender (masculine, feminine, neuter) and the number (singular or plural) of the word to which it refers, for example **die Firma, die...** and **der Mann, der...** But, like English, it takes its case from the role it plays in its own clause:

Das ist der Mann, **den** ich gestern traf.	*That is the man (whom) I met yesterday.*
Dies ist die Firma, bei **der** ich arbeite.	*This is the firm (which) I work at.*

(*i*)   The last example also demonstrates the point that, as in strictly correct English, the preposition governing the relative pronoun precedes it. So that **bei** precedes the dative relative pronoun in this example:

Das Haus, **in dem** ich wohne, ist ganz groß.	*The house I live in is large.*
Die Stelle, **um die** ich mich bewerbe, ist recht gut dotiert.	*The job I am applying for is pretty well paid.*

(*ii*)   In the written language, relative clauses are always marked off by commas.

(*iii*)   The active verb in the relative clause goes to the end of that clause. Check the above examples and the texts for this.

Übungen

1   Check through the two letters and identify all the relative pronouns. For each one, write out why it has the form it has. For example:

der refers to **Brief:** masculine singular. Nominative because it is the subject of its own clause.

Do this for all occurrences.

TEIL B

Dialog

Martina attends her interview on the 18th March. Here are two extracts from her discussions with Frau Feder and Herr Fuchs:

Feder ...Erzählen Sie also etwas von den Aufgaben, die Sie bei Salamander erfüllten.

Dorn Also, der Herr, für den ich arbeitete, Herr Behr, war Einkäufer. Ich habe seine Post gemacht und seinen Kalender geführt. Ich habe auch Lieferanten betreut, die uns ab und zu besucht haben. Die Firma, die übrigens eine internationale Firma ist, hat auch englische Kontakte. Also ich habe die Post in Englisch geführt und englische und amerikanische Lieferanten betreut. Die Abteilung, in der ich arbeitete, war nicht groß aber sehr aktiv.

Feder Und wie stellen Sie sich die Stelle vor, die wir jetzt besprechen?

Dorn Also, die Arbeit wird wahrscheinlich sehr genau und präzise sein. Denn es geht wahrscheinlich um Material, das 100% richtig sein muß. Und ich nehme an, daß wir viele Einzelheiten und Details nachsehen müssen.

Feder Ja, das auf jeden Fall. Und können Sie fließend Englisch?

Dorn Also ja, zum Teil. Das heißt, die Aufgaben, die ich bei Salamander erfüllt habe, haben das von mir verlangt.

erfüllen *fulfil, do*	**annehmen** *suppose, assume*
betreuen *look after, see to*	**die Einzelheit (-en)** *detail*
ab und zu *now and again*	**nachsehen** *look up* (in
übrigens *by the way*	reference work)
die Abteilung (-en) department	**auf jeden Fall** *certainly, of course* (here)
sich (acc.) **vorstellen** *to imagine*	**fließend** *fluent(ly)*
besprechen *discuss*	**zum Teil** *partly, to some extent, sort of*
wahrscheinlich *probably*	**verlangen** *demand*
es geht um *it is about, to do with*	

Dialog

Fuchs Frau Dorn, es freut mich, Ihnen diese Stelle anzubieten.
Dorn Vielen Dank, Herr Fuchs.
Fuchs Nun, wann können Sie anfangen?
Dorn Also, die Wohnung, die wir kaufen wollen, wird am 1.4. frei. Der Einzug dauert ein paar Tage. Ich denke, am

Fuchs	Montag, dem 5. nächsten Monates. Sagt Ihnen das zu? Durchaus. Die Projekte, die jetzt anstehen, sind allerdings dringend. Je früher Sie anfangen, desto besser.
Dorn	Ja, das sehe ich ein. Können wir uns also auf den 5. vereinbaren?
Fuchs	Ja. In Ordnung. Oh, das ist Frau Schmidt, unsere Büroleiterin. Frau Dorn. Frau Dorn wird am 5.April bei uns anfangen.
Schmidt	Sehr angenehm. Ich werde Ihnen Ihr Büro zeigen. Ist Ihnen das recht, Herr Fuchs?
Fuchs	Sicher, Frau Schmidt. Zeigen Sie auch den Haufen Projekte, die sowieso überfällig sind!

es freut mich	*I am pleased*	**dringend**	*urgent*
anbieten	*offer*	**je...desto...**	*the (more)...the*
anfangen	*begin*		*(more)*
die Wohnung	*apartment, flat*	**vereinbaren**	*agree*
der Einzug (⁼e)	*moving in*	**Sehr angenehm**	*Pleased to*
Sagt Ihnen das zu?	*Is that*		*meet you*
	alright by you?	**Ist Ihnen das recht?**	*Is that*
anstehen	*be on the agenda,*		*alright by you?*
	be in hand	**zeigen**	*show*
durchaus	*of course, certainly*	**der Haufen**	*pile*
allerdings	*however*	**überfällig**	*overdue*

Erklärungen

1 **Je...desto...** are each followed by a comparative as in English. For example:

> **Je** früher er kommt, **desto** mehr Zeit haben wir.
> *The earlier he comes, the more time we (shall) have.*
>
> **Je** größer die Bestellung, **desto** kleiner der Stückpreis.
> *The larger the order, the smaller the piece price.*

2 **Sehr angenehm** can be used as *Pleased to meet you.*

Übungen

1 Complete the following:

a) Die Firma, bei ... ich früher arbeitete, heißt Schmidt und Sohn.
b) Das ist doch der Brief, ... ich suchte!
c) Ich mag die Wohnung, in ... ich wohne.
d) Angelika hat die Stelle bekommen, um ... sie sich bewarb.
e) München ist eine Großstadt, ... in Süddeutschland liegt.
f) Frau Schmidt ist die Büroleiterin, für ... Angelika arbeiten wird.
g) Die Projekte, ... Angelika bearbeiten (*work on*) muß, liegen auf dem Schreibtisch.

2   Complete the following telephone conversation between a person asking for details about a job advertised and the organisation advertising the post. You will find the vocabulary you need underneath the dialogue.

Empfang	Firma Sprenkler, Guten Tag?
You	*Say hello, it's about the job which appeared (**erschien**) in the newspaper.*
Empfang	Marketingassistent, meinen Sie?
You	*Confirm this is correct.*
Empfang	Wie kann ich Ihnen helfen?
You	*Say you would like to speak to the person who is responsible for Marketing.*
Empfang	Das ist Frau Stinnes. Sie ist Marketingleiterin. Moment, ich verbinde.
Stinnes	Ja, Sie interessieren sich für die Stelle als Marketingassistent?
You	*Say yes, it is a post which interests you very much.*
Stinnes	Gut. Dann schicken Sie mir Ihren Lebenslauf. Bei welcher Firma arbeiten Sie jetzt?
You	*Say it is a company which produces furniture.*
Stinnes	Und welche Stelle haben Sie dort?
You	*Say you work in the sales office. But you also look after customers and make visits. The boss, who is very nice, demands a lot – and you carry it out.*
Stinnes	Gut. Ich erwarte Ihre Bewerbung also. Auf Wiederhören.
You	*Goodbye, Frau Stinnes.*

erledigen	*to carry out*	**Sich handeln (um)**	*to be about, concern*
die Zeitung	*newspaper*	**zuständig für**	*responsible for*
dafür	*for it*	**das Verkaufsbüro**	*sales office*

12
MAKING
SOCIAL
CONTACTS

TEIL A

Dialog

Martina Dorn has now been selected for the position of buyer at Neumann GmbH in Munich. On her first day she meets some of the people in the company.

Johannes Becker	Hallo, sind Sie die neue Einkäuferin, die letzte Woche angestellt wurde?
Martina	Ja, ich habe erst heute angefangen.
Johannes	Es freut mich, Sie kennenzulernen. Ich heiße Johannes Becker und arbeite in der Verkaufsabteilung.
Martina	Es freut mich auch. Ich bin Martina Dorn.
Johannes	Bei welcher Firma waren Sie vorher tätig?
Martina	Ich war bei Wertheim in der Stadtmitte.
Johannes	Eine gute Firma! Warum wollten Sie nicht mehr dort arbeiten?
Martina	Ich konnte schon alles und es wurde einfach langweilig.
Johannes	Das kann ich verstehen. Hoffentlich werden Sie sich hier nicht langweilen!
Martina	Wie lange sind Sie schon hier?
Johannes	3 Jahre, vorher hatte ich eine Stelle bei einer Textilfirma, die Timmermann OHG hieß, aber

sie war zu klein. Ich arbeite gerne bei einer
größeren Firma; man hat mehr Abwechselung!
Ich finde das Betriebsklima ganz aufregend hier.
Haben Sie schon die anderen Mitarbeiter ken-
nengelernt?

Martina   Nein, noch nicht.
Johannes   Dann muß ich Ihnen die Leute hier gleich vorstellen. Kommen Sie mit!

---

recht haben *to be right*	**die Abwechselung** *variety*
heißen *to be called*	**aufregend** *exciting*
langweilig *boring*	**noch nicht** *not yet*
sich langweilen *to be bored*	

Erklärungen

1   Note that the expressions *to be right* and *to be wrong* are translated
in German using the verb **haben,** *to have,* for example:

Du **hast** recht.   You are right.
Er **hat** unrecht.   He is wrong.

2   **Gerade** is used to express the idea of *have just done,* for example:

Ich bin **gerade** angekommen.   I have just arrived.

Grammatik

1   I was doing (the imperfect tense)

Apart from the few exceptions given in note (*i*) below, the imperfect
tense is in fact little used in speech and letters in German where the
perfect tense is preferred. It is most commonly found in prose writing
where past events are being related. It is formed by adding the
following endings to the verb stem:

---

machen *to do*	
ich mach**te** *I did*	wir mach**ten** *we did*
du mach**test** *you did*	ihr mach**tet** *you did*
Sie mach**ten** *you did*	Sie mach**ten** *you did*
er/sie/es mach**te** *he/she/it did*	sie mach**ten** *they did*

(*i*) There are a number of common verbs which are used in the imperfect in speech. They include **sein, haben, müssen, können** and **wollen.** Of these only **wollen** is regular. Both **können** and **müssen** drop their umlaut. For example:

Wir **konnten** nicht mit dem Auto fahren.	*We couldn't travel by car.*
Ich **mußte** nach Hause gehen.	*I had to go home.*

The forms of **sein** and **haben** are as follows:

sein *to be*		**haben** *to have*	
ich war	*I was*	ich hatt**e**	*I had*
du war**st**	*you were*	du hatt**est**	*you had*
Sie war**en**	*you were*	Sie hatt**en**	*you had*
er/sie/es/war	*he/she/it was*	er/sie/es hatt**e**	*he/she/it had*
wir war**ten**	*we were*	wir hatt**en**	*we had*
ihr wart	*you were*	ihr hatt**et**	*you had*
Sie war**en**	*you were*	Sie hatt**en**	*you had*
sie war**en**	*they were*	sie hatt**en**	*they had*

For example:

Wo **waren Sie** gestern?	*Where were you yesterday?*
Ich hatte einen Termin.	*I had an appointment.*

Note: The endings indicated on the stem **war** are typical for other irregular and strong verbs, for example:

ankommen
Sie **kam**en gestern **an.**   *They arrived yesterday.*
(also **bekommen** changes to **bekamen**)
sehen
Ich **sah** den Film zweimal.   *I saw the film twice.*
(similarly **lesen** becomes **las**)
heißen
Die Firma **hieß** Henkel GmbH.   *The company was called Henkel GmbH.*

Heißen is also commonly used in speech in the imperfect. Study the verb tables for other examples.

2 Seit (since) + present tense

Expressing an idea about something which has been done since a point in time is done using the present tense in German on the understanding that it is an action continuing into the present, for example:

Seit wann **arbeiten** Sie hier?	*Since when (how long) have you worked here?*
Ich **arbeite** hier seit dem 1. Januar.	*I have been working here since the 1st January.*

This structure can also be used to express an action which has been carried out *for* a period of time, for example:

Er studiert schon seit 2 Jahren.	*He has already studied for 2 years.*

Übungen

1 Study the dialogue again and then give the information requested below about Johannes Becker.

    a) In welcher Abteilung arbeitet Johannes Becker?
    b) Seit wann ist er bei der Firma?
    c) Wo hatte er vorher eine Stelle?
    d) Warum wollte er nicht dort bleiben?
    e) Was denkt er über die Firma Neumann?

2 Johannes Becker is describing the company where he used to work. Look at the information below and give his answers to the questions:

Firmenname	Timmermann OHG
Betriebsleiter	Herr Heidegott
Personal	50 Mitarbeiter
Marketingassistent	Johannes Becker
Gehalt	DM 5.000 pro Monat
Urlaub	5 Wochen

    a) Wie hieß Ihre letzte Firma?
    b) Wer war der Betriebsleiter?
    c) Wieviel Mitarbeiter waren da angestellt?
    d) Was für eine Stelle hatten Sie?
    e) Wieviel haben Sie verdient?
    f) Wieviel Wochen konnten Sie in Urlaub fahren?

3 You have just taken a new job in Germany. At the end of the first week you go out for a drink with some of your new colleagues and answer their questions about your past experience. Answer with reference to your own past/present or give an imaginary account.

a) Wo waren Sie vorher?
b) Was für eine Stelle hatten Sie?
c) Warum wollten Sie nach Deutschland kommen?
d) Konnten Sie schon Deutsch?
e) Mußten Sie zuerst in einem Hotel wohnen?

4 You want to ask them some questions, so express the following in German.

a) How long have you worked for the company?
b) Since when have you been exporting to England?
c) How long has the company produced spare parts?
d) Since when has the company had an office in Japan?

TEIL B

Martina has worked for Neumann GmbH for several months now and has just arrived back from a trade fair in Hannover. She now writes the following letter to thank a potential supplier for their hospitality.

Sehr geehrter Herr Bleuel,

Ich danke Ihnen herzlich für den sehr angenehmen Empfang auf Ihrem Stand letzte Woche auf der Hannover Messe. Wir interessieren uns sehr für Ihre Kinderbücher und finden, daß es hier in Süddeutschland sehr gute Absatzmöglichkeiten für dieses Sortiment gibt.

In Bezug auf Ihre Preisliste möchte ich gerne um Ihre 'gelieferten' Preise bitten, so daß wir einen Preisvergleich ausführen können.

Nochmals vielen Dank für Ihre Gastfreundlichkeit und wir freuen uns auf eine angenehme Geschäftsverbindung mit Ihnen.

Mit freundlichen Grüßen,

M.Dorn

M.Dorn

der Empfang *reception*	**der Preisvergleich (-e)** *price comparison*
die Messe (-n) *fair*	**ausführen** *carry out*
das Kinderbuch (¨er) *children's book*	**die Gastfreundlichkeit** *hospitality*
die Absatzmöglichkeiten *marketing possibilities/ potential*	
geliefert *delivered* (i.e. franco domicile)	

Ich würde mich sehr freuen, Dich

am Samstag, den 28.03.92

um 20.30 Uhr

zu einer Weinprobe

bei mir zu sehen.

Bitte gib mir Antwort ob Du kommst.

Martina leaves the following note for Johannes on his desk.

Johannes,

Ich bin vorbeigekommen aber du warst nicht hier! Da ich jetzt meine neue
Wohnung eingerichtet habe, möchte ich eine kleine Einweihungsfete
organisieren. Ich habe Maria, Peter und Georg schon eingeladen und ich
hoffe, daß du auch kommen kannst. Wir essen um acht Uhr!

viele liebe Grüße

Martina
Martina

vorbeikommen *to pass by, pop in*	**die Einweihungsfete** *house-warming party*
die Wohnung (-en) *apartment*	
einrichten *to furnish*	**einladen** *to invite*

-------------------- **Erklärungen** --------------------

1 Note the more casual ending **viele liebe Grüße** which is an
approximate equivalent of *best/warm wishes*.

Übungen

1   You've just returned from a trade fair in Munich where you met
    Frau Oertel a potential supplier of woollen fabrics (**Wollstoffe**)
    which you think will sell very well in Britain. Write a letter similar to
    the sample on page 116 thanking her for her hospitality and
    requesting the latest price list.

2   You leave a note for a German colleague in his/her office to invite
    him/her to a party at your house. Say you popped in at 4 o'clock but
    she/he wasn't there. Say you have organised a party at your home
    to celebrate your birthday and that you hope that she/he will come
    with his wife/her husband. Say you are eating at about nine o'clock.

bei uns zu Hause	*at our home*	**feiern**	*to celebrate*
der Geburtstag(-e)	*birthday*		

13

BUYING
—— AND ——
SELLING

The Essen branch of Thyssen AG, the steel and machine tool manufacturers, wishes to buy some office furniture and telephones Kuhl Möbel GmbH, who are office furniture wholesalers (**Büromöbelgroß-händler**).

Verkäufer	Kuhl Möbel, Guten Morgen.
Einkäufer	Herr Wegener von der Thyssen AG am Apparat. Wir haben Ihren Katalog erhalten und möchten gern Ihre Verkaufsbedingungen erfahren.
Verkäufer	Natürlich. Wir gewähren normalerweise einen Mengenrabatt von 10 Prozent für Aufträge über DM 15.000 und wir wären in der Lage Ihnen ein zusätzliches Skonto von zwei Prozent anzubieten, wenn die Zahlung innerhalb von 30 Tagen nach Empfang der Bestellung erfolgt.
Herr Wegener	Ich möchte auch gerne wissen, was für Zahlungs-arten Sie annehmen?
Verkäufer	Es steht Ihnen frei per Scheck oder Wechsel zu bezahlen. Wenn Sie zum Beispiel durch einen Wechsel per 30 Tage Sicht bezahlten, hätten Sie immer noch Recht auf das 2-prozentige Skonto.
Herr Wegener	Und wie schnell könnten Sie uns beliefern?
Verkäufer	Normalerweise wäre es möglich die Sendung innerhalb von acht Wochen nach Erhalt der Bestell-ung zu versenden.
Herr Wegener	Also, wir brauchen dringend Büromöbel, um unsere neuen Büros in Steele auszustatten. Wenn wir

	Ihnen heute eine Bestellung vom Katalog erteilten, wären Sie bereit uns innerhalb von vier Wochen zu beliefern?
Verkäufer	Wir würden das normalerweise schaffen, aber zur Zeit sind wir mit Aufträgen überhaüft. Ich kann Ihnen nichts versprechen.
Herr Wegener	Ich hätte natürlich früher bestellen sollen, wenn ich nur daran gedacht hätte!
Verkäufer	Wie wäre es mit spätestens sechs Wochen?
Herr Wegener	Ja, schon in Ordnung. Ich schicke Ihnen den Auftrag sofort und hoffe, daß die Waren bis zum 30. Juli ankommen.

erhalten *to receive*
die Verkaufsbedingungen *conditions of sale*
erfahren *to be told, to find out*
gewähren *to grant*
der Mengenrabatt (-e) *bulk discount*
in der Lage sein *to be in a position*
das Skonto (-s) *cash discount*
der Empfang (¨e) *receipt*
die Bestellung (-en) *order*
erfolgen *to ensue, follow, occur*
die Zahlungsart (-en) *means of payment*

der Wechsel (-) *bill of exchange*
per 30 Tage Sicht *at 30 days sight*
Recht haben (auf) *to be entitled (to)*
bereit sein (zu) *to be prepared (to)*
beliefern *to deliver*
die Sendung (-en) *consignment*
der Erhalt (-) *receipt*
ausstatten *to furnish, equip*
dringend *urgently*
erteilen *to place (of order)*
überhäuft *overwhelmed, swamped*

Erklärungen

1 The verb **freistehen** with the dative expresses the idea *to be up to*, for example:

Es **steht** Ihnen **frei**, ob Sie sofort bezahlen oder später. *It is up to you whether you pay immediately or later.*

2 Note the formation of an adjective used in compounds with figures (**2 – prozentig**) by adding **-ig** to the noun. Other examples of this are **...-jährig** and **...-tägig**. For example:

Ein **3-jähriger** Vertrag. *A 3-year contract.*

—— Grammatik ——

☞ 1 Would (the subjunctive)

The subjunctive is used to express thoughts, ideas and hypotheses rather than factual statements. It is thus the mode which is used to express ideas like *What would happen if.../If only...,* etc. It is primarily used in the imperfect tense and is formed by adding the following endings to the stem of the imperfect tense. There are two forms, weak and strong:

Weak **machen** (stem **macht-**)	*Strong* **gehen** (stem **ging-**)
ich macht**e**	ich ging**e**
du macht**est**	du ging**est**
Sie macht**en**	Sie ging**en**
er/sie/es macht**e**	er/sie es ging**e**
wir macht**en**	wir ging**en**
ihr macht**et**	ihr ging**et**
Sie macht**en**	Sie ging**en**
sie macht**en**	sie ging**en**

(*i*) No translation is given since the subjunctive expresses various ideas – see examples below.

(*ii*) The weak imperfect subjunctive is in fact the same as the regular imperfect indicative tense (see Lektion 11).

(*iii*) Strong verbs with the stem vowel **a**, **o** or **u** take an umlaut, for example:

haben	→	hatten (imp.)	→	hätte(n)
sein	→	war (imp.)	→	wäre(n)
geben	→	gab (imp.)	→	gäbe(n)

The subjunctive is most commonly used in the following constructions:

(*a*) I would (the conditional)

The subjunctive often expresses *I would do ...,* etc., for example:

Ich **möchte** eine große Bestellung erteilen.
I would like to place a large order.

Wären Sie in der Lage einen Mengenrabatt anzubieten?
Would you be in a position to offer a quantity discount?

but this can also be achieved using the subjunctive of werden, for example:

Ich **würde** ein Skonto nie anbieten.	*I would never offer a cash discount.*

The subjunctive is also used in conditional sentences expressing *What would happen if ...,* for example:

Würden Sie uns einen Rabatt gewähren, wenn wir 100 Stück bestellten? *Would you grant us a discount if we ordered 100?*

Wir **wären** in der Lage sofort zu liefern, wenn Sie vom Katalog bestellten. *We would be in a position to deliver immediately, if you ordered from the catalogue.*

Note: **bestellten** is also in the subjunctive mood although the form is identical to the imperfect (weak verb).

(b) Wishes

The subjunctive expresses wishes with *If only ...,* for example:

Wenn ich nur gleich bezahlt **hätte!**	*If only I had paid immediately!*
Wenn Sie nur mit einem Wechsel bezahlen **könnten!**	*If only you could pay by bill of exchange!*

(c) What you should/should not have done

To express regret at what you *should have done* or *should not have done,* the subjunctive is used with **sollen,** i.e. **hätte tun sollen** or **hätte nicht tun sollen,** for example:

Ich **hätte** mehr Stühle **bestellen sollen!**	*I should have ordered more chairs!*
Sie **hätten** den Auftrag **nicht annehmen sollen.**	*You shouldn't have accepted the order.*

Übungen

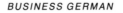

1 Study the dialogue again and then answer the questions below.

a) Was für einen Mengenrabatt gewährt Kuhl Möbel?
b) Wann muß Thyssen AG bezahlen, um das 2-prozentige Skonto zu bekommen?
c) Wann kann Kuhl Möbel die Waren liefern?
d) Warum braucht Thyssen AG die Waren dringend?
e) Über welche Lieferzeit einigen sich die zwei Firmen?
f) Was für Zahlungsarten nimmt Kuhl Möbel an?

sich einigen (über)	*to agree (on)*

2 Study the order form below and answer the questions that follow:

Kuhl Möbel GmbH
Bonnerstr. 46
4300 Essen 1

Ihr Zeichen: HR/90
Unser Zeichen: mp34.1

Auftragnummer: B2453   4. Juni 199

15 Tische 1.60 × 80   Modellnr. 231 zum Preis von DM 550.00 pro Stück
10 Stühle mit Ledersitz   Modellnr. 876 zum Preis von DM 350.00 pro Stück
2 Schränke   Modellnr. 342 zum Preis von DM 990.00 pro Stück

Lieferung: Frei Haus
        Thyssen AG, Rüttenscheiderstr. 7, 4300 Essen 1.

Lieferzeit: 6 Wochen

Zahlung: durch Tratte per 30 Tage Sicht

a) Welche Waren werden bestellt?
b) Wieviel kosten die Stühle pro Stück?
c) Was sind die Zahlungsbedingungen?
d) Wie lang ist die Lieferzeit?
e) Was sind die Lieferungsbedingungen?

3 Your company in Germany requires office supplies (**Büromaterial**) urgently and your usual supplier cannot help you. You telephone another large wholesaler in the area to find out their terms and to order the following:

50 Mappen   *50 folders*
500 Umschläge (weiß)   *500 envelopes (white)*
5 Packungen Schreibmaschinenpapier
   5 packs of typewriting paper
1.000 Büroklammer   *1000 paper clips*

Angestellte	Schmidt GmbH, Guten Morgen.
Sie	*Good morning. Say you are phoning from Volkswagen AG. You need office supplies and you would like to know if they grant quantity discounts.*
Angestellte	Also normalerweise gewähren wir einen Rabatt von 10 Prozent für Aufträge über DM 250.00.
Sie	*Ask if they give discount for prompt payment.*
Angestellte	Nein, unsere Finanzabteilung gewährt kein Skonto.
Sie	*Say that you need the goods urgently and ask them if they would be in a position to send the consignment immediately.*
Angestellte	Im allgemeinen können wir Bestellungen am gleichen Tag versenden, vorausgesetzt, daß wir die Waren auf Lager haben. Was möchten Sie bestellen?
Sie	*Tell him what you want to order.*
Angestellte	Also wir haben große Mengen von diesen Waren, nur bei Mappen könnte es problematisch werden. Wieviel brauchen Sie nochmal?
Sie	*Say you need 50. Ask if they have got enough.*
Angestellte	Ich glaube ja.
Sie	*Say that you will send the order immediately and that you hope the goods will arrive before Friday.*
Angestellte	Machen Sie sich keine Sorgen. Wir werden die Waren sofort versenden.
Sie	*Thank him and say goodbye.*
Angestellte	Nichts zu danken. Auf Wiederhören.

---

ausreichend	*enough/sufficient*	**vorausgesetzt, daß**	*provided that*

---

4 You have just lost a large order and are considering what you should/should not have done. How would you say the following in English?

a)   Wir hätten ihre Bedingungen annehmen sollen!

b) Wenn ich nur ein Skonto angeboten hätte!

c) Der Betriebsleiter hätte keine Anzahlung verlangen sollen.

d) Wenn wir nur eine kürzere Lieferzeit versprochen hätten.

e) Ich hätte einen Mengenrabatt gewähren sollen.

---

die Anzahlung (-en) _the downpayment_	**verlangen** _to demand_

---

5 You are negotiating for the best deal for your company. Express the following queries in German.

a) Could you give us a cash discount if we paid immediately?

b) Would it be possible to grant a bulk discount if we ordered 100 desks?

c) Would you be prepared to accept a cheque?

d) If we paid by bill of exchange, would we have 90 days credit?

e) Would you deliver immediately if we placed an order now?

TEIL B

1 **Antwort auf eine Anfrage über Preise und Zahlungsbedingungen (_Reply to a request for information about prices and terms_).**

Sehr geehrter Herr,

wir danken Ihnen für Ihre Anfrage vom 6. dieses Monats. Wir freuen uns, daß Sie sich für unsere Waren interessieren und legen unseren letzten Katalog und unsere Preisliste bei.

Die Preise verstehen sich frei an Bord deutscher Hafen einschließlich Verpackung. Wir sind aber auch bereit Ihnen einen Mengenrabatt von 10% auf alle Aufträge über DM 1.500 anzubieten.

Für Zahlung innerhalb 30 Tage gewähren wir ein Skonto von 2%. Alle Überweisungen können auf unser Konto nr. 875 34442 1 bei der Deutschen Bank, Flachsmart 11, Köln, vorgenommen werden.

Wir freuen uns auf Ihre Bestellung, die wir prompt und sorgfältig ausführen werden.

mit freundlichen Grüßen

sich verstehen *to be quoted* (of prices)	**die Überweisung (-en)** *transfer*
frei an Bord *free on board* (incoterm)	**das Konto** **(Konten)** *account(s)*
die Verpackung (-en) *packaging*	**vornehmen** *to carry out*
innerhalb *within*	**sorgfältig** *carefully*

Erklärungen

1   **Innerhalb** takes the genitive (see Lektion 6), for example:

innerhalb des nächsten Monats — *within the next month*

Other words which are in this group are **außerhalb,** *outside*; **statt,** *instead*; **trotz,** *despite*; and **während,** *during*, for example:

während des Tages — *during the day*
trotz der Bedingungen — *despite the conditions*

2   Other expressions relating to delivery conditions are:

ab Werk/ab Fabrik *ex works*	**geliefert verzollt** *delivered duty paid*
frei Waggon *free on rail*	
Kosten, Versicherung, Fracht *cost, insurance, freight*	**frei Haus** *franco domicile*

3   Other expressions relating to terms of payment are:

die Vorauszahlung (-en) *payment in advance*	**30 Tage Ziel** *30 days net*
Kasse bei Auftragserteilung *cash with order*	**der kurzfristige/langfristige Kredit** *short-/long-term credit*
Zahlung bei Erhalt der Ware/ gegen Nachnahme *cash on delivery*	

4   **Die Auftragserteilung** *Placing an order*

Sehr geehrte Damen und Herren,

wir danken Ihnen für Ihr Angebot vom 11. Mai und den beigelegten Katalog und möchten Ihnen die folgende Bestellung erteilen:

25 Kofferradios Modellnr. 211 zum Preis von DM 90.00 pro Stück
30 Tonbandgeräte Modellnr. 345 zum Preis von DM 150.00 pro Stück

Frei Haus einschließlich Verpackung
Lieferzeit: 4–6 Wochen
Zahlungsbedingungen: Zahlung bei Erhalt der Ware.

Die Waren sind an unseren Spediteur, Eisenhardt GmbH, Brigittestr. 15, 4300 Essen 1, zu liefern.

Vielen Dank im voraus.

mit freundlichen Grüßen

---

das Kofferradio (-s) *portable radio*
das Tonbandgerät (-e) *tape recorder*
der Spediteur (-e) *forwarding agent*

Vielen Dank im voraus *many thanks in anticipation*

Erklärungen

 1 Note that the expression *is to be done* is rendered simply by **ist zu tun**, for example:

(Auto) **zu** verkaufen
Die Waren **sind** morgen **zu liefern.**
Die Überweisung **ist** auf unser Konto bei der Deutschen Bank **vorzunehmen.**

(car) to be sold (for sale)
The goods are to be delivered tomorrow.
The transfer is to be made to our account with the Deutsche Bank.

Übungen

1 Study the letter on page 125 and make sure that you understand its contents before you place your order.

a) Are these prices free on board or franco domicile?
b) Is it possible to obtain a bulk discount?
c) How promptly must payment be made to receive the cash discount?

   d)   What means of payment is required?

2 Your company has received an order in German (the second letter) and you have been asked to translate it into English.

3 You have received an enquiry on 22.06 and now make your offer enclosing your latest catalogue. Your prices are franco domicile including packaging. You offer a bulk discount of 15% on all orders over DM 2.000 and a cash discount of 3% for payment within 10 days. You ask them to send a cheque on receipt of the goods.

Use the first sample letter on page 125 as a guide.

14

——— IMPORT ———
AND EXPORT

TEIL A

——————— Dialog ———————

John Lister's company manufactures computer components. He wishes to enter the German market. Knowing that agents are a very well established way of working the German market, he has sought the names of potential agents from the British Consulate in Germany, via Export House in London. Mr. Lister is now visiting the second potential agent on his list, Herr Behr, in Frankfurt. We join them in the middle of their discussion.

JB Also, Herr Lister. Welche Informationen brauchen Sie von mir?

JL Ja, Herr Behr. Wie lange sind Sie schon in dieser Branche tätig?

JB Seit acht Jahren. Ich spezialisiere mich auf elektronische Bestand-teile.

JL Und darf ich nach Ihren Qualifikationen fragen?

JB Ich bin Diplomingenieur. Da sehen Sie auf meiner Karte. Ich habe jahrelang bei Semitron in Nürnberg gearbeitet. Ich dachte mir dann: Na, Du machst Dich selbstständig. Durch meine Arbeit bei Semitron hatte ich schon viele Kontakte gemacht. Seit der Zeit bin ich Vertreter.

JL Das hat Ihnen von Anfang an gut gefallen?

JB Doch. Ich hatte mich schon seit Jahren darauf gefreut, selbststän-dig zu sein.

JL Und Sie vertreten ausländische Firmen?
JB Ja. Schon bei Semitron hatte ich mich für das Auslandsgeschäft interessiert. Meine Lieferanten sind überwiegend europäische Firmen.
JL Und wie viele Lieferanten haben Sie?
JB Etwa dreißig. Das sind alles verschiedene Produkte, verstehen Sie.
JL Selbstverständlich. Wie viele Mitarbeiter haben Sie, und wie groß ist das Gebiet, das Sie bearbeiten?
JB Meine Kunden sind alle im Frankfurter Raum. Ich hatte früher viele Kontakte im Nürnberger Raum gehabt, wie gesagt, aber jetzt beschränke ich mich auf Frankfurt. Ich habe zwei Kollegen. Einer ist Diplom Kaufmann und der andere ist ausgebildeter Ingenieur, genau wie ich. Ich habe auch zwei Burokräfte.

---

die Branche(-n) *sector* (of the economy/business)
tätig sein *be active, to operate*
sich spezialisieren auf *to specialise in*
der Bestandteil(-e) *component*
fragen nach *to ask about*
Diplom *degree*, (here: *graduate engineer*)
sich selbstständig machen *to go independent*
der Vertreter(-) *representative, agent*

sich freuen auf *to look forward to*
überwiegend *mainly*
etwa *about*
verschieden *different*
das Gebiet *territory*
bearbeiten *to cover, work* (for example a territory)
sich beschränken auf *to limit oneself to*
ausgebildet *trained, qualified*
die Burokraft (-"e) *office staff*

Grammatik

1 Some verbs are closely associated with a particular following preposition, as often occurs in English, for example:

fragen **nach**	*to ask about*
sich spezialisieren **auf**	*to specialise in*
sich beschränken **auf**	*to limit oneself to*
sich interessieren **für**	*to be interested in*
danken **für**	*to thank (somone) for*
bestehen **auf**	*to insist on*
sich freuen **auf**	*to look forward to*

When followed by a noun, the preposition is treated simply, as illustrated in the passage. When followed by a phrase or clause as below:

I look forward *to meeting him.*
I insist *on visiting him.*
We thank you *for delivering the goods on time.*

the preposition must still appear and is dealt with as follows. Note that the second verb goes to the end of the sentence.

Ich freue mich **darauf, ihn kennenzulernen.**
Ich bestehe **darauf, daß ich ihn besuche.**
Wir danken Ihnen **dafür, daß Sie die Waren rechtzeitig geliefert haben.**

In other words, **da-** or **dar-** (where the preposition starts with a vowel) precedes the preposition, and the complete idea which follows is rendered by a **daß**... clause, or an infinitive phrase with **zu**. So the above sentences would literally be translated by: *I look forward to it, to meet him*; *I insist on it, that I visit him*; *We thank you for it, that you supplied the goods on time.*

2   Es kommt auf (acc.)... **an** (*It depends on...*) is a frequent verb + preposition construction. For example:

Es kommt auf das Wetter **an.**   *It depends on the weather.*
Es kommt auf den Preis **an.**   *It depends on the price.*

With a phrase or clause, **darauf** comes into use, as explained above. For example:

Es kommt **darauf** an, wie hoch der Preis ist.   *It depends on how high the price is.*
Es kommt **darauf** an, wann die Lieferung ankommt.   *It depends on when the delivery arrives.*
Es kommt **darauf** an, ob die Firma die richtigen Maschinen dafür hat.   *It depends on whether this firm has the right machinery for it.*

3   We shall now approach *I had*, known as the pluperfect tense. In Lektion 10 we dealt with the perfect tense which is formed using **haben** or **sein** plus the past participle. For example:

Ich **habe** es **gekauft.**   *I bought/have bought it.*
Er **ist** gestern **abgefahren.**   *He went off yesterday.*

The pluperfect tense represents a further step back in time: *I had done* something: For example: *I **had made*** contacts before I set up my business.

In German this tense is simply made by using **ich hatte** (the imperfect of **haben**) or **ich war** (the imperfect of **sein**), which corresponds exactly to the English. For example:

Ich **hatte** viele Kontakte **gemacht.** *I had made a lot of contacts.*
Ich **hatte mich** für das Auslandsgeschäft **interessiert.** *I had been interested in overseas business.*
Er **war** immer zu anspruchsvoll **gewesen.** *He had always been too demanding.*

(For more on the imperfect tense of **haben** and **sein**, see Lektion 12.)

——————— Übungen ———————

1 Translate the following sentences:
  a) It depends on the price.
  b) It depends on when the goods arrive.
  c) It depends on the quality.
  d) It depends on where the exhibition is taking place (**stattfinden**).
  e) It depends on what you need.
  f) It just depends.

2 Joachim Behr elaborates over lunch on his earlier ambition to set up on his own account. Complete the sentences, using the pluperfect tense:
  a) Bevor ich mich selbstständig machte, ... ich viele Kontakte gemacht.
  b) Ich ... mehrmals versucht, die Firma zu verlassen.
  c) Ich ... sogar mit dem Chef gesprochen.
  d) Ich ... an verschiedene Firmen geschrieben.
  e) Aber alle Versuche ... erfolglos geblieben.

3 Translate this skeleton letter given to you by your boss.
  a) We thank you for your letter of 10. October.
  b) I would like to enquire about electrical contacts (**elektrische Kontakte**).
  c) We are also interested in keyboards (**Tastaturen**).
  d) Do you specialise in other components as well?
  e) I look forward to meeting you next month.

Dialog

Mr. Lister and Herr Behr continue their discussion.

JL Auf welcher Basis rechnen Sie normalerweise ab, Herr Behr?

JB Um ganz ehrlich zu sein, Herr Lister, ist das verschieden. Mit meinen europäischen Lieferanten rechne ich monatlich ab.

JL Monatlich... Hmm. Und Ihre Spesen?

JB Ja, Spesen werden zweimal monatlich abgerechnet.

JL Um ganz ehrlich zu sein, Herr Behr, finde ich das ein bißchen übertrieben. Das ist sehr umständlich, besonders mit Ihren Spesen. Wir müßten noch darüber reden. Und Angebote sind auf Basis FOB, CIF oder Frei Haus?

JB Verstehen Sie, ich konkurriere hier mit anderen deutschen Lieferanten. Um einen Vergleich zu machen, muß der Kunde ein Angebot frei Haus haben.

JL Ja, das sehe ich ein. Das ist kein Problem. Und Ihre Provision?

JB Das kommt darauf an, wer der Lieferant ist; das kommt auch auf das Produkt an; und drittens kommt es auf das Ursprungsland des Produktes an. Aber normalerweise nehme ich eine Provision von 5 Prozent vom gelieferten Preis. Das ist nämlich branchenüblich hier.

abrechnen *to settle accounts*	**Es kommt darauf an** *It depends ...*
um ganz ehrlich zu sein *to be quite honest*	**das Ursprungsland(-¨er)** *country of origin*
die Spesen (pl.) *expenses*	**die Provision** *commission*
übertrieben *exaggerated, a bit much*	**der gelieferte Preis** *the delivery price*
umständlich *complicated, fussy, involved*	**branchenüblich** *usual in the sector, normal*
konkurrieren *to compete*	
der Vergleich *comparison*	

Erklärungen

1 Reference is made to the terms of delivery. **FOB** (Free on Board), **FAS** (Free Alongside Ship) and **CIF** (Cost, Insurance and Freight) are the same as in English. Some other common terms are:

ab Werk   *ex works*
frei Hafen   *delivered to port*
frei Grenze   *delivered at frontier*

But do note that to compete effectively, it is highly probable that a delivered price (**frei Haus** or **ein gelieferter Preis**) will have to be quoted.

TEIL B

John Lister appoints Joachim Behr as his agent. During their discussion on marketing strategy, Lister learns that trade fairs are an important method of market development in Germany. It is important at least to visit major relevant fairs and exhibit at one or two regularly. Behr is flicking through the publication *Internationale Fachmessen* and points out the following fairs as relevant to Lister's interests:

'88: 26.4.-28.4.	INFOBASE	Messe Frankfurt GmbH
'89: 9.5.-11.5.	Internationale Ausstellung und Kongreß für Informationsmanagement	Postfach 97 01 26 D-6000 Frankfurt 97 Tel. (0 69) 75 75-0
	Angebotsschwerpunkte: Informations-software, Hardware, EDV-Software, neue Informationsdienste	Tx. 4 11 558 Telefax (0 69) 75 75-4 33
	Aussteller 1986: 65, davon Ausländer: 14	
	Besucher 1986: 1 875	
	Vermietete Fläche 1986: 1 106 m²	
	FKM-geprüft: ja	

die Ausstellung(-en) *fair, exhibition*	**der Dienst (-e)** *service*
das Angebot (-e) *offer, goods/ services for sale, quote*	**vermietete Fläche** *space let*
der Schwerpunkt (-e) *emphasis*	**FKM** *voluntary control body for exhibitions*
EDV (elektronische Datenverarbeitung) *data processing*	**prüfen** *to check, monitor, control*

'88: 16.3.-23.3.	Hannover-Messe CeBit	Deutsche Messe- und
'89: 8.3.-15.3.	Welt-Centrum der Büro-, Informations- und Telekommunikationstechnik	Ausstellungs-AG Messegelände D-3000 Hannover 82
	Angebotsschwerpunkte: Informations- u. Kommunikationstechnik,	Tel. (05 11) 8 91 Tx. 9 22 728

Telekommunikation,
Mikrocomputertechnik, Software,
Büro- u. Organisationstechnik,
Banken- u. Sicherheitstechnik
Aussteller 1986: 2 142, davon
Ausländer: 680
Besucher 1986: 334 427
Vermietete Fläche 1986: 202 885
m²
FKM-geprüft: ja

die Sicherheit	*security*

'88: 8.11.-12.11. electronica
'89: - Internationale Fachmesse für Bauelemente
und Baugruppen der Elektronik
Angebotsschwerpunkte: Halbleiter-
Bauelemente u. Röhren, passive
Bauelemente, Funktionseinheiten,
elektromechanische Bauelemente u.
Geräteteile, Verbindungsmittel, Gehäuseteile,
Elektronik für die Qualitätssicherung u. das
Entwicklungslabor
Aussteller 1986: 1 865, davon
Ausländer: 801
Besucher 1986: 114 690
Vermietete Fläche 1986: 62 969 m²
FKM-geprüft: ja

die Fachmesse(-n) *specialist fair*
der Anwender (-) *user*
die Lösung (-en) *solution*
einzeln *individual*
der Benutzer(-) *user*
die Dienstleistung(-en)
service

DV (Datenverarbeitung) *data
processing*
das Zubehör *accessories*
die Ausbildung *education,
training*

Übungen

1 J. Behr reminisces about the visits to these fairs which he made while at Semitron, before becoming self-employed. Complete the following, putting the verbs in the perfect (*I have...*) or pluperfect tense (*I had...*)

1989 ... ich auf der INFOBASE gewesen. Und 1988 ... ich auch dort gewesen. 1989 ... ich gute Geschäfte dort gemacht, aber die Hannover-Messe war besser. Ich ... viele Kontakte gemacht, aber die Ausstellungskosten ... in dem Jahr etwas gestiegen.

1988 dagegen ... die Ausstellungskosten etwas niedriger gewesen. Ich ... auch im Jahr 1989 die Systems-Ausstellung in München besucht. Der Schwerpunkt bei Systems ... immer auf DV gewesen. 1989 ... die Ausstellung viele Besucher gehabt.

2 Lister discusses with Behr some issues related to exhibiting at trade fairs. Complete their conversation by inserting the appropriate prepositions.

JL Also Sie glauben, wir sollten uns ... Fachmessen beschränken?

JB Auf jeden Fall. Verstehen Sie, Sie spezialisieren sich ... Bestandteile für Computer. Es hat keinen Zweck auf einer allgemeinen Messe oder gar auf einer Software Messe auszustellen.

JL Nein, das sehe ich ein. Man muß sicher sein, daß sich die Besucher ... Computer wirklich interessieren.

JB Genau. Und denken Sie ..., daß es ein teurer Spaß sein kann.

JL Das wollte ich sagen. Es kommt ... ..., die Kosten pro Besucher auf dem Stand möglichst gering zu halten.

JB Sicherlich, ... kommt es vor allen Dingen ... .

15
MAKING —— COMPLAINTS —— AND APOLOGIES

TEIL A

―――――――― **Dialog** ――――――――

It is the beginning of August and the office furniture ordered by Thyssen AG has not arrived at its destination. Herr Wegener telephones Kuhl Möbel GmbH to complain about the delay.

Empfangsdame Kuhl Möbel, Guten Morgen!

Herr Wegener Guten Morgen. Können Sie mich bitte mit Herrn Buchholz verbinden?

Empfangsdame Kann ich um Ihren Namen bitten?

Herr Wegener Mein Name ist Wegener von der Firma Thyssen.

Empfangsdame Moment, bitte. (*Coming back*) Entschuldigung, sein Anschluß ist besetzt. Möchten Sie einen Moment warten? Bleiben Sie am Apparat!

Herr Wegener Ja, in Ordnung.
(*After a moment Herr Buchholz answers the phone.*)

Herr Buchholz Buchholz am Apparat.

Herr Wegener Guten Morgen, Wegener hier von Thyssen.

Herr Buchholz Ach, guten Tag Herr Wegener. Was kann ich für Sie tun?

Herr Wegener Ja, ich muß Ihnen leider mitteilen, daß unser

	Auftrag noch nicht angekommen ist. Sie haben es mir versprochen, daß die Sendung Ende Juli eintreffen würde. Heute ist bereits der 7. August.
Herr Buchholz	Ja, ich bedauere es sehr, daß wir Sie nicht schon früher davon in Kenntnis gesetzt haben aber wir hatten gerade einen 10-tägigen Streik in unserer Fabrik. Diese Lage hat es uns unmöglich gemacht, unserer Lieferverpflichtungen rechtzeitig nachzukommen. Wir sind jetzt dabei, alle Rückstände so schnell wie möglich zu versenden.
Herr Wegener	Sie müssen doch verstehen, daß diese Lieferungsverzögerung uns in große Verlegenheit bringt. Wir brauchen jetzt dringend eine Teilsendung und dann eine Restlieferung innerhalb von 15 Tagen. Wenn wir innerhalb der nächsten 7 Tage nichts erhalten, werden wir gezwungen sein, den Auftrag zu annulieren.
Herr Buchholz	Machen Sie sich keine Sorgen. Ich bedaure diese Verzögerung sehr und ich werde persönlich dafür sorgen, daß eine Teilsendung in den nächsten Tagen an Sie abgeht.
Herr Wegener	In Ordnung, vielen Dank. Ich wäre Ihnen auch dankbar, wenn Sie mich benachrichtigen könnten, sobald die Waren versandbereit sind und die weiteren Einzelheiten über die Mengen, Verpackung usw. angeben. Sie haben doch meine Telefonnummer, oder?
Herr Buchholz	Ja, kein Problem. Ich werde Sie in den nächsten Tagen anrufen.
Herr Wegener	Das wäre sehr freundlich, vielen Dank.
Herr Buchholz	Nichts zu danken. Aufwiederhören.

---

verbinden (mit) *to connect (with)*
der Anschluß ist besetzt *the line is engaged*
bleiben Sie am Apparat! *Hold the line!*
versprechen *to promise*
eintreffen *to arrive*
in Kenntnis setzen (von) *to make aware (of), inform, advise*

in Verlegenheit bringen *to cause embarrassment*
die Teilsendung (-en) *partial delivery*
die Restlieferung (-en) *the delivery of the balance*
zwingen *to force*
annulieren *to cancel*
sich Sorgen machen *to worry*

der Lieferverpflichtungen nachkommen *to meet delivery commitments*	sorgen (für) *to ensure*
der Rückstand (⁻e) *backlog, arrears*	benachrichtigen *to advise, inform*
die Lieferungsver- zögerung (-en) *delay in delivery*	sobald *as soon as*

Ihre Lieferung vom: 21.02.1992		
Ihre Zeichen: S. / La		
Ihre Rechnung vom: 19.02.1992 Nr.: 890		
Meine Bestellung vom: 12.02.1992 Nr.: 478		

Beim Auspacken Ihrer Sendung stellte ich folgende **Mängel** fest:	Ich bitte um **Gutschrift — Umtausch — Nachlieferung — Ersatzlieferung — Preisnachlaß**
Es fehlen:	
Es sind zerbrochen oder beschädigt: 25 Gläser sind ange- kratzt	Umtausch !
Es wurde falsch geliefert:	
Sonstige Beanstandungen:	

Erklärungen

---

1 Note the following useful phrases for making a complaint:

| die Beschwerde | *the complaint* |
| Ich habe eine Beschwerde. | *I have a complaint.* |

but

| sich beklagen, sich beschweren (über) | *to make a complaint (about)* |

For example:

| Ich möchte **mich über** die Bedienung **beschweren.** | *I'd like to complain about the service.* |
| Ich kann **mich** nicht **beklagen.** | *I can't complain.* |

2 There are also several different ways to apologise:

Es tut mir leid.	*I am sorry.*
leider	*unfortunately*
bedauern	*to regret*
entschuldigen	*to excuse*

For example:

Wir bedauern dieses
  Versehen sehr. *We sincerely regret this oversight.*
Zu unserem **Bedauern** *To our regret*
Zu unserem **Bedauern** müssen wir Ihnen mitteilen, daß wir die
  Waren nicht rechtzeitig liefern können. *We regret to have to inform you that we are unable to deliver the goods on time.*

Entschuldigen Sie, bitte *Please excuse me/us, sorry*
sich **entschuldigen** (wegen + *to excuse oneself, to say sorry*
  gen.) *(for)*
Ich **entschuldige** mich, daß *I am sorry that I didn't come.*
  ich nicht gekommen bin.

3 Note the verb + preposition constructions which we have met here:

sorgen für	*to take care of/ensure*
abhängen von	*to be dependent on*
jemand in Kenntnis setzen von	*to advise someone of*
verbinden mit	*to connect with*

For example:

Ich werde **dafür sorgen**, daß die Waren rechtzeitig geschickt
  werden. *I will ensure that the goods are sent on time.*

——————— Grammatik ———————

1 *Anticipatory* es

Es is frequently used in German to anticipate a subordinate clause, for example:

Ich bedaure **es** sehr, daß die Waren nicht rechtzeitig angekommen

---

sind. *I am very sorry (about it) that the goods didn't arrive on time.*

Sie haben **es** mir versprochen, daß die Waren rechtzeitig ankommen würden. *You promised (it) me, that the goods would arrive on time.*

2 Asking questions

It is also possible to form a question by simply adding a question tag such as **nicht wahr?**, *isn't that true?* and **oder?** *or?*, for example:

Sie können die Waren bis Ende der Woche liefern, **nicht wahr?** *You can deliver the goods by the end of the week, can't you?*

Wir brauchen uns keine Sorgen zu machen, **oder?** *We don't have to worry, do we?*

───────── Übungen ─────────

1 Your company has ordered some goods from a German manufacturer and you have been asked to telephone the German managing director, Herr Schwarz, to complain about a delay in delivery.

Herr Schwarz Schwarz & Kübler OHG, Guten Morgen.
Sie *Ask whether you can speak to Herr Schwarz.*
Herr Schwarz Am Apparat. Wie kann ich Ihnen helfen?
Sie *Say that unfortunately your order hasn't arrived yet and that it was due at the end of the month. Say that you need the goods urgently.*
Herr Schwarz Ich bedaure es sehr aber vor zwei Wochen gab es ein Feuer in unserer Fabrik und viele Waren wurden beschädigt. Wir versuchen noch die Rückstände aufzuarbeiten.
Sie *Say that you are very sorry but you cannot wait any more. You need the goods before the Christmas business starts. Ask whether he can dispatch a partial consignment now and the rest within 10 days. Otherwise you will have to buy elsewhere.*
Herr Schwarz Machen Sie sich keine Sorgen! Wir schicken Ihnen schon diese Woche die Hälfte Ihrer Bestellung und die Restlieferung in zwei Wochen. Als Entschädigung sind wir auch in der Lage Ihnen

Sie	einen Sonderrabatt von 10% zu gewähren. *Ask if he can telephone you when the partial consignment is ready for delivery.*
Herr Schwarz	Ja, natürlich. Ich habe Ihre Telefonnummer und ich könnte Sie auch per Telex benachrichtigen.
Sie	*Say fine. Thank him and say goodbye.*
Herr Schwarz	Nichts zu danken. Ich entschuldige mich nochmals.

---

fällig *due*
aufarbeiten (here) *to clear* (*backlog*)
das Weihnachtsgeschäft *Christmas business*

sonst *otherwise*
anderswo *elsewhere*
die Entschädigung *compensation*

---

2 You are on a business trip in a German speaking country. After spending the first night in your hotel you have several complaints to make.

Sie	*Good morning.*
Empfangsdame	Guten Morgen. Haben Sie gut geschlafen?
Sie	*No. You haven't slept well. You want to complain about your room. It is near the lift and there was a lot of noise yesterday evening. Also the bed wasn't comfortable and the water in the bathroom was cold.*
Empfangsdame	Es tut mir sehr leid aber Sie wollten ein Zimmer auf der zweiten Etage.
Sie	*Say that the floor isn't important and you would be grateful if she could give you another room.*
Empfangsdame	Wir haben ein Zimmer auf der ersten Etage, aber es ist ein bißchen kleiner.
Sie	*Say fine but you hope the bed is comfortable and that the hot water is working.*
Empfangsdame	Ja, es ist ein sehr schönes Zimmer.
Sie	*Ask if you will receive some compensation.*
Empfangsdame	Das muß ich mit dem Direktor besprechen. Vielleicht können wir Ihnen doch einen Rabatt anbieten.

schlafen *to sleep*	**das Bett (-en)** *the bed*
der Fahrstuhl ("e) *lift*	**bequem** *comfortable*
es gab viel Lärm *there was a lot of noise*	

3 Match up the following apologies with the given situations.
1 Es tut mir leid, daß ich nicht kommen konnte.
2 Entschuldigen Sie bitte, aber der Zug hatte Verspätung.
3 Verzeihung.
4 Entschuldigung, was haben Sie gesagt?
5 Ich entschuldige mich wegen der Sprachfehler.
6 Ich bedauere es sehr. Es wird nicht wieder passieren.

a) Apologising for bumping into a stranger in the street.
b) Apologising for your faulty German.
c) Apologising for being late.
d) Apologising to a friend for something you've done wrong.
e) Apologising for being absent.
f) Apologising for not having heard what someone said.

4 You are making a series of complaints to a company with regard to recent orders not carried out to your satisfaction. Use the verb in brackets to complete the sentences.
a) Wir möchten Sie (in Kenntnis setzen von), daß die Waren noch nicht angekommen sind.
b) Es (abhängen von), ob Sie mir einen Rabatt anbieten können.
c) Wir (bedauern) sehr aber wir sind nicht mit den Waren zufrieden.
d) Können Sie (sorgen für), daß die Waren sofort abgeschickt werden.
e) Werden Sie mir (versprechen) eine Ersatzlieferung sofort zu schicken.

TEIL B

1 Read these two extracts from letters of complaint.

Sehr geehrter Herr Bochert,

Zu unserem Bedauern müssen wir Ihnen mitteilen, daß die von Ihnen erhaltenen Waren unserem Auftrag nicht entsprechen...

entsprechen (+ dat.)	*to correspond (to)*

Sehr geehrte Frau Becker,

Wir gestatten uns, Sie darauf aufmerksam zu machen, daß unsere Rechnung vom 4. Mai (Nr. 4547/2) über DM 4.500 noch offensteht. Wir wären Ihnen also sehr dankbar, wenn Sie uns Ihren Scheck umgehend zusenden könnten.

Wenn Ihre Zahlung nicht bis Ende des Monats eingeht, werden wir den fälligen Betrag durch unseren Rechtsanwalt einziehen lassen.

sich gestatten *to allow oneself, take the liberty*	**offenstehen** *be outstanding, unsettled*
aufmerksam machen (auf) *to draw attention (to)*	**eingehen** *to be paid* (into an account)
die Rechnung (-en) *invoice*	**einziehen** *to collect*

———— Erklärungen ————

1 Note that the expression *to have something done* is rendered in German by **etwas machen lassen**. For example:

Ich **lasse** mein Auto **reparieren**.   *I'm having my car repaired.*

Wir werden Ihre Rechnung **überprüfen lassen**.   *We will have your invoice checked.*

2 Read these extracts from letters of apology:

Sehr geehrte Frau Storch,

Wir sind im Besitz Ihres Schreibens vom 26. August und möchten uns wegen des Versehens in Bezug auf Auftragnummer 3454/1 entschuldigen. Leider haben wir Ihre Bestellung falsch gelesen.

Es tut uns sehr leid, Ihnen Unannehmlichkeiten zu bereiten und wir bemühen uns jetzt eine Ersatzlieferung so schnell wie möglich zu versenden.

im Besitz *in possession*	**die Ersatzlieferung** *replacement delivery*
das Versehen (-) *oversight*, (**versehentlich** *by accident*)	**so schnell wie möglich** *as fast as possible*
Unannehmlichkeiten bereiten *to cause difficulties*	**versenden** *to dispatch*
sich bemühen *to endeavour, make every effort*	

Sehr geehrter Herr Klein,

In Bezug auf Ihr Schreiben vom 24. dieses Monats bedaueren wir es sehr, daß die von uns versandten Waren beschädigt ankamen. Dieser Schaden wurde bestimmt während des Seetransports verursacht, da wir immer auf sorgfältige Verpackung geachtet haben.

---

der Schaden (-̈) *damage*	**sorgfältig** *careful*
verursachen *to cause*	**achten (auf)** *to pay attention (to)*

Erklärungen

1 Note that in German whole clauses can be used adjectivally to describe a noun, thus instead of saying

    die Waren, die von Ihnen   *the goods which were received*
      erhalten wurden   *by you*

it is possible to say

    die **von Ihnen erhaltenen** Waren.

In the same way

    die Waren, die von uns   *the goods which were sent by*
      versandt worden sind   *us*

can be replaced by

    die **von uns versandten** Waren.

Note that the participle is acting as an adjective and thus receives the appropriate ending.

Übungen

Write extracts of letters following the instructions below.

1 You are working for a bookshop in your country that specialises in foreign language books. The company has ordered 50 German dictionaries (**Wörterbücher**) but you have only received 35. Write a letter of complaint to the publishers requesting a prompt delivery of the remainder.

2   You are working for a shoe wholesalers (**Schuhgroßhändler**) in Munich. You placed a large order with a manufacturer two months ago but you still haven't received any goods. Advise them that if they do not deliver in the next week you will be forced to look elsewhere.

3   You work for a mail order company (**ein Versandhaus**) and you have received a complaint from a customer who has received the wrong goods. You realise that they have mistakenly been sent somebody else's order and vice versa. Apologise for the oversight and tell them you will forward the correct goods as soon as possible.

16

DIE GEOGRAPHIE ── UND INDUSTRIE ── DEUTSCHLANDS

── Die Geographie ──

Seit der Wiedervereinigung der Bundesrepublik Deutschland mit der Deutschen Demokratischen Republik ist die Gesamtfläche der Bundesrepublik Deutschland um fast 50% gewachsen. Mit mehr als einer Drittelmillion Quadratkilometer ist Deutschland aber immer noch kleiner als Frankreich oder Spanien.

Die deutsche Landschaft ist sehr unterschiedlich. Im Norden ist die Küste, dann ein Tiefland, die Mittelgebirge und schließlich die Alpen im Süden – immer wieder wechselt das Bild der Landschaft. Eine Flugstunde braucht man von der Küste im Norden bis zum Schnee auf den Alpen im Süden. Ungefähr die Hälfte des Bodens ist landwirtschaftlich genutzt, ein knappes Drittel ist von Wald bedeckt. Wichtige Flüsse sind der Rhein (die verkehrsreichste Binnenwasserstraße Europas), die Donau, die Elbe, die Oder, die Spree, die Saale und die Havel).

Im vereinten Deutschland leben 74 Millionen Menschen, wobei 57 aus dem Westen und knapp 17 Millionen aus dem Osten stammen. Die Bevölkerungsverteilung ist aber sehr ungleichmäßig. Die größte Bevölkerungskonzentration befindet sich im Ruhrgebiet, wo auf nur 1% der Staatsfläche 7% der Bevölkerung leben. Jeder dritte Bürger der Bundesrepublik Deutschland lebt in Großstädten mit über 100.000 Einwohnern.

die Gesamtflächte *total surface area*	**die Landwirtschaft** *agriculture*
unterschiedlich *varied*	**landwirtschaftlich** *agriculturally*
das Tiefland *lowland*	**das Volk(ˉer)** *the people, nation*
die Mittelgebirge (-n) *secondary chain of mountains*	**die Bevölkerungs- verteilung** *distribution of the population*
die Landschaft *landscape, countryside*	**ungleichmäßig** *uneven*

Übung

Wahr oder falsch? (Correct any false statements in German.)

1 Deutschland ist größer als Spanien und Frankreich.
2 Die deutsche Landschaft besteht aus Tiefland, Mittelgebirge und Alpen.
3 Es gibt wenig Landwirtschaft in Deutschland.
4 Die deutsche Landschaft ist durch Wald charakterisiert.
5 Die Elbe ist die verkehrsreichste Binnenwasserstraße Europas.
6 Deutschland hat eine hohe Bevölkerungskonzentration.
7 Die größte Bevölkerungsdichte ist im Süden.
8 Die meisten Deutschen wohnen in Kleinstädten.

Die Industrie

Die Schwerpunkte der Industrie in der BRD befinden sich in den Bundesländern Nordrhein-Westfalen, Bayern, Baden Württemberg, Niedersachsen, Hessen und das Saarland. In Nordrhein-Westfalen und im Saarland haben die Kohlevorkommen eine Monostruktur von Kohleförderung und Stahlerzeugung bestimmt. Wegen der internationalen Stahlrezession werden diese Industrien wie überall in Europa zu Problemgebieten. Aus Baden-Württemberg kommen die Zukunftsprodukte, besonders in den Bereichen Datenverarbeitung, Automation und Kommunikation. In Bayern sind viele Fahrzeugbaufabriken und elektrotechnische Firmen herangewachsen.

Der Industriezweig mit dem größten Umsatz und einem Exportanteil von 60% ist der Straßenfahrzeugbau. Nach den USA und Japan ist die BRD der drittgrößte Automobilproduzent der Welt. Die bekanntesten Unternehmen sind die Daimler-Benz AG und die Volkswagen AG.

Nach der Umsatzstärke folgt an zweiter Stelle die chemische Industrie. 80% der Beschäftigten arbeiten in den drei Großunternehmen (BASF AG, Bayer AG, Hoechst AG). Dank modernster Technologien hat die BRD eine führende Position.

Die nächstgrößte Branche ist der Maschinenbau. Hier liegt der Erfolg der Deutschen an ihrer technischen Leistungsfähigkeit, ihrer Pünktlichkeit und ihrer ausgebauten Serviceleistung.

Eine weitere Schlüsselindustrie ist die elektrotechnische Branche, die ein überdurchschnittliches Wachstum aufweist. Hier spielen Mikroelektronik und Informations- und Kommunikationstechniken eine besonders wichtige Rolle für Innovation und Rationalisierung.

der Schwerpunkt (-e) *centre, focus*	**der Exportanteil (-e)**
das Kohlevorkommen (-) *coal deposits*	*proportion of production exported*
die Kohleförderung *coal mining*	**die Stärke (-n)** *strength*
die Stahlerzeugung *steel manufacture*	**dank** (+ dat.) *thanks to*
die Datenverarbeitung *data processing*	**die Leistungsfähigkeit** *efficiency*
der Übergang (-̈e) *transition*	**ausgebaut** *extensive*
	die Serviceleistung *customer service*

---

der Fahrzeugbau *motor*
  vehicle manufacture
der Straßenfahrzeugbau *car*
  manufacture (all road vehicles)
der Industriezweig (-e)
  branch of industry

die Schlüsselindustrie(-n)
  key industry
aufweisen *to show*
überdurchschnittlich *above*
  average

Übung

Bitte beantworten Sie auf Deutsch.

1 Welche Gebiete haben eine Monostruktur von Kohlen- und Stahl-betrieben?

2 Wo werden Produkte der Spitzentechnologien hauptsächlich hergestellt?

3 Bei welcher Industrie gibt es drei Hauptarbeitgeber?

4 Welche Industrie ist ein wichtiges Expansionsgebiet?

5 Welche Industrie hat den höchsten Umsatz?

6 Bei welcher Industrie spielen Pünktlichkeit und Serviceleistung eine große Rolle?

---

die Spitzentechnologie (-n)   *advanced technology*

17

RADIO UND
—— FERNSEHEN IN ——
DER BUNDESREPUBLIK

——————— 1 Radio ———————

In Deutschland werden Radioprogramme von elf Sendern ausgestrahlt. Sieben Länder haben je eine Station; Südwestfunk ist zwischen Baden-Württemberg und Rheinland Pfalz, und Norddeutscher Rundfunk zwischen Schleswig Holstein, Hamburg, und Niedersachsen geteilt. Darüber hinaus sind die Stationen Deutsche Welle und Deutschlandfunk für Auslandsendungen zuständig, die den Interessen der Bundesrepublik als Ganzes dienen.

Die Rundfunkanstalten werden durch Radio- und Fernsehgebühren sowie durch Einkünfte von der Fernsehwerbung finanziert. Die Höhe der Gebühren wird von der Ministerkonferenz der Länder festgesetzt.

——————— 2 Fernsehen ———————

Die Bundesrepublik hat grundsätzlich drei Fernsehprogramme. Das Erste Programm – ARD genannt – bringt Sendungen von den obigen Rundfunkanstalten. Die Redaktion der Nachrichtensendungen erfolgt immer durch den NDR, während der WDR die Redaktion der Sportschau stellt.

Das Zweite Deutsche Fernsehen (ZDF) wird wie das Erste Programm (ARD) bundesweit ausgestrahlt. Beide Programme stehen in einem Kontrast, jedoch nicht in einem Konkurrenzverhältnis zueinander. Die

Sendungen werden von beiden
Programmen im voraus
beraten und abgestimmt, sodaß
verschiedene Wünsche berück-
sichtigt werden können.

Das Dritte Programm wird von
den Sendern der ARD gestellt,
jedoch auf regionaler Basis mit
lokaler Berichterstattung und
Schul- und Studienprogrammen.
Außerdem bringt das Dritte
Programm anspruchsvolle
Diskussionen, Filme und
Dokumentarfilme.

---

3 Kabelfernsehen

Seit Anfang der 80er Jahre baut die Deutsche Bundespost ein Fern-
sehkabelnetz aus. Heute sind über dreieinhalb Millionen Haushalte
diesem Netz angeschlossen. Das erlaubt es ihnen, bis zu siebzehn
Programme öffentlicher und privater Anbieter aus dem In- und Ausland
zu empfangen. Satellitenprogramme werden in das Kabelnetz ein-
gespeist; deshalb lohnt es sich nicht so besonders, die eigene Parabol-
antenne zum Empfang von einzelnen Satellitenprogrammen zu haben.

ausstrahlen *to broadcast*	**die Berichterstattung** *reporting*
teilen *to share*	**außerdem** *apart from that*
darüberhinaus *moreover*	**anspruchsvoll** *demanding,* (here)
zuständig *responsible*	*serious*
die Anstalt *institution*	**angeschlossen** *linked up to*
die Gebühr *fee*	**der Anbieter** *provider*
die Einkünfte (pl.) *income, revenue*	**einspeisen** *to feed in* (to cable
grundsätzlich *basically*	network)
die Redaktion *production*	**deshalb** *therefore*
das Verhältnis *relationship*	**es lohnt sich nicht** *it is not worth it*
beraten *to discuss, consult*	**empfangen** *to receive* (a
abstimmen *to agree, come to an*	programme)
agreement on	

Übung

Antworten Sie auf Englisch.

1 How many radio/TV stations are there in Germany?
2 Do they all belong to individual states? Explain.
3 There are two further stations; what is their task?
4 What is ARD?
5 What is ZDF?
6 What is the difference between ARD and the Third Channel?
7 Why haven't many Germans invested in a dish aerial to receive satellite broadcasts?

Die Stellung der Frau in der Bundesrepublik

'Männer und Frauen sind gleichberechtigt' sagt das Grundgesetz. Aber die Frauen in Deutschland sind doch benachteiligt. Die Lösung dieser Probleme ist nicht nur Aufgabe des Staates, sondern der ganzen Gesellschaft.

Die Frau im Beruf

Frauen, die die gleiche oder eine gleichwertige Arbeit wie Männer verrichten, haben einen Anspruch auf gleiche Bezahlung. Aber oft wird die Arbeit, die typischerweise von Männern und Frauen verrichtet wird, unterschiedlich bewertet: Frauentätigkeit wird oft als sogenannte körperlich leichte Arbeit in der Regel noch unterbewertet.

Allerdings ist im öffentlichen Dienst der Grundsatz 'Gleicher Lohn für gleiche Arbeit' Wirklichkeit. Alle Beamte, Angestellte oder Arbeiter des öffentlichen Dienstes werden in der jeweiligen Lohngruppe gleich bezahlt.

Die Frau und Familie

Die Rolle der Frau in der Familie als Hausfrau und Mutter ist wie eine berufliche Tätigkeit. Deshalb zahlt der Staat für Kinder, die nach 1988 geboren werden, ein Jahr lang ein Erziehungsgeld von monatlich DM600. Während dieser Zeit bleibt dem Vater oder der Mutter der Arbeitsplatz, den er/sie aufgegeben hat, offen.

Die Ehepartner müssen sich nun über ihre Anteile an den Haushalts- und Berufspflichten einigen. Als Familienname ('Ehename') wird jetzt entweder der Name des Mannes oder der Frau bei der Eheschließung festgelegt. Im Fall einer Scheidung muß der wirtschaftlich stärkere Partner für den schwächeren – in der Regel die Frau – so lange sorgen, bis dieser wieder für seine eigene Existenz aufkommen kann.

---

gleichberechtigt *equal, enjoy equal rights*
das Grundgesetz(-e) *basic law, constitution*
benachteiligt *disadvantaged*
die Gesellschaft(-en) *society*
Arbeit verrichten *to carry out work*
unterschiedlich *different(ly)*
der Anspruch(-ë) *claim*
die Tätigkeit(-en) *activity*
körperlich *physical*
die Wirklichkeit(-en) *reality*
der Beamte(-n) *civil servant*
der öffentliche Dienst(-e) *public service*

das Erziehungsgeld(-er) *child allowance (lit. money for bringing up)*
der Anteil(-e) *share*
die Pflicht(-en) *duty*
die Eheschließung(-en) *marriage*
festlegen *to set, fix, decide upon*
im Fall (+ gen.) *in the event of*
die Scheidung(-en) *divorce*
sorgen für *to look after, care for*
aufkommen *to pay for, meet the costs of*

Übung

Antworten Sie auf Englisch.

1 What anomaly is there between the constitution and reality as regards the position of women in society?
2 Even though the same work receives the same reward by law, why do women nevertheless receive on average less than men in pay?
3 Is this true of the public sector? Explain.
4 What is the reasoning behind the award of DM600 per month children's allowance?
5 What does a couple have to decide on?
6 What is said about the name used as the family name by a couple?
7 In the event of a divorce, what legal obligation does the financially stronger partner have?

18

DIE DEUTSCHE WIRTSCHAFT

Industrie–Indikatoren

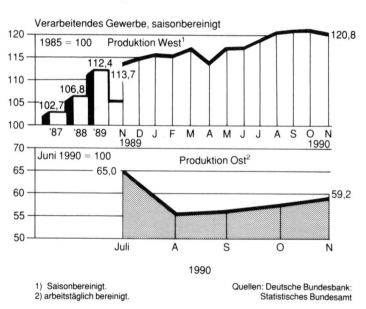

Verarbeitendes Gewerbe, saisonbereinigt

Produktion West[1]

1985 = 100

102,7 106,8 112,4 113,7 120,8

'87 '88 '89 N D J F M A M J J A S O N
            1989   1990

Juni 1990 = 100

Produktion Ost[2]

65,0 59,2

Juli A S O N

1990

1) Saisonbereinigt.
2) arbeitstäglich bereinigt.

Quellen: Deutsche Bundesbank:
Statistisches Bundesamt

Deutschland gehört zu den großen Industrieländern der Welt. Gemessen am Bruttosozialprodukt steht es an vierter Stelle – nach den USA, der Sowjetunion und Japan. Gemessen am Außenhandel hat es sogar den zweiten Platz im Welthandel – nach den USA eingenommen. Da Deutschland aber nur etwa ein Viertel der Einwohnerzahl der USA hat, kann man leicht sehen, wie wichtig der Außenhandel ist. In manchen Branchen wie Chemie, Maschinenbau und Automobilbau ist der Export fast so wichtig wie der Markt im eigenen Land.

Der Erfolg der deutschen Wirtschaft kommt von der marktwirtschaftlichen Ordnung. Nach dem Prinzip 'so wenig Staat wie möglich und soviel Staat wie nötig' sind Privateigentum, Privatinitiative, und Wettbewerb die Treibkräfte der Wirtschaft wobei der Staat auch eine Lenkungsfunktion hat, um Fehlentwicklungen und Ungerechtigkeit zu vermeiden. Heutzutage hat Deutschland ein leistungfähiges System von sozialer Sicherheit, eine der stabilsten Währungen der Welt und einen vorderen Platz in der Weltwirtschaft.

---

gemessen (an + dat.)   *measured by, calculated by*
das Bruttosozialprodukt (-e)   *gross national product*
der Außenhandel   *foreign trade*
einnehmen   *to occupy* (place)
die marktwirtschaftliche Ordnung   *market economy system*
das Privateigentum   *private property*
der Wettbewerb   *competition*
die Treibkraft (-̈e)   *driving force*

die Lenkungsfunktion (-en)   *steering function*
die Fehlentwicklung (-en)   *developments in the wrong direction*
die Ungerechtigkeit (-en)   *injustice*
vermeiden   *to avoid*
leistungsfähig   *efficient*
die Währung (-en)   *currency*
vorder   *in front, ahead*

Übung

Beantworten Sie auf Deutsch.

1   Wie wichtig ist Deutschland als Industrieland?
2   Wie erfolgreich ist es im Welthandel?
3   Wie hoch ist das Bruttosozialprodukt?
4   Wie wichtig ist der Export für Chemie, Maschinenbau und Automobilbau?
5   Was für eine wirtschaftliche Ordnung gibt es in der BRD?
6   Was für eine Rolle spielt der Staat?

Dialog
Außenhandel

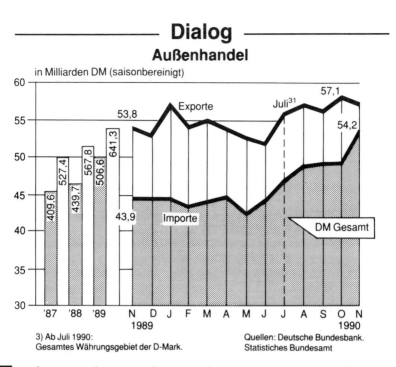

in Milliarden DM (saisonbereinigt)

3) Ab Juli 1990:
Gesamtes Währungsgebiet der D-Mark.

Quellen: Deutsche Bundesbank.
Statistiches Bundesamt

An economic expert discusses the role of foreign trade (**Außenhandel**) in Germany.

Journalist Wie wichtig ist der Außenhandel für die deutsche Wirtschaft?

Experte Der Außenhandel spielt eine entscheidende Rolle im deutschen Wirtschaftsleben, wobei jede vierte Mark im Ausland verdient wird. Auch ist Deutschland der zweitgrößte Exporteur der Welt nach den USA.

Journalist Und warum ist Deutschland so erfolgreich?

Experte Deutscher Erfolg beim Export kommt von einem hohen technologischen Stand, einem breiten Warensortiment, guter Qualität und pünktlicher Lieferung.

Journalist Und wie sieht die Handelsbilanz aus?

Experte Ein Kennzeichen des deutschen Außenhandels ist seit Jahren eine positive Handelsbilanz. Die großen Ausfuhrüberschüsse sind aber nötig um Defizite auf anderen Gebieten wie Tourismus auszugleichen.

Journalist Welcher Anteil der Gesamtproduktion wird exportiert?

Experte Ein Viertel der deutschen Produktion geht in den Export. Dieses Viertel hat eine typische Struktur: Maschinen aller Art, Kraftfahrzeuge, elektronische und chemische Produkte. Dafür werden die folgenden importiert: Energie in Form von Erdöl und Erdgas, Nahrungs- und Genußmittel, Rohstoffe und Halbfabrikate.

Journalist Was ist die deutsche Außenhandelspolitik?

Experte Durch den Abbau von Zöllen und anderen Handelsbeschränkungen setzt sich Deutschland für eine Integration in die Weltwirtschaft und für eine liberale Außenhandelspolitik ein.

Journalist Und was bedeutet die Wiedervereinigung für die deutsche Wirtschaft?

Experte Die Vereinigung mit der DDR bedeutet natürlich eine große Investition und die deutsche Handelsbilanz wird eine Zeitlang unter Druck sein. Sie bietet aber auch eine wertvolle Gelegenheit, Binnen- und Außenhandel noch weiter auszubauen.

---

eine Rolle spielen *to play a role*	**das Erdöl** *mineral oil*
der Binnenhandel *domestic trade*	**die Nahrungsmittel** *foodstuffs*
der Umfang *size, extent*	**die Genußmittel** *luxury goods*
pünktlich *punctual*	**der Rohstoff (-e)** *raw material*
das Kennzeichen (-) *distinguishing feature*	**das Halbfabrikat (-e)** *semi-finished goods*
die Handelsbilanz *balance of trade*	**der Abbau** *reduction*
der Ausfuhrüberschuß (¨sse) *export surplus*	**der Zoll (¨e)** *duty*
das Defizit (-e) *deficit*	**die Handelsbeschränkung (-en)** *trade restriction*
ausgleichen *to compensate for, offset*	**sich einsetzen (für)** *to support, fight (for)*
der Anteil (-e) *share, proportion*	**die Wiedervereinigung** *reunification*
das Kraftfahrzeug (-e) *motor vehicle*	**unter Druck** *under pressure*
	wertvoll *valuable*
	ausbauen *to expand, increase*

--------------- **Übung** ---------------

Now find sentences in the text with an equivalent meaning to those below.

1 A positive balance of payments has been a characteristic of German foreign trade for many years.
2 German success in export comes from a high level of technology, a wide range of goods, good quality and prompt delivery.
3 Germany is in favour of a liberal foreign trade policy via the reduction of duties and other trade barriers.
4 This quarter is typical in structure; machines, motor vehicles and electronic and chemical products.
5 The large foreign trade surpluses are necessary to offset deficits in other areas such as tourism.
6 Unification also offers the opportunity to further expand domestic and foreign trade.

19

_____ MESSEN UND _____
AUSSTELLUNGEN

Messen gibt es seit Jahrhunderten – als Umschlagplätze fur Waren und Güter aller Art, an den geographischen Schnittpunkten der (inter)nationalen Handelsstraßen.

In den ersten Jahren nach dem zweiten Weltkrieg waren Leipzig, Köln, Frankfurt und Hannover Schauplätze von großen Messen. Daneben wurde Nürnberg zu einem Zentrum der Spielzeugindustrie und Offenbach zu einem Standort der Produktion von Lederwaren. In diesen Städten entstanden also die entsprechenden Fachmessen, und München und Düsseldorf entwickelten sich bald zu Fachmessenstädten.

Messen werden heute allgemein als Marktinstitution und wirtschaftliche Kristallisationspunkte angesehen. Darüberhinaus spielen sie eine wichtige Rolle als Branchentreffpunkt, Informationsbörse und wirtschaftspolitisches Forum. Zudem sind sie bedeutende Faktoren im Wirtschaftsleben einer Region.

Deutsche Industriemessen sind international bekannt. Etwa 40% der Firmen, die jährlich auf den hundert wichtigsten Messen der Bundesrepublik ausstellen, kommen aus dem Ausland. Inzwischen sind 41 Länder ständig auf deutschen Messen vertreten. Etwa ein Fünftel kommt aus dem außereuropäischen Ausland. Von den rund 7 Millionen Besuchern deutscher Messen kommen fast 1,5 Millionen aus dem Ausland.

---

das Jahrhundert (-e) _century_ **die Börse (-n)** _exchange, stock_
der Umschlag _transshipment_ _exchange_

der Schnittpunkt (-e) *intersection*	**zudem** *in addition*
der Schauplatz(- e) *showground*	**bedeutend** *significant*
das Spielzeug *toy(s)*	**sich auszeichnen** *to excel, be extraordinary*
daneben *in addition*	**im Vergleich zu** *compared to*
darüberhinaus *moreover*	**ständig** *always, consistently*
der Treffpunkt(-e) *meeting point*	**ein Fünftel** *one fifth*

Übung

 Antworten sie auf Englisch.

1 What has long been the purpose of trade fairs?
2 Where did they tend to be established?
3 What is the difference between the kinds of fair taking place in Hanover and Offenbach?
4 What are the purposes of trade fairs nowadays?
5 What does the figure of 40% in the passage refer to?

Der Verkehr (Teil A)

Das größte Transportunternehmen in der Bundesrepublik ist die Deutsche Bundesbahn (DB). Die Bahn ist besonders wichtig für den Transport von Massengütern und Personen über große Entfernungen. Hohe Zuggeschwindigkeiten sollen den Transport von Personen und Gütern beschleunigen; auf bestimmten Strecken können Züge eine Geschwindigkeit von 250Km/h erreichen. Aber die Bahn ist auch wichtig für den Pendelverkehr. Pendler sind Leute, die in einer Stadt arbeiten, die aber außerhalb der Stadt wohnen. In den Ballungsräumen um Berlin, Hamburg, Frankfurt, Stuttgart, München und das rheinisch-westfälische Industriegebiet ist ein ausgebautes Personennahverkehrsnetz heute unentbehrlich.

Jeder kennt das Wort 'Autobahn'. Deutschland hat ein dichtes Netz von Autobahnen – fast 10.000 Kilometer – das nicht nur dem Innenverkehr sondern auch dem Transitverkehr dient. Es gibt in der Bundesrepublik über 40 Millionen zugelassene Fahrzeuge, und vier Fünftel des Personenverkehrs wird mit dem eigenen Wagen bewältigt. Das Kraftfahrzeug bleibt auch in Zukunft Hauptverkehrsmittel.

das Unternehmen(-) *company, organisation*	**unentbehrlich** *indispensible*
die Entfernung(-en) *distance*	**jeder** *everyone*
die Geschwindigkeit(-en) *speed*	**dienen** *to serve*
beschleunigen *to accelerate*	**das Fahrzeug(-e)** *vehicle*
die Strecke *stretch, distance (of track)*	**zugelassen** *registered*
der Ballungsraum (-¨e) *conurbation, densely populated area*	**das Fünftel(-)** *fifth*
ausgebaut *complete, extensive*	**bewältigen** *to cover, master, come to terms with*
	die Zukunft *future*
	Haupt- *main*
	das Verkehrsmittel(-) *means of transport*

Übung

1 In what area of transport is the railway particularly important?
2 In what way is the railway effective in the transport of passengers over shorter distances?
3 Was the Autobahn network developed solely for German users? Explain.
4 Illustrate the importance of the car in passenger transport in Germany.

Der Verkehr (Teil B)

Deutschland hat eine Handelsflotte von 1500 Schiffen; man legt großen Wert auf die eigene Flotte, die auch in Krisenzeiten die Versorgung sichern kann. Die deutschen Seehäfen – Hamburg, Bremen, Bremerhaven, Lübeck, Wilhelmshafen und Rostock – liegen zwar nicht so verkehrsgünstig zu den Industriezentren Westeuropas, haben aber durch große Investitionen in der Technik, Containereinrichtungen usw. diesen Wettbewerbsnachteil ausgleichen können. Die Binnenschiffahrt läuft über ein Netz von 5.000 Kilometern, bestehend aus Kanälen, Flüssen und Seen. Die Qualität des Wasserstraßennetzes wird weiterhin verbessert. Die Saar wird kanalisiert und die Verbindung zwischen dem Rhein und der Donau wird über den Main-Donau-Kanal jetzt hergestellt. Auf den Wasserstraßen können insbesondere Massengüter – Baumaterial, Mineralölprodukte, Erze und Kohle – kostengünstig transportiert werden.

Lufthansa ist die nationale Luftverkehrsgesellschaft. Condor, LTU, und Hapag Lloyd sind Charterverkehrsgesellschaften, die sich meistens mit dem Ferienverkehr befassen. Frankfurt ist nach London der zweitgrößte Flughafen Europas; andere sind Berlin-Tegel, Bremen, Düsseldorf, Hamburg, Hannover, Köln-Bonn, München, Nürnberg, Saarbrücken und Stuttgart.

man legt großen Wert auf... *great store is set by ...*	**der Nachteil(-e)** *disadvantage*
eigen *own* (adj.)	**binnen-** *inland*
die Versorgung *provision, supply*	**bestehen (aus)** *to consist (of)*
die Krise (-n) *crisis*	**die Verbindung wird hergestellt** *the link/ connection is made*
günstig *favourable, good, convenient*	**das Erz(-e)** *ore*
die Einrichtung(-en) *equipment*	**die Gesellschaft** *company*
der Wettbewerb *competition*	**sich mit** (dat.) **befassen** *to deal with*

Übung

Antworten Sie auf Englisch.

1 Why does Germany set store by having its own merchant fleet?
2 What competitive disadvantage do German ports suffer from?
3 How has this in part been overcome?
4 Illustrate how the inland waterways have been improved recently.
5 What kind of goods can be transported economically by inland waterway?

20

SOZIALE SICHERHEIT —— UND BERUFLICHE —— AUSBILDUNG

A German civil servant (**der Beamte**) discusses the social security services available to German citizens (**die deutschen Bürger**).

Journalist	Inwiefern garantiert die BRD die soziale Sicherheit ihrer Bürger?
Beamte	Deutschland ist ein demokratischer und sozialer Bundesstaat. Der Staat ist also verpflichtet, seine Bürger vor sozialer Unsicherheit zu schützen. Um diese Aufgabe auszuführen, gibt es ein weitgespanntes Netz sozialer Gesetze.
Journalist	Können Sie uns vielleicht ein Beispiel dieser Sozialleistungen geben?
Beamte	Zum Beispiel sind fast alle deutschen Bürger gegen Krankheit versichert. Der Arzt rechnet die ärztliche Behandlung, Medikamente, Operationen usw. direkt mit der Kasse ab. Der Patient braucht also nicht zu bezahlen.
Journalist	Und wenn man auch nicht arbeiten kann?
Beamte	Jeder Arbeitnehmer, der krank wird, hat ein Recht auf Weiterzahlung seines Verdienstes durch den Arbeitgeber. Danach zahlen die Krankenkassen bis zu 78 Wochen lang Krankengeld, das bis zu 80% des normalen Verdienstes betragen kann.
Journalist	Hilft der Staat auch Leuten, die arbeitslos werden?
Beamte	Alle Arbeiter und Angestellten sind gegen Arbeitslosigkeit versichert. Wer arbeitslos ist, erhält ein Arbeits-

losengeld, das rund zwei Drittel seines letzten Verdienstes ausmacht. Danach bekommt man Arbeitslosenhilfe, die zwischen fünfzig und sechzig Prozent des Verdienstes beträgt.

Journalist Und wenn man alt wird und nicht mehr arbeiten will?

Beamte Jeder Bürger hat das Recht mit 65 für Männer, oder 63 für Frauen, in den Ruhestand zu treten.

Journalist Und was für finanzielle Hilfe bekommt man?

Beamte Jeder Rentner bekommt eine Rente, die sich nach der Versicherungsdauer und der Höhe des Arbeitsentgelts richtet. Außerdem sorgt das Prinzip der Rentendynamik dafür, daß die Renten mit dem wirtschaftlichen Wachstum Schritt halten.

---

verpflichtet *obliged*
schützen *to protect*
weitgespannt *wide-ranging, comprehensive*
das Gesetz (-e) *law*
die Sozialleistung *social services*
versichert (gegen) *insured (against)*
die Krankheit (-en) *illness*
der Arzt ("e) *doctor*
abrechnen (sep.) *to settle (payment)*
ärztlich *medical*
die Behandlung *treatment*
die Krankenkasse (-n) *body which administers health insurance*
der Arbeitnehmer/geber (-) *employee/er*
ein Recht haben (auf) *to have a right (to)*
der Verdienst (-e) *earnings*
das Krankengeld *equivalent of sick pay*

arbeitslos *unemployed*
die Arbeitslosigkeit *unemployment*
das Arbeitslosengeld *unemployment benefit*
ausmachen (here) *to amount to*
die Arbeitslosenhilfe *equivalent of supplementary benefit*
in den Ruhestand treten *to retire*
der Rentner (-) *pensioner*
die Rente (-n) *pension*
die Versicherungsdauer *length of time insured*
das Arbeitsentgeld (-e) *remuneration, earnings*
sich richten nach *to be determined by, to be based on*
die Rentendynamik *principle linking pensions to economic growth (average wage increase)*
Schritt halten (mit) *to keep pace (with)*

Übung

✓ Using the text translate the following sentences into German.

1 German citizens are insured against illness and don't need to pay for medical treatment, medication or operations.

2 An employee who falls ill also has a right to continued payment of his earnings by the employer and then by the health insurance.

3 Anyone who is unemployed receives unemployment benefit which amounts to approximately two thirds of his earnings for one year.

4 German citizens can retire at between 60 and 65 and have a right to a pension.

5 Pensions in Germany are determined by the length of insurance contribution and the level of earnings.

6 German pensioners receive 'dynamic' (index linked) pensions which keep pace with economic growth.

───── Berufliche Ausbildung ─────

Für die meisten Jugendlichen führt nach Haupt- oder Realschule der Weg weiter zur Berufsschule und in eine berufliche Ausbildung. Nach dem deutschen Modell der Berufsausbildung im 'dualen System' lernen sie die Theorie in der Schule und die Praxis im Betrieb.

Es gibt etwa 450 anerkannte Ausbildungsberufe. Sie sind bei den Jugendlichen unterschiedlich beliebt: in zwanzig bevorzugten Berufen konzentrieren sich fast 60% der männlichen Auszubildenden; bei den weiblichen Auszubildenden sind es sogar 80%. Die Jungen wollen am liebsten Kraftfahrzeugmechaniker, Elektroinstallateur und Maschinenschlosser werden, die Mädchen Verkäuferin, Friseuse und Bürokauffrau.

Die praktische Ausbildung im Betrieb (oft 'Lehre' genannt) dauert je nach dem Beruf zwei bis dreieinhalb Jahre. Neben der Ausbildung im Betrieb muß der Lehrling drei Jahre lang ein- bis zweimal in der Woche eine Berufschule besuchen.

der Jugendliche (-n) *young person*	**der Kraftfahrzeugmechaniker**
die Berufsschule (-n) *general*	**(-)** *motor mechanic*
equivalent of technical college	**der Elektroinstallateur (-)**
where students attend on day	*electrical fitter*
release	**der Maschinenschlosser (-)**
anerkannt *recognised*	*machine fitter*
beliebt *popular*	**die Friseuse (-n)** *hairdresser*

bevorzugt *preferred* **männlich** *male* **weiblich** *female* **der Auszubildende (-n)** *trainee/apprentice*	**die Bürokauffrau (en)** *office* *clerk* **die Lehre (-n)** *general term* *for apprenticeship* **der Lehrling (-e)** *apprentice*

Übung

Answer the following questions in German.

1. Welche Ausbildung bekommen die meisten Jugendlichen in der BRD?
2. Was bedeutet das 'duale' System?
3. Sind alle Ausbildungsberufe gleich beliebt von männlichen Auszubildenden und woran ist das zu sehen?
4. Was sind typische weibliche Lehren?
5. Wie lange dauert eine Lehre normalerweise?
6. Wie oft müssen die Lehrlinge die Berufschule besuchen?

Schematische Gliederung des Bildungswesens

21

AUSLÄNDISCHE ARBEITNEHMER

Dialog

A journalist from the BBC, Bill Davis, is interviewing Andreas Fischer, a social worker in Frankfurt, on the subject of foreign workers in Germany.

BD Herr Fischer, warum sind die Gastarbeiter überhaupt hier?

AF Es ist so. In den fünfziger und sechziger Jahren brauchte Deutschland viele Arbeitskräfte, um das Wirtschaftswunder zu verwirklichen. Arbeiter kamen aus ärmeren Ländern wie Spanien, Jugoslawien, Griechenland, Italien, aber vor allem aus der Türkei, um in Deutschland verhältnismäßig hohe Löhne zu verdienen.

BD Also, sie sind aus vielen verschiedenen Ländern, und sind teilweise schon seit langem hier?

AF Ja. Die ausländischen Arbeitnehmer mit ihren Familienangehörigen bilden heutzutage die größte Minderheit in der Bundesrepublik. Nahezu 60% der Ausländer halten sich schon zehn Jahre und länger in Deutschland auf. Mehr als zwei Drittel der ausländischen Kinder sind bereits hier geboren.

BD Herr Fischer, Sie haben von Minderheiten gesprochen. In dieser Beziehung gibt es in jedem Land kulturelle Probleme. Ist es in Deutschland auch so?

AF Verstehen Sie, die Gastarbeiter haben einen großen Beitrag zum wirtschaftlichen Aufstieg geleistet, aber das Zusammenleben ist nicht frei von Reibungen, besonders in manchen Großstädten, wo der Anteil der Ausländer an der Bevölkerung in einigen Fällen über 20% liegt. Die größte Gruppe, die 1,4 Millionen Türken, finden es besonders schwer, sich in Deutschland – in einem fremden Kulturkreis – zurechtzufinden.

BD Um ganz konkret zu sein, was für Probleme haben diese Leute?

AF Unter der Arbeitslosigkeit haben die ausländischen Arbeitnehmer mehr zu leiden als ihre deutschen Kollegen. Und die sogenannten Gastarbeiterkinder, die in Deutschland groß werden, sind in der Schule und in ihren Berufsaussichten im Vergleich zu deutschen Kindern im Nachteil.

BD Und was wird getan, um diese Probleme zu lösen?

AF Die Ausländer, die schon in Deutschland sind, haben die Möglichkeit, an dem wirtschaftlichen, sozialen und kulturellen Leben voll beteiligt zu sein. Aber der weitere Zuzug von ausländischen Arbeitnehmern aus nicht-EG Staaten wird begrenzt; und man hilft Ausländern, die es wollen, in ihr Heimatland zurückzukehren.

BD Vielen Dank für dieses Gespräch.

---

der Gastarbeiter (-) *guest/immigrant worker*
überhaupt *at all*
die fünfziger Jahre *the fifties*
verwirklichen *realise, bring about*
verhältnismäßig *relatively*
der Lohn(-¨e) *wage*
vor allem *mainly*
der Familienangehörige(-n) *dependent*
die Minderheit(-en) *minority*
sich aufhalten *stay, sojourn*
in dieser Beziehung *in this respect/ connection*
einen Beitrag leisten *make a contribution*

der Aufstieg (-e) *development, progress*
die Reibung(-en) *friction*
der Anteil(-e) *share, proportion*
sich zurechtfinden *find one's way about/feel at home*
leiden *to suffer*
die Berufsaussichten (pl) *career prospects*
der Nachteil(-e) *disadvantage*
beteiligt sein (an) *take part/ participate in*
der Zuzug(-¨e) *influx*
begrenzt *limited*

Übungen

1 True or false? (Correct the false statements.)

a) Many guest workers arrived in Germany in the fifties and sixties.

b) They came because Germany was reputedly a land whose

streets were paved with gold.

c) Foreign workers make up around 60% of the population.

d) More than ⅔ of the children of immigrant workers were born in Germany.

e) Only the Turks find it difficult to integrate.

f) There is not much unemployment among immigrant workers, as there are always unpleasant jobs to be done.

g) The children of immigrant workers are at a disadvantage at school and in the job market as compared to German youngsters.

h) Special trains are put on to take home immigrant workers who wish to leave.

2 Antworten Sie auf Deutsch!

a) Wann sind viele Gastarbeiter nach Deutschland gekommen?

b) Woher sind sie gekommen?

c) Welcher Prozentsatz der Ausländer halten sich weniger als 10 Jahre in Deutschland auf?

d) Warum finden es die Türken besonders schwer, sich in Deutschland zurechtzufinden?

e) Was für Probleme haben die ausländischen Arbeitnehmer und ihre Familien?

f) Welche Schritte unternimmt die Regierung, um zu verhindern, daß das Problem größer wird?

———— Deutschland und ———— Europa

Für die deutsche Wirtschaft und für die deutsche Politik ist die Entwicklung der EG von wesentlicher Bedeutung. Hierzu einige Informationen und ein Gespräch mit einem deutschen Betriebsleiter.

Die Entwicklung der Europäischen Gemeinschaft

1957 Der Römer Vertrag wurde unterzeichnet. Dadurch wurden die EWG (Europäische Wirtschaftsgemeinschaft) und Euratom (Europäische Atomgemeinschaft) gegründet.

1968 Die Zölle innerhalb der Gemeinschaft der Sechs wurden abgeschafft; die Zollunion wurde damit vollendet.

1973 Durch den Beitritt von Dänemark, Großbritannien und Irland erhöhte sich die Zahl der Mitglieder auf neun.

1975 Im Abkommen von Lomé, das die EG mit 46 Entwicklungs-ländern Afrikas, der Karibik und des Pazifik schloß, wurden die Beziehungen zwischen den europäischen Industriestaaten und den Ländern der Dritten Welt auf festen Boden gesetzt.

1979 Die ersten Direktwahlen in den neun EG-Mitgliedstaaten zum Europäischen Parlament fanden statt.

1981 Griechenland wurde der 10. Mitgliedstaat der EG.

1985 Der Europäische Rat einigte sich auf die Einheitliche Europäis-che Akte. Diese sollte zur Gründung des Binnenmarktes im Jahre 1993 und zur Währungsunion führen.

1986 Spanien und Portugal traten der EG bei. Die Gemeinschaft der 12 besteht seit 1.1.1986.

1987 Der Europäische Rat einigte sich über das Delors-Paket zur Stärkung der Zusammenarbeit auf wirtschaftlicher sowie auf politischer Ebene in Europa.

von wesentlicher Bedeutung *of fundamental importance*	**auf festen Boden setzen** *to firm up*
die Entwicklung(-en) *development*	**die Wahl(-en)** *election, choice*
der Vertrag(-̈e) *treaty, contract*	**das Mitglied(-er)** *member*
unterzeichnen *sign*	**der Europäische Rat** *Council of Ministers*
dadurch *thereby*	**sich einigen auf/über** *to agree on/about*
die Gemeinschaft(-en) *community*	**die Einheitliche Europäische Akte** *the Single European Act*
abschaffen *to abolish*	**der Binnenmarkt** *the Single Market*
vollenden *to complete*	**die Währung(-en)** *currency*
sich erhöhen *to rise, increase*	**auf wirtschaftlicher Ebene** *at an economic level*
der Beitritt *(here) entry*	
das Abkommen(-) *agreement*	
schließen *to close,* (here) *conclude*	

Übung

Antworten Sie auf Deutsch.

1 Wann konnte man zuerst Abgeordnete zum Europäischen Parlament wählen?

2 Welches Abkommen befaßt sich mit den Beziehungen zwischen der EG und der Dritten Welt?

3   Wie und wann wurde die Gemeinschaft der Sechs zur Gemeinschaft der 12?
4   Wozu sollte die Einheitliche Europäische Akte führen?
5   Was geschah 1957?

Dialog

Herr Bodo Schulze, Betriebsleiter der Firma B. Schulze KG, Stuttgart, spricht über die Bedeutung der EG für die deutsche Industrie. Hier ein Auszug aus seiner Rede.

'Mehr als ein Viertel der deutschen Produktion wird in andere Länder ausgeführt. Die Bundesrepublik Deutschland ist neben den USA und Japan eines der größten Exportländer der Welt. Das heißt aber auch, daß jeder vierte deutsche Arbeitsplatz von einem sicheren Weltmarkt abhängt. Deutschland braucht daher einen großen, sicheren Absatzmarkt.

Europa bietet diesen Markt; rund die Hälfte unseres Exports geht in die EG. Es ist wichtig, diesen Markt auszubauen und zu sichern. Die Wirtschaftsgrenzen müssen ganz beseitigt werden, nicht nur damit ein deutsches Unternehmen nach Paris oder Rom ebenso unkompliziert und sicher verkaufen kann wie ein Hamburger Betrieb nach München oder Frankfurt, sondern damit die europäischen Unternehmen künftig besser technologisch zusammenarbeiten können. Dies wird ihnen helfen, im Konkurrenzkampf zu bestehen...'

der Auszug(-¨e) *extract*	**die Grenze** *border, barrier*
der Absatzmarkt *market*	**damit** *so that (for the purpose*
ausbauen *to develop, build up*	*of)*
beseitigen *to eliminate*	**künftig** *in future*
die Hälfte(-n) *half*	**bestehen** *(here) to survive*
sichern *to secure*	

Übung

Answer in English.

1   How much of total German production is exported?

2 What is said about the USA and Japan?
3 What is the implication of this level of export for the German job market?
4 To what does the proportion of one half relate in the passage?
5 Name two results of the abolition of economic barriers in Europe.

22

DIE DEUTSCHSPRACHIGEN LÄNDER EUROPAS

Die Schweiz

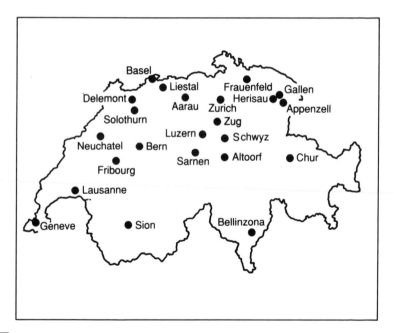

Die Schweiz liegt mitten in Europa und besteht zu zwei Dritteln aus Gebirge mit Schnee. Sie ist also ein Land der Enge, nur ein Viertel ist landwirtschaftlich bebaubar und kaum ein Viertel kann besiedelt werden.

Auch in Bezug auf Rohstoffe hat die Schweiz wenig, wovon sie leben kann; etwas Uran, ein bißchen Eisenerz und Salz ist vorhanden. Von Anfang an gab es immer nur eines: Transit und Warenexport und dabei muß sie mehr Güter einführen, als sie ausführen kann. Die Schweiz ist also von dem wachsenden Tourismus und dem erfolgreichen Dienstleistungssektor von Banken und Versicherungen abhängig, um diese Bilanz zu verbessern. Die Schweizer sind die Pioniere der Hotellerie.

Erfolgreiche Industrien gibt es aber natürlich auch; zum Beispiel ist die traditionelle Branche des Uhrmachers zu einer hochentwickelten Industrie geworden. Im Uhrforschungslabor in Neuenburg haben Schweizer die Quarzuhr erfunden. Auch sind Schweizer Textilmaschinen weltberühmt und dadurch haben sich auch die Farbchemie und der Maschinenbau entwickelt.

Was die Schweiz jetzt exportiert ist ihre industrielle Erfahrung, und ihr technisches Können.

Politisch gesehen ist die Schweiz ein Bund von 23 Kantonen, der verschiedene Republiken mit eigener Geschichte und verschiedenen Sprachen vereinigt. Die offiziellen Sprachen sind Deutsch, Französisch, Italienisch und Rätoromanisch. So lautet der Spruch 'Einheit, ja; Einheitlichkeit, nein'.

das Gebirge (-) *chain of mountains*	**der Dienstleistungssektor (-en)** *services industry*
die Enge *lack of space*	
bebaubar *suitable for cultivation*	**der Uhrmacher (-)** *clock maker*
besiedelt *populated*	**das Uhrforschungslabor (-)** *clock research laboratory*
der Rohstoff (-e) *raw material*	
das Uran *uranium*	**erfinden** *invent*
das Eisenerz (-e) *iron ore*	**die Farbchemie** *chemical dyes*
vorhanden sein *to be present, exist*	**das Können** *know-how*
einführen *to import*	**die Einheit** *unity*
ausführen *to export*	**die Einheitlichkeit** *uniformity*
(von)etwas abhängig sein *to be dependent on something*	

Übung

Wahr oder falsch?
Correct any false statements.

1 Die vielen Alpen bedeuten, daß es wenig Platz gibt, um Wohnungen zu bauen und Lebensmittel zu kultivieren.

2 Die Schweiz hat viele Rohstoffe einschließlich Uran, Eisenerz und Salz.

3 Die Schweizer Handelsbilanz für Güter weist ein Defizit auf.

4 Der Dienstleistungssektor spielt eine unwichtige Rolle.

5 Wichtige Branchen in der Schweiz sind Elektrotechnik und Fahrzeugbau.

6 Die Schweiz ist eine Vereinigung von vielen verschiedenen Völkern.

7 Die Schweizer haben viel Erfahrung in der Hotellerie.

8 Die Uhrmacherindustrie existiert nicht mehr in der Schweiz.

Österreich

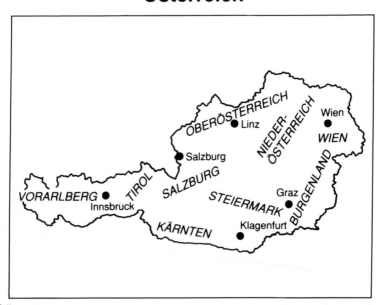

Österreich ist ein Bundesstaat, der aus neun Bundesländern – Burgenland, Kärnten, Niederösterreich, Oberösterreich, Salzburg, Steiermark, Tirol, Vorarlberg, Wien – besteht. Es hat eine Bodenfläche von 83.855 Km².

Österreich ist ein rohstoffreiches Land mit Vorkommen von Eisen, Metallen und wertvollen Mineralien. Heutzutage gibt es auch ausgedehnte Erdöl – und Erdgaslager, die sich von West nach Ost den Nordalpenrand entlang erstrecken. Dieser natürliche Reichtum ist die Basis der österreichischen Industrie.

Eisen- und Stahlhütten verarbeiten eigenes und importiertes Eisenerz zu hochspezialisierten Produkten wie Maschinen, Anlagen und Edelstahl-Fertigteilen. Der Anlagenbau und die Fertigung von 'maßgeschneiderten' Investitionsgütern haben besondere Bedeutung erreicht.

Reichliche Rohstoffe, insbesondere Holz, Mineralöl und Erdgas haben auch die Entwicklung einer sehr expansiven Chemieproduktion ermöglicht. Hier spezialisiert man sich auf synthetische Fasern, Düngemittel, Plastikwaren und pharmazeutische Produkte.

Österreich ist aber nicht nur ein industrielles Land. Man darf nicht vergessen, daß Österreich auch seit Jahrhunderten für seinen Beitrag zu der Welt von Theater, Musik und Oper bekannt ist.

rohstoffreich *rich in raw materials*		**der Anlagenbau** *manufacture of equipment*	
das Vorkommen (-) *deposit*		**maßgeschneidet** *tailor-made*	
ausgedehnt *extensive*		**die Investitionsgüter** *capital goods*	
der Lager (-) *bed* (of oil)		**das Holz** *wood*	
der Reichtum (¨er) *wealth*		**ermöglichen** *to make possible*	
Eisen/Stahlhütte (-n) *iron/steel works*		**die Faser (-n)** *fibre*	
der Edelstahl (¨e) *high grade steel*		**das Düngemittel (-)** *fertilizer*	
der Fertigteil (-e) *finished part*			

Übung

Bitte beanworten Sie auf Deutsch.

1 Wie groß ist Österreich im Vergleich zu Deutschland?
2 Was für Rohstoffe hat Österreich?
3 Inwiefern sind die vorhandenen Rohstoffe wichtig für Industrie?
4 Wie hoch ist der technologische Stand in Österreich.
5 Was hat zu der Entwicklung der chemischen Industrie geführt?
6 Welche Fachbereiche haben die größte Bedeutung in Österreich?

23

—— FÖDERALISMUS ——

Die Bundesrepublik Deutschland besteht aus sechszehn Ländern (siehe Karte), die in einem föderalistischen Verhältnis ('Bund') zueinander stehen. Die föderative Struktur ist eine alte deutsche Verfassungstradition, die nur durch das Hitler-Regime unterbrochen wurde. Heute macht es diese Struktur möglich, regionalen Eigenheiten, Wünschen und Problemen gerecht zu werden.

Die Länder sind verantwortlich für Teilbereiche des Umweltschutzes und des Polizeiwesens. Im kulturellen Bereich sind die Länder für alle Schulen, großenteils für Hochschulen und Universitäten, und für Erwachsenenbildung zuständig. Die Länder sind auch die zuständigen Behörden für die Verwaltung und Ausführung von Bundesgesetzen.

Um diese Aufgaben zu erfüllen, verfügen die Länder über gewisse Steuereinnahmen, insbesondere über einen Teil der Einkommensteuer, und die Gemeinden erhalten einen Teil der Gewerbesteuer, Grundsteuer und anderer Steuer für die Erfüllung ihrer Aufgaben auf Ortsebene.

Die Befürworter des Föderalismus sagen, daß es volksnäher ist, als zentralisierte Systeme: die Landesregierung erscheint dem Bürger näher und vertrauter als die Regierung in der Bundeshauptstadt; politische Parteien, die auf nationaler Ebene in der Opposition stehen, sind oft in mehreren Ländern Regierungsparteien; durch den Bundesrat können die Länder auch in Bundesangelegenheiten mitwirken.

---

das Verhältnis(-se) *relationship, proportion*

die Einnahme(-n) *income, revenue*

die Steuer(-n) *tax*

die Verfassung(-en) *constitution*	**die Gemeinde(-n)** *parish, lowest level of state administration*
unterbrechen *to interrupt*	
die Eigenheit *individuality, character*	**die Gewerbesteuer(-n)** *trading tax*
etwas(dat.) **gerecht werden** *cater for, take account of*	**auf Ortsebene** *at local level*
	der Befürworter(-) *protagonist, supporter*
der Bereich(-e) *area*	
der Teil(-e) *part*	**volksnah** *close to the people*
der Umweltschutz *environmental protection*	**erscheinen** *to appear, seem*
	vertraut *trustworthy*
das Wesen *system*, (here) *policing*	**der Bundesrat** *second chamber of parliament*
die Erwachsenenbildung *adult education*	
	die Bundesangelegenheit(-en) *federal matter, affair*
die Verwaltung *administration*	
die Ausführung *execution*	
das Gesetz(-e) *law*	
verfügen über *to have* (*available/at one's disposal*)	

Übung

True or false? Here are some statements about the German constitution and political scene. Indicate which are true and which false.

1 The German for *federal* is **Bund-**.
2 The federal system was introduced for the first time after the overthrow of the Hitler regime.
3 The Länder have similar areas of competence to the British regions and County Councils.
4 The Länder have more autonomy than their British counterparts because they have direct fiscal revenues.
5 Länder have parliaments with ruling parties and opposition parties.
6 The ruling party in the Länder must be the same as the ruling party in the Bundestag (national parliament).
7 The Länder have a voice in national policy through the second chamber (Bundesrat).

Dialog
Die politischen Parteien

Bill Davis now visits the **Zentrale für Politische Bildung** in Bonn, putting together material for a programme on political union in Europe. He speaks here with Klaus Schneider, a spokesman for the Zentrale für Politische Bildung.

BD In Großbritannien haben wir noch das Zweiparteiensystem. Wieviel politische Parteien haben Sie hier in Deutschland, Herr Schneider?

KS Im Bundestag sind heute sechs Parteien vertreten: die Sozialdemokratische Partei Deutschlands (SPD), die Christlich-Demokratische Union (CDU), die Christlich-Soziale Union in Bayern (CSU), die Freie Demokratische Partei (FDP), die Grünen und die PDS. Die letzten zwei Parteien sind aus dem östlichen Teil Deutschlands; die PDS war früher die SED, die Sozialistische Einheitspartei Deutschlands, die die Regierung der ehemaligen DDR stellte. Im Bundestag bilden die CDU und die CSU eine gemeinsame Fraktion.

BD Und wo liegen diese Parteien auf dem politischen Spektrum?

KS Die vier Parteien SPD, CDU, CSU und FDP entstanden 1945 bis 1947 in den westdeutschen Ländern. Die SPD war eine Wiedergründung der gleichnamigen sozialistichen Partei, die 1933 vom Hitler-Regime verboten worden war. Die anderen Parteien waren Neugründungen. CDU und CSU sprechen konservative Wähler aus beiden christlichen Konfessionen an, während die FDP sich als Erbe des deutschen Liberalismus sieht.

BD Und was ist mit den Grünen?

KS Als vierte Fraktion sind 1983 zum ersten Mal die Grünen in den Bundestag eingezogen. Die Partei ist aus einer Umweltschutzbewegung hervorgegangen und vereinigt heute Atomkraftgegner und andere Protestgruppen, und vertritt pazifistische Tendenzen.

BD Gibt es in der Bundesrepublik auch kleine Parteien und unabhängige Mitglieder des Bundestags?

KS Keine Partei darf in den Bundestag einziehen, die weniger als 5% der Stimmen im jeweiligen Wahlgebiet erhalten hat. Diese '5% Sperrklausel' soll verhindern, daß rechts- oder linksradikale Parteien im Bundestag vertreten werden, und soll dafür sorgen, daß eine Partei oder eine Koalition regierungsfähig ist. In der Wahl vom 2. Dezember, 1990, wurde dieses Gesetz in den östlichen Wahlgebieten aufgehoben, sodaß kleine Parteien der ehemaligen DDR weiterhin vertreten werden konnten. So wurden die B90/Grünen (Ost) in dieser Wahl gewählt, aber die Grünen (West) haben die 5% Klausel nicht überwunden. Und die PDS (früher SED) hat damals auch nur 2,4% der Stimmen erhalten, aber hat Sitze im Parlament bekommen.

BD Können Parteien von jeder politischen Prägung in Deutschland tätig sein?

KS Eigentlich nein. Parteien, die darauf ausgehen, die demokratische Grundordnung zu beseitigen, oder den Bestand der Bundesrepublik Deutschland zu gefährden, können aufgelöst werden. So wurden 1952 die Sozialistische Reichspartei (rechtsextremist) und 1956 die Kommunistische Partei Deutschlands (linksextremist) verboten.

BD Herr Schneider, haben Sie vielen Dank für dieses Gespräch.

---

vertreten *to represent*
gemeinsam *joint*
die Fraktion(-en) *faction*
entstehen *to emerge, develop from*
gleichnamig *of the same name, eponymous*
verbieten *to forbid, ban*
ansprechen *to address, speak for*
der Erbe *heir*
zum ersten Mal *for the first time*
einziehen (here) *to be elected to, enter*
die Bewegung(-en) *movement*
hervorgehen aus *to develop from*
vereinigen *to unite*
der Atomkraftgegner(-) *opponent of nuclear power*

das Gebiet(-e) *area, territory*
die (Sperr)klausel(-n) *(legal) clause, provision*
sorgen für *to see to it that*
regierungsfähig *able to govern*
aufheben *to lift, remove*
ehemalig *former*
der Bestand *existence*
gefährden *to jeopardise, endanger*
auflösen *to dissolve*
auf etwas ausgehen *to be out to/ intend to do something*
(weiterhin) bestehen *to (continue to) exist*
voraussichtlich *forseeably, probably*

Übung

Translate the following into German.

1 The CDU/CSU and the FDP form a coalition.
2 The CDU, CSU and the FDP were founded after the war for the first time, whereas the SPD had existed previously.
3 Six parties are represented in the **Bundestag**.
4 The Green Party overcame the 5% clause in 1983 and entered parliament for the first time.
5 Parties whose intention is to destroy the state can be dissolved.
6 After the election of 2nd December, 1990, small parties from the East could still be represented.
7 The Green Party developed from an environmental movement and brings together various protest groups.
8 In 1952 and 1956, extremist parties were banned.

KEY
TO
THE EXERCISES

Lektion 1

Teil A

1 (*a*) Die (*b*) Das (*c*) Der (*d*) Die. **2** (*a*) Unsere (*b*) Mein (*c*) Seine (*d*) Ihr (*e*) Ihr. **3** (*a*) geht (*b*) gehe (*c*) Gehen (*d*) gehen (*e*) bin (*f*) sind (*g*) Sind (*h*) ist. **4** Ich bin (your name). Ich bin Vertreter(in) bei der Firma Johnson in London. Wir sind ein Verlag. Ist Frau Schmidt da?/Ich wohne im Hotel Adler. Ich bin in Zimmer 20./Hier ist die Telefonnummer. Vielen Dank/Auf Wiedersehen. **5** (*a*) 1 (*b*) 4 (*c*) 5 (*d*) 6 (*e*) 2 (*f*) 3.

Teil B

1 (*a*) 1. Januar 1992 (*b*) 2. März 1993 (*c*) 3. Juni 1994 (*d*) 15. September 1995 (*e*) 20. November 1996 (*f*) 31. Dezember 1997 **2** (*a*) Sehr geehrte Herren (*b*) Sehr geehrte Frau Braun (*c*) Es freut mich Ihnen mitzuteilen, daß (*d*) mit freundlichen Grüßen. **3** (*a*) verkaufe (*b*) vertreten (*c*) arbeitet (*d*) besucht (*e*) kommt (*f*) Nehmen. **4** Ich vertrete (die Firma) Smiths Ltd./Unsere Firma ist im Norden/Wir verkaufen Ersatzteile/Ihr Vertreter kommt morgen/Unsere Produkte sind sehr gute Qualität/Wir besuchen unsere Kunden jede Woche.

Lektion 2

Teil A

1 München ist in Süddeutschland und ist die Hauptstadt von Bayern. München ist ungefähr 400 Kilometer von Bonn entfernt. München hat 1,2 Millionen Einwohner. Sie liegt an der Isar. Die wichtigsten Industrien dort sind Maschinenbau, Elektrotechnik und Tourismus. München hat gute Flug-, Bahn-, und Straßenverbindungen mit anderen deutschen Städten und mit Südeuropa. **2** München liegt in Süddeutschland/Sie liegt in Bayern/München ist ungefähr 1.000 Kilometer von Hamburg/München hat 1,2 Millionen Einwohner/Die wichtigsten Industrien sind Maschinenbau, Elektrotechnik und Tourismus. **3** In der

Vorstadt/Im Westen/Die Verkehrsverbindungen sind sehr gut/Die Buslinie 12/Zwanzig Kilometer/Ja, es gibt ein Restaurant dort/Ja, es gibt
auch eine Bank dort/Ja, man kann dort Geld wechseln. **4** das, ein,
einen, eine, ein, eine, einen, einen, eine. **5** denken, glaube, kommt,
fährt, Trinken, bringt, haben, verstehe. **6** Nein, ich habe keinen
Koffer/Nein, ich fahre nicht nach München/Nein, es gibt hier kein
Restaurant/Nein, das Hotel hat keinen Fitneßraum/Nein, das Zimmer
hat kein Radio.

Teil B
2 (a) Sehr geehrter Herr Braun, (b) es freut uns, Ihnen mitzuteilen,
daß…, (c) wir freuen uns auf Ihren Besuch, (d) Sie finden die Firma in
der Ludwigstraße, Nummer 10, (e) mit freundlichen Grüßen.

Lektion 3

Teil A
1 See model passage. **2** Friedrich Krupp AG ist in der Maschinenbau, Anlagenbau und Stahlbranchen tätig und produziert Maschinen und Anlagen. Der Hauptsitz liegt in Essen. Sie ist eine sehr
große Firma mit ungefähr 64.000 Mitarbeitern und hat einen hohen
Umsatz von mehr als DM 20.000 Millionen. Das Gesamtsortiment
umfaßt Kunstoffmaschinen, Werkzeuge, Magnete, Lokomotive, petro-
chemische Anlagen und Zement- und Förderanlagen. Der wichtigste
Markt für Friedrich Krupp AG ist Westeuropa. **3** größte, höher,
erfolgreicher, niedriger, schlechter. **4** Ich arbeite für Carter
Machines Ltd in der Maschinenbaubranche in England/Sie ist die größte
Maschinenbaufirma in England und hat den höchsten Umsatz/Er ist/liegt
in London aber wir haben Zweigstellen in vielen Ländern/Es gibt 3.000
Mitarbeiter in London/Ja, die meisten sind Engländer aber es gibt
Mitarbeiter aus allen Ländern/Ich spreche Französisch und Deutsch/
Vielen Dank. **5** Möchten Sie sich setzen/Ich informiere mich über Ihre
Firma/Interessieren Sie sich für unsere Produkte?/Ich freue mich auf
die Besichtigung/Verabreden wir uns am Montag, sagen wir um 9
Uhr?/Wo befindet sich Ihr Büro?/Sie informieren sich am besten beim
Portier. **6** (a) Wie groß ist die Firma? (b) Wo liegt der Hauptsitz? (c)
Wann erweitert sich die Firma? (d) Wer ist Betriebsleiter? (e) Wieviele
Mitarbeiter hat die Firma? (f) Was produziert die Firma?

Teil B
1 Ja, wir haben eine sehr gute Geschäftsverbindung/Ja, sie sind sehr
zuverlässig/Ihre Produkte sind von guter Qualität/Ihre finanzielle Lage

ist günstig/Meiner Meinung nach bringt eine Zusammenarbeit kein Risiko.

2 Sehr geehrte Damen und Herren!
Wir danken Ihnen für Ihre Anfrage vom 2. Juni über die Firma Davies & Co. Unserer Meinung nach ist die Firma sehr zuverlässig und hat einen guten Ruf. Ihre finanzielle Lage ist günstig.

Alle Einzelheiten sind natürlich vertraulich.
Mit freundlichen Grüßen,

Lektion 4

Teil A
1 For example: Ingrid ist Diplom Kaufmann. Sie fährt oft zu den Lieferanten, etc. **2** Ich bin Kaufmann von Beruf und bin jetzt Verkaufsleiter bei der Firma Stemag in Hannover. Ich fahre oft zu den Kunden überall in Europa. Manchmal vertrete ich meine Firma auch in den USA. Ich beginne meine Arbeit in Hannover sehr früh morgens. Ich habe Feierabend kaum vor 7 Uhr abends. Ich habe oft Sitzungen mit anderen leitenden Angestellten. **3** (*a*) Ich arbeite bei der Firma... (*b*) Ich bin...von Beruf. (*c*) Die Firma liegt... (*d*) Ich bin verantwortlich für.... (*a*) Ja, ich studiere. (*b*) Ich studiere... (*c*) Ich studiere auf der Universität/Fachhochschule/auf dem College... (*d*) Ich studiere am liebsten...**4** For example: (*a*) Sie gefällt mir gut. (*b*) Es gefällt mir nicht gut. (*c*) Er gefallt mir gut. (*d*) Das gefällt mir gut. **5** der, dem, dem, der, dem, der, dem, der, der, dem.

Teil B
1 For example: Angelika arbeitet als Marketingassistentin in der Pharmazeutikabranche. Die Arbeit gefällt ihr gut..., etc. **2** For example: ....Meine neue Arbeit gefällt mir gut. Sie ist interessant und das Gehalt ist gut. Ich beginne die Arbeit um acht Uhr und habe um 4.30 Feierabend. Ich übersetze die Post aus Deutschland und mache die Post für den Marketingdirektor. Ich fahre auch oft zu den Lieferanten mit dem Chef. Das Betriebsklima ist gut und ich esse im Firmenrestaurant zu Mittag... **3** weißt, reise, arbeitest, übersetze, gehen, ist, telefoniere, gibt.

Lektion 5

Teil A
1 (*a*) Herr Sieg will ein schnelles Auto kaufen. (*b*) Der Verkäufer

empfiehlt das neue Opel Modell. (*c*) Das neue Opel hat ABS Bremsen, Allradsteuerung und Zentralverriegelung. (*d*) Der Wagen kostet DM 35.000 oder DM 33.750 für Firmen. (*e*) Herr Sieg will bar bezahlen. (*f*) Er bekommt 5% Rabatt. (*g*) Das Auto hat fünf Gänge. (*h*) Das Auto hat ABS Bremsen. **2** Ich will ein neues Auto kaufen. Möchten Sie mitkommen?/Ja, aber ich versuche auch ein preisgünstiges Auto zu finden/Ich möchte ein elegantes Auto aber bequem mit Allradsteuerung/ Ungefähr einhundertzwanzig mit Hinterradantrieb/Ich weiß, ich muß in Raten zahlen! Haben Sie ein Auto? **3** The new electronic typewriter TIPP208 from Grundig uses the latest technology. It is simple to use, small, light and elegant. It operates from the mains at home or in the office and with batteries for the business trip. The TIPP208 keyboard is international and reacts quietly and quickly. The TIPP208 has all the advantages of the latest technology: a memory, a correcting system and interchangeable typefaces for your personal style. THE NEW SMALL TIPP208. EVEN THE PRICE IS MODEST! **4** helfen, möchte, empfehlen, Möchten, empfehle, ist, anschauen, kommen, kostet, verkaufen, nehme. **5** (*a*) Ich denke, daß das Opel Modell sehr elegant ist. (*b*) Das VW Modell ist sehr bequem obwohl es kleiner ist. (*c*) Mir gefällt das Merzedes Modell, weil es sehr groß ist. (*d*) Ich weiß nicht, ob dieses Modell preisgünstig ist.

Teil B
1 Sehr geehrte Damen und Herren! Wir danken Ihnen für Ihr Interesse und können Ihnen folgendes über unsere Firma/Produkte berichten. Unsere Maschinenwerkzeuge werden hauptsächlich in Shef-field produziert. 25% der Gesamtproduktion wird exportiert. Die Waren werden nach Europa über Rotterdam transportiert. Bitte wenden Sie sich an uns, wenn Sie weitere Informationen brauchen. **2** Zuerst werden die Bestandteile produziert/Sie werden zuerst kontrolliert und dann werden sie mit Computer montiert/Alle Teile werden mit Wasser während der Montage bespritzt/Dann werden die Fertig-produkte nach der Versandabteilung transportiert und werden überall in die Welt geschickt. **3** (*a*) Man produziert die Autos in Hamburg. (*b*) Man exportiert 40% der Gesamtproduktion. (*c*) Man kauft die Autos wegen Ihrer Qualität. (*d*) Man schickt 30% der Exporte nach den USA.

Lektion 6

Teil A
2 (*a*) Wir bitten um Zusendung Ihres Katalogs. (*b*) Wir bitten um Zusendung Ihrer Preisliste. (*c*) Wir bitten um Angabe Ihrer Zahlungs-bedingungen. (*d*) Wir bitten um Angabe Ihrer Lieferbedingungen. (*e*)

Wir bitten um Angabe Ihrer Lieferzeit. **3** (*a*) das Auto der Firma (*b*) die Sekretärin des Chefs (*c*) das Büro der Sekretärin (*d*) das Computer des Einkaufsleiters (*e*) der Name des Generaldirektors (*f*) die Tür des Büros. **4** -e, -es, -es, -s, -en, -e, -en, -en, -en, -en, -en, -s.

Teil B
1 Grüß Gott. Mein Name ist… Ich bin von der Firma… Ich möchte den Einkaufsleiter sprechen./Leider habe ich keine Verabredung, aber ich bin auf der Durchreise./Ich möchte einen Termin machen, bitte./Ich bin morgen um drei Uhr frei./Bitte können Sie das wiederholen?/Ja das geht in Ordnung./(Spell your name.)/Auf Wiederhören.

Lektion 7

Teil A
1 (*a*) Klaus muß mit Ingrid über ihre Geschäftsreise nach Österreich sprechen. (*b*) Ingrid trifft sich um elf Uhr mit dem Vertreter von der pharmazeutischen Firma. (*c*) Sie will ihn mindestens eine Stunde sprechen. (*d*) Klaus möchte das neue Restaurant um die Ecke ausprobieren. (*e*) Klaus will schwimmengehen, Fußball schauen und ein Weinkeller besuchen. (*f*) Ingrid fährt am Montag. **2** (*a*) Ich fahre am 6. Juni nach Österreich (*b*) Ich besuche Wien zuerst. (*c*) Ich wohne im Hotel Ibis. (*d*) Ich komme am 14. Juni in Salzburg an. (*e*) Ich verbringe 3 Tage dort. (*f*) Ich fliege am 17. Juni zurück. **3** Ich gehe Samstag morgen schwimmen. Am Nachmittag gehe ich einkaufen. Ich muß Geschenke für meine Frau/meinen Mann und meine Kinder kaufen. Am Abend möchte ich das Restaurant um die Ecke ausprobieren. /Am Sonntag miete ich ein Auto, um die Umgebung zu besuchen. Möchten Sie mitkommen? **4** (*a*) Ich treffe sie um 10 Uhr. (*b*) Ich muß mit ihm um halb 12 sprechen. (*c*) Ich will sie um viertel nach eins besuchen (*d*) Ich möchte mich mit ihnen um 3 Uhr treffen. (*i*) Sie. (*ii*) Ihnen. (*iii*) Sie. (*iv*) Ihnen. **5** (*a*) Er schlägt vor, daß er Montag fährt. (*b*) Er zieht das große Auto vor. (*c*) Er kommt um vier Uhr nachmittags an. (*d*) Er nimmt an, daß die Besprechung drei Stunden dauert. (*e*) Er kommt am Donnerstag zurück.

Teil B
1 (*a*) Falsch – er soll heute kommen. (*b*) Wahr. (*c*) Falsch – er möchte im Hotel Adler wohnen. (*d*) Wahr. (*e*) Falsch – sie soll ihn anrufen/er gibt seine Telefonnummer. **2** An Hilde Werner – Der Techniker ist heute nicht frei aber er kann das Fotokopiergerät morgen reparieren. Er kommt um 2 Uhr. An Peter Braun – Ihre Platznummer für den Flug nach Linz ist 25B. Das Hotel Adler reserviert ein Einzelzimmer Nr. 215

für den 7. – 9. März inklusiv. An Johannes Berg – Können Sie Klaus Schmidt anrufen, um die Geschäftsreise zu bestätigen. Er will unbedingt morgen wissen.

Lektion 8

Teil A

1 (*a*) Sie wird am 6. Juni nach Wien fliegen. (*b*) Sie wird am 11. Juni nach Linz fliegen. (*c*) Sie wird um 10 Uhr abends im Hotel ankommen. (*d*) Der Agent wird sie um Viertel vor acht abholen. (*e*) Sie wird fünf Nächte im Hotel Ibis bleiben. (*f*) Der Agent holt sie vom Hotel ab. **2** Guten Tag. Ich möchte bitte zwei Einzelzimmer reservieren./Für den fünften Marz./Ich brauche das Zimmer für fünf Nächte./Mit Bad./ (Name.)/Ja, ich kann das schriftlich bestätigen./Ich werde um sechs Uhr abends ankommen./Auf Wiedersehen. **3** Ja. Ich werde am Freitag, dem dreizehnten um sechs Uhr morgens von Birmingham abfliegen und werde um neun Uhr in Berlin ankommen. Ja. Ich werde im Hotel Kempinski wohnen. Das Zimmer ist bestätigt. Doch, ich werde Herrn Schramm besuchen. Er wird mich vom Flughafen abholen. Er wohnt in der Nähe des Flughafens. Wir werden zu Siemens fahren. Dann werde ich zwei neue Kunden in Berlin besuchen. Danke schön.

Lektion 9

Teil A

1 Wie komme ich am besten zum Hauptmarkt/zum Karl Marx Haus/zur Porta Nigra/zum Hafen? **2** Gehen sie die Ostallee entlang; an den Kaiserthermen rechts. Die Europahalle ist an der zweiten Kreuzung./Gehen Sie die Theodor Heuss Allee entlang; an der Porta Nigra links bis zum Hauptmarkt. Dann halb rechts./Gehen Sie die Reichsabtei entlang, bis zur Schönbornstraße; dann links. Die St. Paulin ist links an der nächsten Ecke./Gehen Sie die Theodor Heuss Allee entlang. Gehen Sie immer geradeaus weiter bis zur Mosel. Gehen sie dann links in die Uferstraße. Sie sehen dann den Alten Kran auf der rechten Seite. **3** (*a*) right. (*b*) wrong. (*c*) wrong. (*d*) wrong. (*e*) right. (*f*) wrong. **4** (*a*) Kommen Sie herein! (*b*) Bitte legen Sie ab! (*c*) Bitte nehmen Sie Platz! (*d*) Bringen Sie bitte zwei Kaffee! (*e*) Vergiß das Bier nicht! (*f*) Gib mir die Adresse! (*g*) Bitte entschuldigen Sie die Unterbrechung!

Teil B

1 Platz nehmen; bitte nicht rauchen; bitte den Platz nicht verlassen; aufpassen bitte; ein Trinkgeld fur unseren Fahrer nicht vergessen! **2** Herzlich Willkommen in –./Mein Name ist – und ich möchte ein paar

Worte sagen./Bitte in diesem Raum nicht rauchen./Heute abend ist eine Party./Morgen um 10 Uhr ist eine Rundfahrt und morgen nachmittag ist ein Besuch in..../Ich wünsche Ihnen einen schönen Aufenthalt in – und jetzt bitte bedienen Sie sich!

Lektion 10

Teil A

1 (*a*) Ich habe die Anzeige in der Süddeutschen Zeitung gesehen. (*b*) Es ist eine Stelle als Einkäufer. (*c*) Ich brauche Erfahrung im internationalen Einkaufsmarketing. (*d*) Ja, ich soll Englisch perfekt beherrschen. (*e*) Ich soll Kenntnisse in den Bereichen Wertanalyse, Lieferantenbewertung und Kalkulation haben. (*f*) Die Firma bietet gute Entwicklungschancen an. **2** (*a*) Wir haben eine neue Zweigstelle in Hamburg gegründet. (*b*) Der Betriebsleiter hat 50 Mitarbeiter engagiert. (*c*) Die Firma hat drei Büros gemietet. (*d*) Sie haben schon viel Erfolg gehabt. (*e*) Sie haben viele Produkte verkauft. (*f*) Ich habe die Zweigstelle letzte Woche besucht. **3** Check using sample letter.

Teil B

1 (*a*) Martina ist am 10. Oktober 1966 geboren. (*b*) Ihr Vater ist Bildredakteur von Beruf. (*c*) Sie hat das Gymnasium von 1978 bis 1985 besucht. (*d*) Sie hat ihr Studium im Jahre 1990 abgeschlossen. (*e*) Sie hat von September 1990 bis Oktober 1991 bei Salamander gearbeitet. (*f*) Sie hat ihre Stelle bei Wertheim in Oktober 1991 gefunden. **2** Was für ein Diplom hat er abgeschlossen?/Wo hat er bis jetzt gearbeitet?/Was für Arbeit hat er gemacht?/Hat er Erfahrung in Verhandlung gehabt? **3** Wo bist du am Wochenende gewesen?/Ich bin nach Hause gefahren./Hast du Freunden besucht?/Nein, ich habe eine Geschäftsreise gemacht./Hast du Erfolg gehabt?/Ja, die Firma hat 100 Maschinen gekauft. **4** Refer to sample application form.

Lektion 11

Teil A

1 der – masculine nominative; das – neuter nominative; der – masculine nominative; den – masculine accusative; der – masculine nominative.

Teil B

1 (*a*) der (*b*) den (*c*) der (*d*) die (*e*) die (*f*) die (*g*) die **2** Guten Tag. Es handelt sich um eine Stelle, die in der Zeitung erschien./Ja. Das ist richtig./Ich möchte die Person sprechen, die für Marketing zuständig ist./Ja. Ich interessiere mich für die Stelle. Das ist eine Firma, die Möbel herstellt./Ich arbeite im Verkaufsbüro. Aber ich betreue auch

Kunden und mache Besuche./Der Chef, der sehr nett ist, verlangt viel – und ich erledige es./Auf Wiedersehen.

Lektion 12

Teil A

1 (*a*) Johannes Becker arbeitet in der Verkaufsabteilung. (*b*) Er ist schon 3 Jahre bei der Firma. (*c*) Vorher hatte er eine Stelle bei einer Textilfirma/bei Timmermann OHG. (*d*) Er wollte bei einer größeren Firma arbeiten. (*e*) Er findet das Betriebsklima ganz aufregend. **2** (*a*) Meine letzte Firma hieß Timmermann OHG. (*b*) Der Betriebsleiter war Herr Heidegott. (*c*) 50 Mitarbeiter waren da angestellt. (*d*) Ich hatte eine Stelle als Marketingassistent. (*e*) Ich habe DM 5.000 im Monat verdient. (*f*) Ich konnte 5 Wochen in Urlaub fahren. **3** (*a*) Ich habe bei…gearbeitet. (*b*) Ich hatte eine Stelle als… (*c*) Weil ich mein Deutsch verbessern wollte/weil… (*d*) Ich konnte schon ein bißchen/ziemlich viel deutsch. (*e*) Ich mußte die ersten Tage/die erste Woche/in einem Hotel wohnen. **4** (*a*) Seit wann arbeiten Sie bei der Firma? (*b*) Seit wann exportieren Sie nach England? (*c*) Wie lange produziert die Firma schon Ersatzteile? (*d*) Seit wann hat die Firma ein Büro in Japan?

Teil B

1 Follow the model letter page, inserting: auf der Münchener Messe…interessieren uns sehr für Ihre Wollstoffe…finden, daß es hier in Großbritannien…Können Sie uns bitte Ihre neuste/letzte Preisliste schicken… **2** Ich bin um 4 Uhr vorbeigekommen aber du warst nicht hier. Wir haben eine Fete am Freitag bei uns zu Hause organisiert, um meinen Geburtstag zu feiern. Ich hoffe, daß du mit deiner Frau/deinem Mann kommen kannst. Wir essen um 9 Uhr.

Lektion 13

Teil A

1 (*a*) Kuhl Möbel gewährt einen Mengenrabatt von 10 Prozent für Aufträge über DM 15.000. (*b*) Thyssen muß innerhalb von 30 Tagen nach Empfang der Bestellung bezahlen. (*c*) Kuhl Möbel kann die Waren normalerweise in acht Wochen liefern. (*d*) Thyssen braucht die Waren dringend, um ihre neuen Büros in Steele auszustatten. (*e*) Die zwei Firmen einigen sich über eine Lieferzeit von sechs Wochen. (*f*) Kuhl Möbel nimmt Schecks oder Wechsel an. **2** (*a*) Tische, Stühle und Schränke werden bestellt/Büromöbel wird bestellt. (*b*) Die Stühle kosten DM 350.00 pro Stück. (*c*) Die Zahlungsbedingungen sind durch Tratte per 30 Tage Sicht. (*d*) Die Lieferzeit ist 6 Wochen. (*e*) Die Lieferungsbedingungen sind Frei Haus. **3** Guten Morgen. Herr/

Frau... von Volkswagen AG am Apparat. Wir brauchen Büromaterial und möchten gerne wissen, ob Sie Mengenrabatt gewähren/Geben Sie Skonto für prompte Bezahlung?/Wir brauchen die Waren dringend. Wären Sie in der Lage die Sendung sofort zu schicken?/Wir möchten 50 Mappen, 5 Packungen Schreibmaschinenpapier, 500 weiße Umschläge und 1.000 Büroklammer./Wir brauchen 50. Haben Sie ausreichend?/Wir werden den Auftrag sofort schicken und hoffen, daß die Waren bis Freitag ankommen!/Vielen Dank. Aufwiederhören. **4** (*a*) We should have accepted their terms. (*b*) If only I had offered a cash discount. (*c*) The managing director shouldn't have demanded a downpayment. (*d*) If only we had promised a shorter delivery period. (*e*) I should have granted a bulk discount. **5** (*a*) Könnten Sie uns ein Skonto gewähren, wenn wir sofort bezahlten? (*b*) Wäre es möglich einen Mengenrabatt zu gewähren, wenn wir 100 Schreibtische bestellten? (*c*) Wären Sie bereit einen Scheck anzunehmen? (*d*) Wenn wir per Wechsel bezahlten, könnten wir 90 Tage Kredit haben? (*e*) Würden Sie sofort liefern, wenn wir einen Auftrag jetzt erteilten.

Teil B

1 (*a*) They are free on board prices. (*b*) Yes, 10%, for orders over DM 1.500. (*c*) Within 30 days. (*d*) Bank transfer. **2** We thank you for your offer of 11th May and the enclosed catalogue and should like to place the following order: 25 portable radios Model No. 211 at DM 90.00 each, 30 tape recorders Model No. 345 at DM 150.00 each, Franco domicile including packaging Delivery period: 4-6 weeks, Terms of payment: Payment on receipt of goods, The goods are to be delivered to our forwarding agents: Eisenhardt GmbH, Brigittestr. 15, 4300 Essen 1. Thanking you in anticipation. Yours faithfully. **3** Follow sample letter 1. For payment write 'Bitte schicken Sie uns einen Scheck bei Erhalt der Waren'.

Lektion 14

Teil A

1 (*a*) Es kommt auf den Preis an. (*b*) Es kommt darauf an, wann die Waren ankommen. (*c*) Es kommt auf die Qualität an. (*d*) Es kommt darauf an, wo die Ausstellung stattfindet. (*e*) Es kommt darauf an, was Sie brauchen. (*f*) Es kommt darauf an. **2** (*a*) hatte (*b*) hatte (*c*) hatte (*d*) hatte (*e*) waren **3** (*a*) Wir danken Ihnen für Ihr Schreiben vom 10. Oktober. (*b*) Ich möchte mich über Ihre elektrischen Kontakte erkundigen/informieren. (*c*) Wir sind auch an Tastaturen interessiert. (*d*) Spezialisieren Sie sich auch auf andere Bestandteile? (*e*) Ich freue mich darauf, Sie nächsten Monat zu treffen. Mit freundlichen Grüßen.

Teil B
1   bin, war, habe, habe, waren *or*: sind, waren, habe, war, hat.
2   auf, auf, für, daran, darauf an, darauf, an.

Lektion 15

Teil A
1   Kann ich Herrn Schwarz sprechen?/Leider ist unser Auftrag noch
nicht angekommen. Er war am Ende des Monats fällig. Wir brauchen
die Waren dringend./Es tut mir sehr leid aber wir können nicht länger
warten. Wir brauchen die Waren, bevor das Weihnachtsgeschäft
anfängt. Können Sie uns eine Teilsendung jetzt und die Restlieferung
innerhalb von 10 Tagen schicken. Sonst werden wir gezwungen sein,
anderswo zu kaufen./Können Sie uns telephonieren sobald die Teilsendung versandbereit ist?/In Ordnung. Vielen Dank. Auf Wiederhören.
2   Nein, ich habe nicht gut geschlafen. Ich möchte mich über das
Zimmer beschweren. Es ist neben dem Fahrstuhl und gestern abend
gab es viel Lärm. Auch war das Bett nicht bequem und das Wasser im
Badezimmer war kalt./Die Etage ist nicht so wichtig. Ich wäre Ihnen
dankbar, wenn Sie mir ein anderes Zimmer geben könnte./In Ordnung,
aber ich hoffe, daß das Bett bequem ist und daß es warmes Wasser
gibt./Werde ich eine Entschädigung bekommen? 3   1 (*e*), 2 (*c*), 3 (*a*),
4 (*f*), 5 (*b*), 6 (*d*) 4   (*a*) Wir möchten Sie davon in Kenntnis setzen,
daß ... (*b*) Es hängt davon ab, ob ... (*c*) Wir bedauern es sehr aber ...
(*d*) Können Sie dafür sorgen, daß ... (*e*) Werden Sie es mir versprechen ...

Teil B
Possible replies: 1   Wir gestatten uns, Sie darauf aufmerksam zu
machen, daß wir nur 35 von den 50 bestellten Wörterbüchern erhalten
haben. Wir brauchen die Waren dringend und wären Ihnen deshalb
dankbar, wenn Sie uns die Restlieferung prompt/umgehend liefern
könnten. 2   In Bezug auf unseren Auftrag vom 6. 12. 9 x vor zwei
Monaten, müssen wir Ihnen leider mitteilen, daß wir die Waren immer
noch nicht erhalten haben. Wenn Sie nicht innerhalb der nächsten
Woche liefern, werden wir gezwungen sein, anderswo zu bestellen.
3   Wir sind im Besitz Ihres Schreibens vom 7.7 und bedauern es sehr,
daß Sie die falschen Waren erhalten haben. Leider haben wir Ihre
Waren versehentlich an einen anderen Kunden geschickt. Wir möchten
uns wegen dieses Versehens entschuldigen und werden uns bemühen,
Ihnen die richtigen Waren so schnell wie möglich zu schicken.

Lektion 16

Die Geographie Deutschlands
1 Falsch. Deutschland ist kleiner. **2** Wahr. **3** Falsch. Die Hälfte des Bodens ist landwirtschaftlich benutzt. **4** Wahr. **5** Falsch. Der Rhein ist es. **6** Wahr. **7** Falsch. Die größte Konzentration befindet sich im Ruhrgebiet. **8** Wahr.

Die Industrie
1 Das Ruhrgebiet und das Saarland. **2** In Baden-Württemberg und Bayern. **3** Bei der chemischen Industrie; Hoechst, Bayer und BASF. **4** Die elektotechnische Branche. **5** Der Straßenfahrzeugbau. **6** Bei Maschinenbau.

Lektion 17

Radio und Fernsehen
1 At the time of writing, eleven. **2** Most do, but NDR is shared between Schleswig Holstein, Hamburg and Niedersachsen, and SWF between Baden-Württemberg and Rheinland Pfalz. **3** Overseas broadcasts, representing a German view. **4** Channel 1. Member organisations also produce Channel 3. Organisationally, ARD is not totally dissimiliar to the IBA. **5** Channel 2. ZDF is a single broadcasting company. **6** Channel 3 is more local in character. **7** Because cable TV is widespread, which makes satellite broadcasts available via the cable network.

Die Stellung der Frau
1 The constitution states that women have equal rights, but in reality they are disadvantaged. **2** Often the work done by women is classed as light work, so paid less. **3** No. In the public sector, all employees on the same pay grade are paid the same, irrespective of gender. **4** The job of housewife and mother should be rewarded like any other job. **5** The shareout of domestic and wage-earning responsibilities. **6** That a couple may choose the family name of either partner as their family name. **7** To support the financially weaker partner until she/he can support him/herself.

Lektion 18

Die deutsche Wirtschaft
1 Deutschland ist eines der größten Industrieländer der Welt. **2** Deutschland hat den zweiten Platz im Welthandel – nach den USA. **3** Das Bruttosozialprodukt ist das vierthöchste der Welt. **4** In diesen Branchen ist Export fast so wichtig wie der Markt im eigenen

Land. **5** Es gibt eine marktwirtschaftliche Ordnung. **6** Der Staat hat eine Lenkungsfunktion, um Fehlentwicklungen und Ungerechtigkeit zu vermeiden.

Außenhandel
1 Ein Kennzeichen des deutschen Außenhandels ist seit Jahren eine positive Zahlungsbilanz. **2** Deutscher Erfolg beim Export kommt von einem hohen technologischen Stand, einem breiten Warensortiment, guter Qualität und pünktlicher Lieferung. **3** Deutschland setzt sich für eine liberale Außenhandelspolitik, durch den Abbau von Zöllen und anderen Handelsbeschränkungen ein. **4** Dieses Viertel hat eine typische Struktur: Maschinen, Kraftfahrzeuge, elektronische und chemische Produkte. **5** Die großen Ausfuhrüberschüsse sind aber nötig, um Defizite auf anderen Gebieten wie Tourismus auszugleichen. **6** Die Vereinigung bietet auch eine wertvolle Gelegenheit Binnen- und Außenhandel noch weiter auszubauen.

Lektion 19

Messen
1 The transshipment of goods of all kinds. **2** At the intersection of major trade routes. **3** The Offenbach Fair is a specialist fair for leather, whereas the Hanover Fair is a general trade fair. **4** As a marketing tool, a meeting place for specific industries, an information exchange, and an economic forum. **5** 40% of the exhibiting companies at major fairs are foreign.

Der Verkehr (Teil A)
1 Long distance transport of goods and passengers. **2** For commuters in large conurbations. **3** Germany is a thoroughfare so many foreign vehicles use her motorways. **4** 4/5 passenger transport is by car; there are 40 million registered vehicles.

Der Verkehr (Teil B)
1 For security during times of crisis. **2** They are not conveniently situated in relation to the industrial centres of Europe. **3** By investment, for example in container technology. **4** The Saar is being canalised and the Main-Danube canal links the industrial areas of Germany with the Black Sea. **5** Bulk goods like oil products, ore, coal and building materials.

Lektion 20

Soziale Sicherheit
1 Deutsche Bürger sind gegen Krankheit versichert und brauchen nicht für ärztliche Behandlung, Medikamente und Operationen zu

bezahlen. **2** Ein Arbeitnehmer, der krank wird, hat auch das Recht auf Weiterzahlung seines Verdienstes durch den Arbeitgeber und danach durch die Krankenkasse. **3** Wer arbeitslos ist, erhält ein Arbeitslosengeld, das rund zwei Drittel seines letzten Verdienstes ausmacht. **4** Deutsche Bürger können zwischen 60 und 65 in den Ruhestand treten und haben ein Recht auf eine Rente. **5** Renten in Deutschland richten sich nach der Versicherungsdauer und der Höhe des Arbeitsentgelts. **6** Deutsche Rentner bekommen dynamische Renten, die mit dem wirtschaftlichen Wachstum Schritt halten.

Berufliche Ausbildung
1 Die meisten Jugendlichen bekommen eine berufliche Ausbildung. **2** Das 'duale' System bedeutet, daß man die Theorie in der Schule studiert und die Praxis in einem Betrieb ausübt. **3** Nein, es gibt 20 bevorzugte Berufe. **4** Typische weibliche Lehren sind Verkäuferin, Friseuse und Bürokauffrau. **5** Eine Lehre dauert normalerweise zwei bis dreieinhalb Jahre. **6** Die Lehrlinge müssen die Schule ein bis zwei Mal in der Woche besuchen.

Lektion 21

Ausländische Arbeitnehmer
1 (*a*) True (*b*) False, there was much rebuilding and general work to be done after the war. (*c*) False; 60% have been in Germany longer than 10 years. (*d*) True. (*e*) False (other groups do, too). (*f*) False. Foreign workers are particularly hard hit by unemployment. (*g*) True. (*h*) False. Foreign workers are given assistance to return home if they wish, but not in the way suggested.
1 (*a*) In den 50er und 60er Jahren. (*b*) Sie sind aus armen Ländern wie Spanien, Jugoslawien, Griechenland, Italien und der Türkei gekommen. (*c*) 40%. (*d*) Weil sie sich in einem fremden Kulturkreis befinden. (*e*) Arbeitslosigkeit; die Kinder sind in der Schule schon wegen der Sprache im Nachteil. (*f*) Der weitere Zuzug von Ausländern wird begrenzt und man hilft Ausländern, die es wollen, ins Heimatland zurückzukehren.

Deutschland und Europa
1 1979. **2** Das Abkommen von Lomé. **3** Durch den Beitritt von Dänemark, GB und Irland im Jahre 1981, und von Spanien und Portugal 1986. **4** Sie sollte zur Gründung des Binnenmarktes im Jahre 1993 führen. **5** Der Römer Vertrag, der die EG gründete, wurde unterzeichnet.

Dialog
1 1/4. **2** Germany is one of the top exporters alongside the USA and

Japan. **3** One in four jobs depends on secure export markets. **4** One half of Germany's exports goes to other EC countries. **5** European countries will be able to cooperate more closely, and therefore compete more effectively.

Lektion 22

Die Schweiz

1 Wahr. **2** Falsch. Die Schweiz hat nur wenig Rohstoffe. **3** Wahr. **4** Falsch. Der Dienstleistungssektor ist sehr erfolgreich. **5** Falsch. Wichtige Branchen sind die Farbchemie und Maschinenbau. **6** Wahr. **7** Wahr. **8** Falsch. Diese Branche ist zu einer hochentwickelten Industrie geworden.

Österreich

1 Österreich ist viel kleiner als Deutschland. **2** Österreich hat Eisen, Metallen, Mineralien, Erdöl und Erdgas. **3** Diese Rohstoffe sind die Basis der Industrie. **4** Der technologische Stand in Österreich ist sehr hoch. **5** Die chemische Industrie ist wichtig geworden, weil die nötigen Rohstoffe vorhanden sind. **6** Synthetische Fasern, Düngemittel, Plastikwaren und pharmazeutische Produkte haben die größte Bedeutung in Österreich.

Lektion 23

Föderalismus

1 True. **2** False. Federalism has a long tradition in Germany. **3** True. **4** True. **5** True. **6** False. **7** True.

Die politischen Parteien

1 Die CDU/CSU und die FDP bilden eine Koalition. **2** Die CDU, CSU und die FDP waren Neugründungen nach dem Krieg, aber die SPD bestand schon früher. **3** Sechs Parteien sind im Bundestag vertreten. **4** Die Grüne Partei überwindete die 5% Klausel im Jahr 1983 und zog zum ersten Mal in den Bundestag ein. **5** Parteien, die darauf ausgehen, die Grundordnung/den Staat zu beseitigen, können aufgelöst werden. **6** Nach der Wahl vom 2. Dezember 1990 konnten kleine Parteien aus dem Osten noch vertreten werden (z.B. B90/Grünen). **7** Die Grüne Partei ist aus einer Umweltschutzbewegung hervorgegangen und vereinigt verschiedene Protestgruppen. **8** 1952 und 1956 wurden extreme Parteien verboten.

APPENDIX 1

Die Zahlen (Numbers)

0	null	7	sieben	14	vierzehn
1	eins	8	acht	15	fünfzehn
2	zwei	9	neun	16	sechzehn
3	drei	10	zehn	17	siebzehn
4	vier	11	elf	18	achtzehn
5	fünf	12	zwölf	19	neunzehn
6	sechs	13	dreizehn		

As you can see, for numbers 13–19 **-zehn** is simply added with the exception of **sechzehn** where the **-s** is dropped and **siebzehn** where the **-en** is dropped.

Numbers 20–29 are as follows:

20	zwanzig	25	fünfundzwanzig
21	einundzwanzig	26	sechsundzwanzig
22	zweiundzwanzig	27	siebenundzwanzig
23	dreiundzwanzig	28	achtundzwanzig
24	vierundzwanzig	29	neunundzwanzig

Beyond 20 the units always come first with **und** linking them to the tens as in *four and twenty*. Remember also that **eins** drops its **-s** in the middle of compounds as in **einundzwanzig**.

Here are some more numbers:

30	dreißig	70	siebzig	100	hundert
40	vierzig	80	achtzig	1.000	tausend
50	fünfzig	90	neunzig	1.000.000	eine
60	sechzig				Million

All tens add **-zig** with the exception of **dreißig**. **Sechzig** and **siebzig** again drop the **-s** and **-en** respectively. Also remember that numbers are all written as one word! For example:

1992	neunzehnhundertzweiundneunzig
264.854	zweihundertvierundsechzigtausend-achthundertvierundfünfzig

Die Ordinalzahlen (Ordinal numbers)

To express *first* to *nineteenth*, simply add **-te**, as below:

erste	*first*	sechste	*sixth*
zweite	*second*	siebte	*seventh*
dritte	*third*	achte	*eighth*
vierte	*fourth*	neunte	*ninth*
fünfte	*fifth*	zehnte	*tenth*

Note the irregular forms **erste** and **dritte** and remember that **siebte** and **achte** again drop **-en** and **-t** respectively.

To express twentieth and upwards, add **-ste**, as below:

einundzwanzigste	*21st*	fünfundvierzigste	*45th*
hundertste	*100th*		

Ordinal numbers can be **der**, **die** or **das** depending on what they are describing, for example:

der erste Mann	*the first man*
die zweite Frau	*the second woman*
das dritte Haus	*the third house*

———— Die Tage der Woche ————
(The days of the week)

Montag	*Monday*	Freitag	*Friday*
Dienstag	*Tuesday*	Samstag	*Saturday*
Mittwoch	*Wednesday*	Sonnabend*⎭	
Donnerstag	*Thursday*	Sonntag	*Sunday*

*Used in North Germany.

Some expressions which you may find useful are:

am Montag	*on Monday*
montags	*on Mondays*
jeden Montag	*every Monday*

———— Die Monate des Jahrs ————
(The months of the year)

Januar	*January*	Juli	*July*
Februar	*February*	August	*August*
März	*March*	September	*September*
April	*April*	Oktober	*October*
Mai	*May*	November	*November*
Juni	*June*	Dezember	*December*

Some expressions which you may find useful are:

im Januar	*in January*
der 20te Juni	*the 20th June*
am 17te April	*on the 17th April*

Asking and Telling The Time

Some phrases which you may find useful are:

Wie spät ist es? Wieviel Uhr ist es?	*What time is it?*
Es ist ein Uhr.	*It is one o'clock.*
Es ist viertel nach eins.	*It's a quarter past one.*
Es ist halb zwei.	*It's half past one.*
Es ist viertel vor zwei.	*It's a quarter to two.*
Es ist zehn nach zwei.	*It's ten past two.*
Es ist zwei Uhr vierzig.	*It's two-forty.*

Remember that in German *half **past** one* is seen as *half **to** two*.

Some other useful expressions are:

Es ist zehn vor elf morgens.	*It's ten to eleven in the morning.*
Um vier Uhr nachmittags.	*At four o'clock in the afternoon.*
Um sieben Uhr morgen abend.	*At seven o'clock tomorrow evening.*

Farben (Colours)

gelb	*yellow*	blau	*blue*
weiß	*white*	grau	*grey*
braun	*brown*	orange	*orange*
schwarz	*black*	rot	*red*
grün	*green*	lila	*purple*

Light and *dark* are **hell** and **dunkel** respectively. For example:

hell grün	*light green*
dunkel rot	*dark red*

APPENDIX 2

Table of Common Irregular Verbs

The irregular form is shown in each tense in he/she/it form (the third person singular). The forms of compound verbs (i.e. verbs with prefixes, for example **abhängen**, **verstehen**) are the same as for the simple verb (for example **hängen**, **stehen**) and are therefore not indicated separately.

Infinitive	Present	Imperfect	Present Perfect
anfangen (*to begin*)	fängt ... an	fing...an	hat angefangen
beginnen (*to begin*)	beginnt	begann	hat begonnen
bekommen (*to receive*)	bekommt	bekam	hat bekommen
bieten (*to offer*)	bietet	bot	hat geboten
bitten (*to ask for*)	bittet	bat	hat gebeten
bleiben (*to stay*)	bleibt	blieb	ist geblieben
bringen (*to bring*)	bringt	brachte	hat gebracht
denken (*to think*)	denkt	dachte	hat gedacht
dürfen (*to be able*)	darf	durfte	hat gedurft*
empfehlen (*to recommend*)	empfiehlt	empfahl	hat empfohlen
essen (*to eat*)	ißt	aß	hat gegessen

fahren (*to drive*)	fährt	fuhr	ist gefahren
fallen (*to fall*)	fällt	fiel	ist gefallen
finden (*to find*)	findet	fand	hat gefunden
geben (*to give*)	gibt	gab	hat gegeben
gehen (*to go*)	geht	ging	ist gegangen
haben (*to have*)	hat	hatte	hat gehabt
halten (*to hold, consider*)	hält	hielt	hat gehalten
hängen (*to hang*)	hängt	hing	hat gehangen
heißen (*to be named, mean*)	heißt	hieß	hat geheißen
helfen (*to help*)	hilft	half	hat geholfen
kennen (*to know (person, place)*)	kennt	kannte	hat gekannt
können (*to be able*)	kann	konnte	hat gekonnt*
kommen (*to come*)	kommt	kam	ist gekommen
lassen (*to leave*)	läßt	ließ	hat gelassen
laufen (*to walk, run*)	läuft	lief	ist gelaufen
lesen (*to read*)	liest	las	hat gelesen
liegen (*to lie*)	liegt	lag	hat gelegen

mögen (*to like*)	mag	mochte	hat gemocht*
müssen (*to have to*)	muß	mußte	hat gemußt
nehmen (*to take*)	nimmt	nahm	hat genommen
nennen (*to call, name*)	nennt	nannte	hat genannt
raten (*to advise*)	rät	riet	hat geraten
rufen (*to call, shout*)	ruft	rief	hat gerufen
schließen (*to close*)	schließt	schloß	hat geschlossen
schreiben (*to write*)	schreibt	schrieb	hat geschrieben
sehen (*to see*)	sieht	sah	hat gesehen
sein (*to be*)	ist	war	ist gewesen
sitzen (*to sit*)	sitzt	saß	hat gesessen
sprechen (*to speak*)	spricht	sprach	hat gesprochen
stehen (*to stand*)	steht	stand	hat gestanden
steigen (*to climb, rise*)	steigt	stieg	ist gestiegen
tragen (*to carry*)	trägt	trug	hat getragen
treffen (*to meet*)	trifft	traf	hat getroffen
treten (*to step*)	tritt	trat	hat getreten
trinken (*to drink*)	trinkt	trank	hat getrunken
tun (*to do*)	tut	tat	hat getan

verbinden (*to connect, link*)	verbindet	verband	hat verbunden
verlieren (*to lose*)	verliert	verlor	hat verloren
wachsen (*to grow*)	wächst	wuchs	ist gewachsen
werden (*to become*)	wird	wurde	ist geworden
wissen (*to know*)	weiß	wußte	hat gewußt
wollen (*to want*)	will	wollte	hat gewollt*
ziehen (*to pull*)	zieht	zog	hat gezogen

* The past participle of these modal verbs is replaced by the infinitive when following another infinitive form. For example:

ich habe fahren dürfen   *I was allowed to drive*

ENGLISH–GERMAN GLOSSARY OF COMMERCIAL TERMS

account   das Konto (Konten)
advertise   werben
advertising agency   die Werbeagentur (-en)
appointment   die Verabredung (-en), der Termin (-e)

balance sheet   die Bilanz (-e)
bank   die Bank (-en)
bill of exchange   der Wechsel (-)
bill of lading   das Konnossement (-s)
board of directors   der Vorstand (¨e)
branch   die Zweigstelle (-n)
brand   die Marke (-n)
broker   der Makler (-)
budget   das Budget
business   das Geschäft
businessman/woman   der Geschäftsmann/die Geschäftsfrau (die Geschäftsleute)
business trip   die Geschäftsreise (-n)
buy   kaufen
buyer   der Käufer (-)

capital   das Kapital, *of town* die Hauptstadt (¨e)
capital goods   die Investitionsgüter
cash   bar, *to pay in cash*   bar bezahlen
cash (of cheque)   einlösen
cash payment   die Barbezahlung
catalogue   der Katalog (-e), die Broschüre (-n)
certificate of origin   das Ursprungszeugnis (-se)

client   der Kunde (n)
commerce, trade   der Handel
commercial agent   der Händler (-)
company   die Firma (Firmen)
competition   der Wettbewerb, die Konkurrenz
competitors   der Konkurrent (-en)
competitive   konkurrenzfähig
computer   der Computer (-)
consignment note   der Frachtbrief (-e)
consume   verbrauchen
consumer   der Verbraucher (-)
consumer goods   die Verbrauchsgüter
contract   der Vertrag (¨e)
costs   die Kosten
cost   kosten
credit   der Kredit (-e)
creditor   der Gläubiger (-)
current account   das Girokonto (konten)
customer   der Kunde (-n)
customs duty   der Zoll (¨e)

dealer   der Händler (-)
debit   belasten
debtor   der Schuldner (-)
deliver   liefern
delivery   die Lieferung
demand (for)   die Nachfrage (nach)
discount   *(cash)* das Skonto (Skonten), *(bulk)* der Mengenrabatt (-e)
discount   diskontieren
dispatch   der Versand
dispatch   senden, versenden
distributor   der Großhändler

domestic trade   der Binnenhandel
duty   der Zoll (¨e)

earn   verdienen
earnings   der Verdienst (-e)
estimate   der Voranschlag (¨e)
executive   der leitende
   Angestellte (-n)
expenditure   die Ausgaben
expenses   die Spesen
export   der Export (-e)
export   ausführen
external trade   der Außenhandel

factory   die Fabrik (-e)
finance   finanzieren
financial   finanziell
fiscal year   das Finanzjahr (-e)
foreign exchange/currencies   die
   Devisen
foreign trade   der Außenhandel
freight(costs)   die Fracht(kosten)

goods   die Waren
gross   Brutto- (in compounds)
gross national product   das
   Bruttosozialprodukt

head office   der Sitz (-e)
hire   mieten
hire-purchase   der Ratenkauf (¨e)
home trade   der Binnenhandel

import   der Import (-e)
import   einführen
income   das Einkommen (-)
income tax   die
   Einkommensteuer (-)
industry   die Industrie (-n)
industrial   industriell
instalments, buying or selling
   in   der Ratenkauf, der
   Ratenverkauf (¨e)
instalments, to pay in   in Raten
   zahlen
insurance   die Versicherung (-en)

insurance agent, broker   der
   Versicherungsmakler (-)
insurance policy   die
   Versicherungspolice (-n)
insure   versichern
interest   die Zinsen
interest rate   der Zinsensatz (¨e)
invest   investieren
investment   die Investition (-en)
investor   der Investor
invoice   die Rechnung (-en)

joint-stock company   die
   Aktiengesellschaft (-en)

labour   die Arbeit
launch (a product)   einführen
liabilities   die Schulden
limited liability company   die
   Gesellschaft (-en) mit
   beschränkter Haftung (GmbH)
liquid assets   flüssige Mittel
loan   das Darlehen (-)
loan   leihen

management   die Führung
manager   der Betriebsleiter (-)
managing director   der leitende
   Direktor (-)
manufacture   herstellen
manufactured goods   die
   Fertigwaren
manufacturer   der Hersteller (-)
market   der Markt (¨e)
market research   die
   Marktforschung
merchant   der Händler (-)
middleman   der Vermittler (-)
monopoly   das Monopol (-e)
multinational   multinational

negotiate   verhandeln
negotiation   die Verhandlung (-en)

offer   das Angebot (-e)
offer   (an)bieten

operating costs   die Betriebskosten
output   der Output, die Produktion
overhead expenses   die allgemeinen Unkosten
overtime   die Überstunden

packaging   die Verpackung
partner   der Partner (-)
pay   bezahlen
payment   die Bezahlung
personnel   das Personal
personnel manager   der Personalleiter (-)
price   der Preis (-e)
price list   die Preisliste (-n)
produce   herstellen, produzieren
producer   der Hersteller (-)
product   das Produkt (-e)
production   die Produktion
production manager   der Produktionsleiter (-)
productivity   die Produktivität
profit   das Gewinn (-e)
profit margin   die Gewinnspanne
profitable   rentabel
profitability   die Rentabilität
purchase   der Kauf (-̈e)
purchase   kaufen

quality   die Qualität
quality control   die Qualitätskontrolle

rate   der Satz (-̈e)
raw material   der Rohstoff (-e)
retailer   der Einzelhändler (-)
retail trade   der Einzelhandel
retire   in den Ruhestand treten
risk   das Risiko (Risiken)

salary   das Gehalt (-̈er)
sale   der Verkauf (-̈e)
sales assistant/man   der Verkäufer (-)

sales manager   der Verkaufsleiter (-)
sell   verkaufen
seller   der Verkäufer (-)
share (company)   die Aktie (-n)
shareholder   der Aktionär (-e)
software   das Software
stock (in)   auf Lager
stockbroker   der Börsenmakler (-)
stock exchange   die Börse (-n)
strike   streiken
supply and demand   das Angebot und die Nachfrage

tax   die Steuer (-)
tax free   steuerfrei
terms   die Bedingungen
terms of payment   die Zahlungsbedingungen
trade   der Handel
trade fair   die Messe (-n)
trademark   die Handelsmarke (-n)
trade union   die Gewerkschaft (-en)
transport   der Transport
turnover   der Umsatz (-̈e)

value   der Wert (-e)
VAT   MWS (die Mehrwertssteuer)

wage   der Lohn (-̈e)
wholesale   der Großhandel
wholesaler   der Großhändler (-)
worker   der Arbeiter

GERMAN–ENGLISH VOCABULARY

ab und zu *now and again*
der Abbau (-e) *reduction, cut*
der Abend (-e) *evening*
aber *but*
der Abflug(-̈e) *departure*
abhängig sein *be dependent on*
abholen *to pick up, meet*
abrechnen *to settle accounts*
abreisen *to depart*
der Absatz (-̈e) *sales*
der Absatzmarkt(-̈e) *market*
abschaffen *to abolish*
abstimmen *to agree, come to an agreement on*
die Abteilung (-en) *department*
die Abwechselung *variety*
achten (auf + acc.) *to pay attention (to)*
alle *all*
allerdings *however*
allgemein *general*
alt *old*
die Ampel (-n) *traffic light*
an *to, on*
anbieten *to offer*
der Anbieter(-) *provider*
andere (r,s) *other*
anderswo *elsewhere*
anerkannt *recognised*
anfangen *to start*
die Anfrage (-n) *enquiry*
die Angabe (-n) *data, information*
das Angebot (-e) *offer*
angeschlossen *linked to*

ankommen *to arrive*
die Ankunft (-̈e) *arrival*
der Anlagenbau *plant manufacture*
sich anmelden *check in, register*
annehmen *to suppose, accept*
annulieren *to cancel*
anrufen *to telephone*
die Anschrift (-en) *address*
ansprechen *to address, speak for*
der Anspruch (-̈e) *claim,*
anspruchsvoll *demanding, discriminating*
die Anstalt (-en) *institution*
anstehen *to be on the agenda, be in hand*
der Anteil (-e) *share, proportion*
die Antwort(-en) *answer*
der Anwender (-) *user*
anwesend *present*
die Anzahlung (-en) *downpayment*
die Anzeige (-n) *advertisement*
arbeiten *to work*
der Arbeitgeber (-) *employer*
der Arbeitnehmer (-) *employee*
arbeitslos *unemployed*
die Arbeitslosigkeit *unemployment*
die Art (-en) *type, sort*
der Arzt (-̈e) *doctor*
die Aufenthalt(-e) *stay*
die Aufgabe (-n) *task, job*
sich aufhalten *to stay, sojourn*
aufheben *to lift, remove*
aufkommen *to pay for, meet the costs of*

auflösen   *to dissolve*
aufmerksam machen   *to draw attention to*
die Aufmerksamkeit   *attention*
aufpassen   *pay attention, take care*
aufregend   *exciting*
der Aufstieg (-e)   *development, progress, upward trend*
der Auftrag (¨e)   *order*
ausgebildet   *trained, qualified*
ausbauen   *to expand, increase*
ausführen   *to carry out, to export*
die Ausführung   *execution, model, version*
ausgezeichnet   *excellent*
die Auskunft (¨e)   *information*
auslegen   *to set out*
ausliefern   *to deliver*
ausreichend   *sufficient*
ausrichten   *to pass on (a message)*
sich ausruhen   *to relax, rest*
die Ausstattung   *fittings, equipment*
aussteigen   *to alight*
die Ausstellung(-en)   *exhibition*
ausstrahlen   *to broadcast*
austauschbar   *interchangeable*
der Auszubildende (-n)   *trainee, apprentice*
sich auszeichnen   *to excel, be extraordinary*
der Auszug(¨e)   *extract*
der Außenhandel   *foreign trade*
außerdem   *apart from that*

die Bahn   *railway*
der Bahnhof(¨e)   *station*
bald   *soon*
baldig   *early, soon*
bar bezahlen   *to pay in cash*
der Beamte(-n)   *official*
bearbeiten   *to cover, work (e.g. a territory)*
bedauern   *to regret*

sich befassen (mit)   *to deal (with)*
sich befinden   *to be situated*
begrenzt   *limited*
die Behandlung   *treatment*
behilflich   *helpful*
beide   *both*
beigelegt   *enclosed*
der Beitritt (-e)   *entry (e.g. into EC)*
bekannt   *well-known*
beklagen   *to complain*
benachrichtigen   *to advise, inform*
benachteiligt   *disadvantaged*
benutzen   *to use*
der Benutzer(-)   *user*
das Benzin   *petrol*
bequem   *comfortable*
beraten   *to consult, discuss*
der Bereich (-e)   *domain, field*
bereit   *ready, prepared*
der Bericht (-e)   *report*
berichten   *to report*
die Berichterstattung (-en)   *reporting*
der Beruf (-e)   *profession*
beruflich   *professional*
die Berufsaussichten (pl.)   *career prospects*
die Beschaffung   *procurement*
beschäftigen   *to employ*
beschäftigt   *busy*
bescheiden   *modest*
beschleunigen   *to accelerate*
sich beschränken (auf)   *to limit o.s. (to)*
die Beschwerde (-n)   *complaint*
beschweren   *to complain*
beseitigen   *eliminate, build up*
besiedelt   *populated*
besonders   *especially*
besprechen   *to discuss*
bestätigen   *to confirm*
der Bestandteil (-e)   *component*
bestehen   *to survive*

bestehen (aus)   *to consist (of)*
bestellen   *to order*
die Bestellung (-en)   *order*
bestimmt   *for sure*
der Besuch (-e)   *visit*
besuchen   *to visit*
beteiligt sein   *to take part in, participate in*
betreuen   *to look after, see to, take care of*
der Betrieb (-e)   *company, factory*
das Betriebsklima   *working environment*
der Betriebsleiter (-)   *managing director*
die Bevölkerung   *population*
bevor   *before*
bewältigen   *to cover, master, come to terms with*
beweisen   *to prove*
bewerben (um)   *to apply for*
bezahlen   *to pay*
in Bezug auf   *with reference to*
bezugnehmend auf   *with reference to*
bieten   *to offer*
die Bildung   *education*
billig   *cheap*
der Binnenmarkt   *the Single Market*
bis   *until*
bitte   *please*
bitten (um)   *request*
bißchen   *a little*
bleiben   *to stay, remain*
die Börse(n)   *exchange, stock exchange*
die Branche (-n)   *sector of industry*
branchenüblich   *usual in the sector, normal*
brauchen   *to need*
die Bremse (-n)   *brake*
der Brief (-e)   *letter*
die Brücke(-n)   *bridge*

der Bundesrat   *second chamber of parliament*
die Bürokraft(¨e)   *office staff*
das Büro(-s)   *office*
die Büroklammer (-)   *paperclip*
die Büromaschine (-n)   *office equipment*

die Chemie   *chemistry*
die Chemikalien   *chemicals*

dürfen   *to be allowed to*
daß   *that*
da   *as*
damit   *so that (for the purpose of)*
daneben   *in addition*
dankbar   *grateful*
Danke   *thank you*
danken (+ dat.)   *to thank*
dann   *then*
darüberhinaus   *moreover*
die Datenverarbeitung   *data processing*
das Defizit (-e)   *deficit*
denken   *to think*
deshalb   *therefore*
deswegen   *therefore*
deutsch   *German*
dienen   *to serve*
der Dienst(-e)   *service*
die Dienstleistung(-en)   *service*
dies   *this*
das Diplom   *degree*
die Disposition   *production control*
dringend   *urgently*
durchaus   *of course, certainly*
der Durchschnitt   *average*
die Dusche(n)   *shower*

ebenfalls   *similarly, also*
die Ecke (-n)   *corner*
EDV (elektronische Datenverarbeitung)   *data processing*

ehemalig *former*
die Eheschließung *marriage*
ehrlich *honest*
eigen *own (adj.)*
eigentlich *actually, in fact*
das Eigentum *property*
sich einigen (auf) *to agree (on)*
ein paar *a few*
einführen *to import*
einfach *simple*
eingehen *to arrive (of goods, mail)*
die Einheit (-en) *unit, unity*
einige *some*
der Einkauf(-̈e) *purchase*
einkaufen gehen *to go shopping*
der Einkaufsleiter (-) *purchasing manager*
die Einkünfte *income*
einladen *to invite*
die Einplanung *planning*
die Einrichtung(-en) *equipment, facility*
einschließlich *inclusive*
einsteigen *to board*
eintreffen *to arrive*
einverstanden *agreed*
der Einwohner(-) *inhabitant*
die Einzelheit (-en) *detail*
einzeln *individual*
das Einzelzimmer(-) *single room*
das Eisen *iron*
die Elektrotechnik *electronic engineering*
der Empfang (-̈e) *reception, receipt*
empfangen *to receive (e.g. TV)*
empfehlen *to recommend*
die Entfernung *distance*
die Entschädigung *compensation*
entscheiden *to decide*
die Entscheidung (-en) *decision*
entschuldigen *to excuse*
die Entschuldigung (-en) *sorry, apology*

entstehen *to emerge, develop from*
das Erdöl *mineral oil*
die Erfahrung (-en) *experience*
erfinden *to invent*
der Erfolg (-e) *success*
erfolgreich *successful*
erfüllen *to fulfil, do*
erhalten *to receive*
erkundigen (über) *to enquire (about)*
erledigen *sort out, do, carry out*
ermöglichen *to make possible*
der Ersatzteil (-e) *spare part*
erscheinen *to appear, seem*
erteilen *to place (of order)*
der Erwachsene (-n) *adult*
erwarten *to await, expect*
erweitern *to expand*
das Erz (-e) *ore*
es kommt darauf an *it depends on*
essen *to eat*
etwa *about*
etwas *something*
der Europäischer Rat *European Council*

Fach- (in compounds) *specialist*
die Fachmesse(-n) *specialist fair*
fahren *to go, travel*
der Fahrstuhl (-̈e) *lift*
das Fahrzeug(-e) *vehicle*
fällig *due*
der Familienangehörige(-n) *dependant*
die Farbe (-n) *colour*
der Feierabend *end of the working day*
feiern *to celebrate*
festlegen *to set, fix, decide upon*
finden *to find*
die Firma (-en) *company*
fließend *fluently*

der Flug (¨e) *flight*
der Flughafen(¨) *airport*
folgen *to follow*
folgendes *the following*
die Fracht *freight*
fragen (nach) *ask (for)*
die Fraktion(-en) *faction, political grouping*
Frankreich *France*
die Frau (-en) *woman, Mrs*
frei *free*
freuen *to be glad*
sich freuen (auf) *to look forward (to)*
der Freund (-e) *friend*
führen *to manage, lead*
funktionieren *to operate*
das Fünftel *a fifth*
für *for*

der Gang (¨e) *gear*
der Gast (¨e) *guest*
der Gastarbeiter(-) *guest, immigrant worker*
die Gastfreundlichkeit *hospitality*
das Gebiet(-e) *area, territory*
der Geburtstag (-e) *birthday*
das Gebäude(-) *building*
die Gebühr (-en) *fee*
gefährden *jeopardize, endanger*
der Gehalt (¨er) *salary*
gehen *to go*
gehören (zu) *belong (to)*
die Gemeinde(-n) *parish*
gemeinsam *joint, together*
die Gemeinschaft (-en) *community*
genau *exactly*
geradeaus weiter *straight on*
gern geschehen *don't mention it*
gern(e) *gladly*
Gesamt- (in compounds) *total*
das Geschäft (-e) *business*
die Geschwindigkeit *speed*
die Gesellschaft(-en) *society*

das Gesetz (-e) *law*
das Gespräch (e) *conversation, interview*
gesund *healthy*
gewähren *to grant*
glücklicherweise *fortunately*
glauben *to think, believe*
gleich *very soon, immediately*
gleichberechtigt *equal, enjoying equal rights*
gleichfalls *likewise*
gleichzeitig *simultaneously*
die gleitende Arbeitszeit *flexitime*
gründen *to found*
die Grenze(-n) *border*
groß *big*
Großbritannien *Great Britain*
das Grundgesetz *basic law*
grundsätzlich *basically*
der Gruß (¨e) *greeting*
gut *good*
günstig *favourable, good, convenient*

haben *to have*
der Hafen (¨) *port*
der Handel *trade*
handeln *to deal with*
der Haufen (-) *pile*
Haupt- (in compounds) *main*
hauptsächlich *primarily*
der Hauptsitz (-e) *head office*
die Hauptverwaltung(-en) *main office*
die Hausfrau (-en) *housewife*
heißen *to be called*
helfen *to help*
hoch *high*
hoffentlich *hopefully*
die Hälfte(-n) *half*

das Industriegebiet (-e) *industrial zone*
innerhalb (+ gen.) *within*

insbesondere   *in particular*
das Jahr (-e)   *year*
das Jahrhundert (-e)   *century*
jetzt   *now*
der Jugendliche (-n)   *young person*
kaputt   *broken*
kaufen   *to buy*
kaum   *hardly*
kennen   *to know, be acquainted with (person, place)*
kennenlernen   *to meet, get to know*
in Kenntnis setzen (von)   *to make aware (of), inform*
die Kenntnisse (pl.)   *knowledge*
klein   *small*
der Koffer (-)   *suitcase*
kommen   *to come*
konkurrieren   *to compete*
das Können   *know-how*
können   *to be able to*
das Konto (Konten)   *account*
kontrollieren   *to check, supervise*
kosten   *to cost*
kraftvoll   *powerful*
die Krankheit (-en)   *illness*
die Krise(-n)   *crisis*
der Kunde (-n)   *customer*
kurz   *short*
kurzfristig   *short term*
körperlich   *physical*
künftig   *future (adj.)*

die Lage   *situation, position*
das Lager (-)   *warehouse*
das Land (¨er)   *country, state*
die Landschaft   *landscape, countryside*
die Landwirtschaft   *agriculture*
lang   *long*
langfristig   *long term*
langweilig   *boring*
leer   *empty*
die Lehre   *apprenticeship*
der Lehrling (-e)   *apprentice*

leicht   *light, easy*
leiden   *to suffer*
leider   *unfortunately*
die Leistung (-en)   *achievement, service*
leistungsfähig   *efficient*
der Leiter(-)   *leader, manager*
lesen   *to read*
Lieblings- (in compounds)   *favourite*
die Lieferbedingung (-en)   *term of delivery*
der Lieferschein (-e)   *delivery note*
liefern   *to deliver*
die Lieferung (-en)   *delivery*
der Lieferwagen(-)   *delivery lorry/van*
die Lieferzeit   *period of delivery*
liegen   *to lie, be situated*
links   *to the left*
der Lohn(¨e)   *wage*
die Lösung(-en)   *solution*

maßgeschneidet   *tailor-made*
machen   *to do*
das Mal (-e)   *time*
man   *one*
der Mann (¨er)   *man*
männlich   *male*
die Mappe (-n)   *folder*
der Markt (¨e)   *market*
der Maschinenbau   *mechanical engineering*
mehrere   *several*
die Meinung (-en)   *opinion*
die meisten   *most, majority*
der Mengenrabatt (-e)   *bulk discount*
die Messe (-n)   *trade fair*
mieten   *to hire*
die Minderheit(-en)   *minority*
mit   *with*
der Mitarbeiter (-)   *employee, colleague*

das Mitglied(-er) *member*
mitteilen *to advise, inform*
mittelgroß *medium-sized*
mögen *to like*
die Möglichkeit (-en) *possibility*
der Monat (-e) *month*
die Montage *assembly*
montieren *to assemble*
der Morgen *morning*
morgen *tomorrow*
das Möbel *furniture*
müssen *to have to*

nach *after, according to*
nachdem *after*
der Nachmittag *afternoon*
nachsehen *to look up (a reference)*
nächst *next, nearest*
der Nachteil (-e) *disadvantage*
nachteilig *disadvantageous*
der Name (-n) *name*
nehmen *to take*
das Netz(-e) *network*
der Netzanschluß *mains*
neu *new*
nicht *not*
nichts *nothing*
niedrig *low*
noch *still*
noch nicht *not yet*
nochmal *again*
der Norden *north*
die Norm (-en) *standard*
normalerweise *normally*
nur *only*

ob *whether*
obwohl *although*
öffnen *to open*
öfters *frequently*
der Osten *east*

die Pflicht(-en) *duty*
der Platz (¨e) *seat*
der Preis (-e) *price*

preisgünstig *value for money, inexpensive*
produzieren *to produce*
die Provision *commission*
prüfen *to check, monitor, control*
pünktlich *punctual*

die Qualität *quality*
die Querstraße(-n) *crossroads*

der Rabatt (-e) *discount*
die Rate (-n) *instalment*
ratsam *advisable*
die Rechnung (-en) *invoice*
das Recht (-e) *right*
ein Recht haben (auf) *to be entitled (to)*
recht haben *to be right*
rechts *to the right*
rechtzeitig *on time*
die Redaktion *production*
die Reibung(-en) *friction*
die Reise (-en) *journey*
die Rente (-n) *pension*
der Renter (-) *pensioner*
reparieren *to repair*
richtig *correct, right*
das Risiko (Risiken) *risk*
der Rohstoff (-e) *raw material*
rohstoffreich *rich in raw materials*
die Rolle (-n) *role*
der Rückstand (¨e) *backlog, arrears*
der Ruf (-e) *reputation*
der Ruhestand *retirement*
rund *about, approximately*
rückwendig *by return*

schätzen *to protect*
der Schaden (¨) *damage*
die Scheidung(-en) *divorce*
schicken *to send*
der Schiff (-e) *boat*
schlecht *bad*

der Schlüssel   *key*
der Schnittpunkt(-e)   *intersection*
der Schrank(¨e)   *cupboard*
die Schreibmaschine (-n)
   typewriter
der Schwerpunkt(-e)   *emphasis*
sehen   *to see*
sehr   *very*
sein   *to be*
seit   *since*
die Sekretärin (-nen)   *secretary*
sich selbstständig machen   *to go
   independent*
selbstverständlich   *of course*
die Sendung (-en)   *consignment*
sicher   *sure, confident*
die Sicherheit   *safety, security*
sichern   *to secure*
das Skonto   *cash discount*
sobald   *as soon as*
solch   *such*
sollen   *to be to, should*
Sonder- (in compounds)   *special*
sonst   *otherwise*
die Sorge (-n)   *worry*
sorgen (für)   *to ensure, care for,
   sort out*
sorgen (um)   *take care (of)*
sorgfältig   *carefully*
das Sortiment (-e)   *range of goods*
die Sozialleistungen   *social services*
spät   *late*
der Spediteur (-e)   *forwarding
   agent*
der Speicher (-)   *memory (of
   computer)*
die Spesen (pl.)   *expenses*
sich spezialisieren (auf)   *to
   specialise (in)*
spielen   *to play*
das Spielzeug(-e)   *toy*
die Sprache (-n)   *language*
sprechen   *to speak*
die Stärke (-n)   *strength*

der Stahl   *steel*
stattfinden   *to take place*
die Stelle (-n)   *post, job*
das Stellenangebot(-e)   *job vacancy*
die Steuer(-n)   *tax*
die Strecke(-n)   *stretch, distance
   (of track)*
das Studium (Studien)   *studies*
die Stunde (-n)   *hour*
ständig   *always, consistently*
suchen   *to look for*
der Süden   *south*

der Tag (-e)   *day*
tätig sein   *to be active/operate (in
   an area)*
die Tätigkeit(-en)   *activity*
teilen   *to share*
teilnehmen an (dat.)   *to take part in*
das Telefon (-e)   *telephone*
teuer   *expensive*
treffen   *to meet*
der Treffpunkt(-e)   *meeting point*
trinken   *to drink*
das Trinkgeld (-er)   *tip*
tun   *to do*

die U-bahn(-en)   *underground*
über   *over, via*
überall   *everywhere*
überfällig   *overdue*
überhaupt   *at all*
der Überschuß (¨sse)   *surplus*
übersetzen   *to translate*
übertrieben   *exaggerated,
   a bit much*
die Überweisung (-en)   *transfer*
überwiegend   *mainly*
üblich   *customary, usual*
übrigens   *by the way*
um   *around*
umfassen   *to include*
der Umsatz (¨e)   *turnover*

der Umschlag (¨e) *envelope, transshipment*
umständlich *complicated, fussy, involved*
die Umwelt *environment*
der Umweltschutz *environmental protection*
unbedingt *at all costs, definitely*
unentbehrlich *indispensible*
ungefähr *about*
unrecht haben *to be wrong*
unterbrechen *interrupt*
unterschiedlich *different(ly), varied, various*
unterwegs *en route*
unterzeichnen *to sign*
das Ursprungsland(¨er) *country of origin*

verabreden *to make an appointment*
verantwortlich *responsible*
verbieten *to forbid*
verbinden (mit) *to connect, link (with)*
die Verbindung (-en) *link, connection, relationship, communication*
verbrauchen *to consume, use*
verbringen *to spend time*
verdienen *to earn*
der Verdienst (-e) *earnings*
vereinbaren *to agree*
die Verfassung(-en) *constitution*
sich verfehlen *to miss one's way*
verfügen über *to have (available/ at one's disposal)*
vergessen *to forget*
der Vergleich (-e) *comparison*
verhandeln *to negotiate*
das Verhältnis *relationship, proportion*
verhältnismäßig *relatively*
verkaufen *to buy*

die Verkaufsbedingungen *conditions of sale*
der Verkaufsleiter (-) *sales manager*
das Verkehrsmittel *means of transport*
der Verlag(-e) *publishing house*
verlangen *to demand*
verlassen *to leave*
vermeiden *to avoid*
die vermietete Fläche *space let*
die Verpackung (-en) *packaging*
der Versand *despatch*
verschieden *different*
verschonen *spare, save*
versenden *to send*
versichert (gegen) *insured (against)*
die Versicherung (-en) *insurance*
die Versorgung *provision, supply*
versprechen *to promise*
Verspätung haben *to be late*
verstehen *to understand, to be quoted (of prices)*
versuchen *to try*
vertraulich *confidential*
vertraut *trustworthy, familiar*
vertreten *to represent*
der Vertreter (-) *representative*
verursachen *to cause*
die Verwaltung(-en) *administration*
verwenden *to use*
verwirklichen *realise, bring about*
die Verzögerung (-en) *delay*
die Verzeihung *pardon*
verzollt *duty paid*
viel(e) *much* (many)
vielleicht *perhaps*
das Volk (¨er) *the people, nation*
voll *full*
vollenden *to complete*
vollständig *complete*
von *from, by*
voraus *in advance*

vorausgesetzt, daß *provided that*
voraussichtlich *foreseeably, probably*
die Vorauszahlung (-en) *payment in advance*
vorbeigehen (an + dat.) *to go past*
vorbeikommen *pop in*
vorbereiten *to prepare*
vorbereitet *prepared*
vorhaben *to plan*
vorhanden sein *to be present, exist*
vornehmen *to carry out*
vorschlagen *to suggest, propose*
vorsprechen *to present o.s. (for a meeting)*
die Vorstadt(⸚) *suburbs*
(sich) vorstellen *to introduce (oneself)*
sich (dat.) vorstellen *to imagine*
der Vorteil (-e) *advantage*
vorteilhaft *advantageous*
vorziehen *to prefer*

wählen *to choose, select*
die Wahl(-en) *election*
während *during*
wahrscheinlich *probably*
die Währung (-en) *currency*
die Ware (-n) *good(s)*
warum *why*
was *what*
das Wasser *water*
der Wechsel (-) *bill of exchange*
wechseln *change (e.g money)*
weg *away*
wegen (+ gen.) *because of*
weiblich *female*
weil *because*
weiter *further*
weiterbefördern *to forward*
die Welt *world*
wenden (an + acc.) *contact*
wenig *little, few*

wenn *if, when*
wer *who*
werden *to become*
der Werft(-e) *wharf, dock*
das Werkzeug (-e) *tool*
wertvoll *valuable*
das Wesen *system, being, soul*
der Westen *west*
der Wettbewerb *competition*
wichtig *important*
wie *how, like*
wie weit *how far*
wieder *again*
wiederholen *to repeat*
die Wiedervereinigung *reunification*
wieviel *how much*
die Wirklichkeit *reality*
der Wirtschaftsprüfer(-) *accountant*
wissen *to know (fact)*
wo *where*
die Woche (-n) *week*
das Wochenende (-) *weekend*
die Wohnung (-en) *flat, apartment*
wollen *to want to*
wünschen *to wish*

die Zahlung (-en) *payment*
die Zahlungsbedingung(-en) *term of payment*
das Zeichen (-) *reference*
zeigen *to show*
die Zeitschrift(en) *magazine*
ziemlich *rather, more or less, quite*
das Zimmer (-) *room*
der Zoll (⸚e) *duty*
zu *to*
die Zubehör *accessories*
zudem *in addition*
zuerst *firstly*
zugelassen *registered (of vehicle)*
die Zukunft *future*
der Zulieferant(-en) *supplier*

zunächst   *first of all*
sich zurechtfinden   *to find one's*
    way about/feel at home
zurückkommen   *to come back,*
    return
zurückrufen   *to call back*
die Zusammenarbeit   *cooperation*
zuständig   *responsible*
die Zuverlässigkeit   *reliability*
der Zuzug(ⁱe)   *influx*
der Zweigstelle (-n)   *branch*
zwingen   *to force*

Grammatical Index